TOWARD A MORE PERFECT UNION

Dr. Edward O. Guerrant
Chairman of the Department of History
California State College at Los Angeles

Dr. Kenneth A. Martyn
Vice President for Academic Affairs and Professor of Special Education
California State College at Los Angeles

TOWARD A MORE

PERFECT

D. C. HEATH AND COMPANY   BOSTON

UNION

The Constitution
in Historic Perspective

Preface

TOWARD A MORE PERFECT UNION is a collection of documents related to the origin and development of the Constitution of the United States. The stuff of history is the written record—the published documents, the letters (official or personal), the newspapers, the speeches—and from them this volume of readings has been compiled. The readings are intended to enrich and supplement any curriculum dealing with history, government, and the American Constitution. They will aid the creative teacher in introducing his students to a variety of primary sources used by historians in writing history; they provide a supplement to strained school libraries that are trying to meet the demands of new social studies curriculum guides; and they illustrate the Constitution as a changing, living instrument of American government.

The first chapter consists of the entire Constitution, including the recent Twenty-fifth Amendment. The student thus has in its entirety, with some explanatory comment, the single document on which the remainder of the book is focused. The remaining chapters of the book include selections which illustrate the origins of the Constitution, its historical development, and its relevance today to various areas of controversy:

The readings in Chapters 2–5 carry it from its English and colonial roots through the Civil War and repercussions of the War. Each selection illustrates one important historical event. The student is then able to decide for himself the impact of this particular document and its ideas on the framers and interpreters of the Constitution.

Then Chapters 6–10 relate this historical background to five specific areas. These are areas in which constitutional interpretations are often controversial and in which attitudes shift and evolve: suffrage, government regulation and reform, social welfare, civil rights, and foreign policy.

The documents chosen relate primarily to American political history, but many have social and economic importance as well. Since they are arranged in chronological order within each chapter, the historical perspective is preserved. Also, recent topics such as civil rights legislation and debate on Vietnam show the relevance of historical background to modern-day problems.

The book is organized with an introduction to each document, giving its background and pointing up highlights to direct the student in his reading. Questions and cross-references constantly direct the student's thoughts back to other documents he has read and to the Constitution itself, encouraging him to do the critical thinking necessary to grasp the document's broader implications. In addition, chapter introductions help to bridge any historical gaps and provide a theme for the readings in that chapter.

In order to stimulate inductive reasoning on the part of the student, he is encouraged to digest and compare the documents himself. Often he is provided with opposing points of view to be weighed in his own mind. Also, a glossary is provided at the end of many documents to enable the student to understand some of the obscure or obsolete usages which may be found in the text.

It is hoped that this book will stimulate the student with a variety of primary sources: little-known readings as well as the more accessible major documents. Each selection will teach a greater respect for the methods of the historian and will enrich class and individual study. Thus, each selection will encourage a deeper understanding of the Constitution — its development and its historic perspective.

Contents

I

What Does the Constitution Say? 1
  CONSTITUTION OF THE UNITED STATES 10

II

What Ideas in the Constitution Came from England? 52
  Divine Right of Kings, 1609 52
  Protest to King James I, 1621 54
  Petition of Right, 1628 55
  The Poor in England, 1649 57
  Habeas Corpus Act, 1679 59
  English Bill of Rights, 1689 62
  John Locke on Representation and Democracy, 1689 64

III

How Did Colonial Experience Shape the Constitution? 67
  The Mayflower Compact, 1620 67
  Representative Government in Virginia, 1621 68
  Church and State, 1636–1644 69
  Maryland Toleration Act, 1649 72
  The Zenger Case, 1735 73
  The Albany Plan of Union, 1754 77
  Letters from a Farmer in Pennsylvania, 1767 80
  The Intolerable Acts, 1774 82
  First Continental Congress, 1774 84
  Rights of British Americans, 1774 85
  The Virginia Bill of Rights, 1776 88
  The Declaration of Independence, 1776 91

IV

What Were the Problems of the Early Government? 96

Articles of Confederation, 1777 96
Northwest Ordinance, 1787 100
Shays' Rebellion, 1786 102
The Virginia Plan, 1787 105
The New Jersey Plan, 1787 108
Richard Henry Lee on the Constitution, 1787 111
Federalist 10, 1787 114
Jefferson on the Bill of Rights, 1789 118
*Jefferson and Hamilton on the Meaning of
    the Constitution, 1791* 120
The Whiskey Rebellion, 1794 122
Marbury v. Madison, 1803 123

V

States' and Federal Rights: What Is the Balance of Power? 126

The Kentucky Resolution, 1798 126
The Hartford Convention, 1815 129
South Carolina's Nullification Ordinance, 1832 131
Jackson's Proclamation on Nullification, 1883 134
The Compromise of 1850 136
Southern Support of the Compromise of 1850 138
The Impending Crisis of the South, 1858 139
Alabama Ordinance of Secession, 1861 141
Jefferson Davis' Farewell Address to the Senate, 1861 142
Economic Effects of Secession, 1861 144
Reconstruction Follows War, 1867 145
Amnesty for the South, 1871 147
An Attitude Toward Governmental Power Today, 1965 148

VI

Should Suffrage Be Limited? 151

An Argument Against Universal Suffrage, 1821 152
An Argument for Universal Suffrage, 1828 153
Democracy in America, 1835 155
Declaration of Women's Rights, 1848 158
For the Right to Vote, 1908 160
Against Woman Suffrage, 1918 162
John Austin Moon on Woman Suffrage, 1918 163
The Voting Rights Act of 1965 165
The Supreme Court Decision on the Voting Rights Act, 1966 168

VII

Should Government Protect the Individual by
Regulating Business?   170

William Graham Sumner on Wealth and Individualism, 1902   172
Munn v. Illinois, 1877   173
The Growth of the Standard Oil Company, 1883   174
Andrew Carnegie Defends Trusts, 1889–1900   176
Ida Tarbell on Standard Oil, 1904   179
The New York Tenements in the 1890's   182
The Sherman Anti-Trust Act, 1890   183
Theodore Roosevelt's New Nationalism, 1910   184
Child Labor in 1918   187
Reuben Dagenhart's Opinion of Hammer v. Dagenhart, 1924   189
Woodrow Wilson's New Freedom, 1912   190

VIII

What Role Should Government Play in
Individual Welfare?   194

The Stock Market Crash, 1929   195
Unemployment During the Great Depression, 1932   197
The American Farmer and the Great Depression, 1932   200
Roosevelt's Idea of Government, 1932   202
Hoover's Commentary on the New Deal, 1934   205
The National Recovery Administration, 1935   207
Social Security, 1935   209

IX

What Are an Individual's Civil Rights?   211

The Dred Scott Decision, 1857   212
The Constitutionality of the 1875 *Civil Rights Act*, 1883   215
Plessy v. Ferguson, 1896   216
The Grandfather Clause, 1915   219
School Desegregation, 1954   221
Declaration of Constitutional Principles, 1956   223
The Civil Rights Act, 1957   226
Desegregation Difficulties, 1962   227
Civil Rights Act of 1964   230
Heart of Atlanta Motel v. United States, 1964   232

X

How Does the Constitution Affect Foreign Policy?   236

Washington's Farewell Address, 1796   237
Jefferson on the Louisiana Purchase, 1802   240
The Monroe Doctrine, 1823   242

The Spanish-American War, 1898   243
The Responsibility of an American President, 1917   244
Wilson's Call to Arms, 1917   246
Woodrow Wilson's Support of the League of Nations, 1919   249
Recognition of the Soviet Union, 1933   251
Destroyer-Bases Agreement, 1940   253
The Yalta Agreement, 1945   257
The Charter of the United Nations, 1945   259
North Atlantic Treaty Organization, 1949   264
Vietnam Resolution of Support, 1964   265
Senate Debate on Vietnam, 1966   267

Acknowledgments

For permission to reproduce copyrighted material, grateful acknowledgment is made to the following:

American Public Health Association for permission to use material from *The Child and the State* by Grace Abbott, published by the University of Chicago Press and copyright 1938 by the American Public Health Association.

Appleton-Century-Crofts for permission to use material from *Northern Editorials on Secession,* edited by Howard Cecil Perkins and copyright 1942 by D. Appleton-Century Co.

Columbia University Press for permission to use material from *The Papers of Alexander Hamilton,* edited by Harold C. Surett and copyright 1965.

Cornell University Press for permission to use material from *The Works of Gerrard Winstanley,* edited by George H. Sabine. Copyright, 1941, by Cornell University. Used by permission of Cornell University Press.

Dale D. Drain, executor of the estate of Edith Bolling Wilson, for permission to use material from *The New Freedom* by Woodrow Wilson, published 1913 by Doubleday, Page & Co.

E. P. Dutton & Co., Inc., for permission to use material from the book *Cobb of "The World"* by John L. Heaton. Copyright, 1942, by E. P. Dutton & Co., Inc. Reprinted by permission of the publishers.

Harvard College Library for permission to use material from the *Papers of General Benjamin Lincoln* in the Sparks Manuscripts. By permission of the Harvard College Library.

Harvard University Press for permission to use materials from *The History of the Colony and Province of Massachusetts* by Thomas Hutchinson, edited by Lawrence Shaw Mayo, copyright 1936; and from *The Political Works of James I,* edited by Charles Howard McIlwain, copyright 1918.

The New York Times for permission to use an article appearing in the *Times* of October 25, 1929. © 1929 by The New York Times Company. Reprinted by permission.

Prentice-Hall, Inc., for permission to use material from William E. Leuchtenburg, Editor, *The New Nationalism, Theodore Roosevelt,* © 1961. Reprinted by permission of Prentice-Hall, Inc., Englewood Cliffs, New Jersey.

Princeton University Press for permission to use material from *The Papers of Thomas Jefferson,* edited by Julia P. Boyd. Reprinted by permission of the Princeton University Press, copyright 1950.

Random House, Inc., for permission to use two selections from *The Public Papers and Addresses of Franklin D. Roosevelt,* edited by Samuel I. Rosenman and copyright 1938.

Charles Scribner's Sons for permission to use material from *Challenge to Liberty* by Herbert Hoover, copyright 1934.

Yale University Press for permission to use material from *Commons Debates, 1621,* edited by Wallace Notestein, Frances Helen Relf, and Hartley Simpson and copyright 1935; and from *The Challenge of Facts and Other Essays* by William Graham Sumner, edited by Albert Galloway Keller and copyright 1914.

I
What Does
the Constitution Say?

The American Revolution was ignited by a minor incident in April, 1775. The first shots were exchanged between Lexington's and Concord's minutemen and the British troops who were sent to seize military supplies collected by the colonists.

The fighting might have remained a local incident, but King George III had observed in 1774 that the "Colonies must either submit or triumph." News of this attitude reached America just at the time the colonists met in Philadelphia for the Second Continental Congress in May of 1775.

This group of distinguished men included many of those who later signed the Declaration of Independence. While proclaiming the justice of their cause and the necessity of defending themselves, they did not want to sever ties with Britain even then. The Continental Congress appointed George Washington of Virginia as commander-in-chief of the Continental Army, and in June, 1775, he left the Congress in Philadelphia to gather and lead the army.

Washington faced unbelievable difficulties. The troops were poorly paid, badly clothed, and ill fed. There were American victories at Bunker Hill, Saratoga, Kings Mountain, Yorktown, and other places. But Americans lost New York City, Philadelphia, and Charleston to the British, as well as battles at Long Island, Brandywine Creek, Germantown, and Camden. Final victory came in 1781 when Washington's forces besieged those of Lord Cornwallis at the Battle of Yorktown.

While Washington was striving to win independence on the field of battle, the Continental Congress moved gradually toward a complete break with England and the establishment of an American government. Seeing no hope of reconciliation with George III's government in 1775 or 1776, American leaders became convinced that they must proclaim their independence to the world.

1

The Declaration of Independence (*see pp. 91–95*) was adopted on July 4, 1776, but even before that historic event the Continental Congress had advised the colonies to establish their own independent governments. Many of the state constitutions contained a Bill of Rights which listed privileges they felt had been denied them by Britain. These governments also provided for the separation of powers among the executive, judicial, and legislative branches of government to better secure liberties. The constitutions, of course, varied from state to state. For example, the Pennsylvania constitution was the most democratic in allowing voting rights; there was no property requirement for voting or for office holding. States such as South Carolina required men to own fifty acres as a voting prerequisite; the governor and other high officials must have property valued at £10,000.

The Continental Congress also provided for a federal government by adopting the Articles of Confederation (*see pp. 96–100*). This experimental government was largely the work of John Dickinson (*see pp. 80–82*). The Congress of the Confederation, however, did not officially come into existence until the last of the thirteen states ratified it in 1781.

The Articles were the basis of government for the United States until the inauguration of George Washington in 1789. The states were wary of surrendering any of their dearly won independence to a strong central government; the Confederation was a loose alliance of independent states. There was no national executive and no federal judiciary. Congress had no power to levy taxes and it could not control commerce among the states. Congress had the power to declare war, to raise an army, to borrow money, and to conclude treaties with foreign nations.

Yet from 1781 until 1787 it became clear to many Americans that the Articles were not strong enough to preserve order in the states and to help build a strong nation.

A meeting was held in Alexandria, Virginia, to discuss the rights of Maryland and Virginia in the use of the Potomac River. After arriving at a settlement between these two states, they issued an invitation to all the states to send delegates to a convention to be held in Annapolis, Maryland, in 1786 for the purpose of discussing trade problems common to all. Although only five states responded to the call, the Annapolis Convention adopted a resolution drafted by Alexander Hamilton asking all states to send delegates to Philadelphia in 1787 to consider measures to meet the "exigencies of the Union." Early in 1787 the Congress of the Confederation followed suit and invited the states to send delegates to "revise the Articles of Confederation."

Despite the limited authorization from Congress, a number of delegates from the larger states met privately in Philadelphia before the Convention opened on May 25, 1787, to discuss plans for a new document.

The Philadelphia (or Constitutional) Convention, at which twelve of the thirteen states were represented, met in the Old State House, already famous as the place where the Declaration of Independence had been proclaimed. A total of fifty-five men attended. George Washington was selected as the presiding officer. The convention drew the most outstanding men of the times, whose accomplishments and wisdom have continued to merit the admiration of much of the world since then. Benjamin Franklin, Alexander Hamilton, James Madison, James Wilson, John Dickinson, Charles Pinckney, William Paterson, Gouverneur Morris, and Robert Morris were merely a few of the distinguished thirty-nine men whose names later appeared at the bottom of the historic document.

These men were particularly well suited to their work. Most were college graduates at a time when such an education was a most unusual accomplishment. Five were college presidents or college professors. Over half had served in the Congress of the Confederation, and the rest had been members of state legislatures. Many of the men were young, in their mid-thirties, and only four of the group were over sixty years of age. They were well versed in the history of ancient and modern governments, and were the most respected leaders of the colonial, revolutionary, and post-revolutionary period.

For several weeks the delegates debated first the Virginia (or large-state) Plan (*see pp. 105–108*), then the New Jersey (or small-state) Plan (*see pp. 108–111*). The Virginia Plan called for proportional representation in both houses, with the lower house electing members of the upper house. The New Jersey Plan proposed that each state should be equally represented in Congress. The smaller states feared domination by the larger states. Domination had not been a problem under the Articles, since each state had one vote. While some delegates felt that a real source of conflict might develop between sectional lines or between differences in economic interests, the major contest within the Convention was between the large and small states. The meeting was saved by the Great (or Connecticut) Compromise of mid-July, which provided for equal representation in the Senate and proportional representation in the House.

There were many other disputes that followed. The Southern states wanted to count the slaves as part of their total population for purposes of representation in the House, but not if direct taxes were to be levied on the basis of population. The Northern states wished just the reverse: to count slaves for taxes but not for representation. The three-fifths compromise solved this dilemma; five slaves were counted as three persons for both purposes.

The Southern states, economically dependent on export of their agricultural produce, favored a two-thirds majority for the passage of tariff and commerce laws. They feared that Northern commercial interests might bring pressures to tax their exports or to place a prohibitive tariff on the importation of slaves. Consequently, the convention compromised; the Southern states agreed to a simple majority in Congress for the regulation of commerce in return for the prohibition of any export tax and a provision to prevent Congress from abolishing the importation of slaves before 1808.

The finished Constitution was endorsed by unanimous vote of all the states present on September 17, 1787. As soon as nine states ratified the Constitution, a new form of government would go into effect. From the sovereign states of 1787 delegates had fashioned a union in which the federal government was given certain specified powers, and yet the states retained many powers not yielded to the central government.

The Convention had hardly finished its work before the Great Debate began: should this document become the basis of a new government? The supporters of the Constitution were called Federalists. They had the support of respected men like George Washington and Benjamin Franklin and the brilliance of such younger men as James Madison, Alexander Hamilton, John Jay, and others. In support of ratification of the Constitution the last three wrote the *Federalist Papers* (*see pp. 114–118*), which remain unsurpassed as commentaries on the nature of the Constitution. Most Federalists contended that without ratification the experiment in independence and union might well fail.

Anti-Federalists, including such well-known persons as Patrick Henry, Richard Henry Lee (*see pp. 111–114*), George Clinton of New York, and Elbridge Gerry (who attended the Convention), opposed adoption of the new Constitution. But Anti-Federalists differed among themselves in their reasons for their opposition. Some believed the states should have retained the right to levy import duties. Others believed too much power was given the federal government and too little was left to the states. Most condemned the lack of a Bill of Rights, which they insisted was necessary to guarantee individual liberties against the power of the federal government.

The contests in the ratification conventions in many states were bitter and prolonged. Many Federalists gained support for their cause by agreeing to add a Bill of Rights to the Constitution. New Hampshire was the ninth state to ratify. The Virginia Convention ratified by the narrow margin of ten votes. Hamilton led the fight for ratification in New York, where only three votes carried the day for the Federalists. When Washington was inaugurated as President, North Carolina and Rhode Island still had not agreed to join the union.

4

They ratified only after Congress had submitted a Bill of Rights to the states for approval.

The Constitution itself provided that its ratification should be by state conventions elected by the people for that specific purpose; thus the Constitution was to be the will of the people. Thomas Jefferson discussed the nature of a constitution as a fundamental charter. The will of the people, he said, established a government that could be changed only by the people themselves by the process defined in the Constitution. Jefferson recognized the need to alter the Constitution of the United States from time to time to keep pace with changes in our society. In a letter written to a friend Jefferson remarked, "Some men look at constitutions with sanctimonious reverence, and deem them like the ark of the covenant, too sacred to be touched. . . . I know that age well; I belonged to it and labored with it. . . . But I know also that laws and institutions must go hand in hand with the progress of the human mind."[1] And in 1824, just two years before his death, Jefferson again commented to a friend that "The real friends of the constitution in its federal form, if they wish to be immortal, should be attentive to amendments to make it keep pace with the advance of the age in science and experience."[2]

The Constitution is still the basis of the government today because it was flexible enough to have met the needs of succeeding generations in a nation that has seen rapid changes. In 1789 the Constitution served a nation that was largely agricultural and provincial. The young nation had little influence in world affairs, and British troops even occupied a few posts on American soil. Today, with a population fifty times greater, with some metropolitan areas larger than the entire population of the nation in 1789, with airplanes crossing the nation in a few hours and spacecraft circling the world in ninety minutes, with vast factories producing wealth undreamed of in the past, and with a position as the most powerful nation in the world, the Constitution is still the basic framework of our government.

The Constitution has survived as the framework of the government because, as Jefferson suggested, the document has kept pace with the "advances in science and experience." Jefferson suggested that change take place by adding amendments. But since the Bill of Rights was added shortly after the adoption of the Constitution only fifteen amendments have been added. These few amendments suggest that the Constitution is flexible for other reasons, too.

Part of the flexibility of the Constitution is in the language of the document. When the framers had very specific situations

---

[1]Andrew A. Lipscomb, ed., *The Writings of Thomas Jefferson* (The Thomas Jefferson Memorial Association of the United States, Washington, D.C., 1905), XV, 40–41.
[2]*Ibid.*, p. 15.

in mind, the language of the Constitution is very precise. The three-fifths slave compromise in Article 1, Section 2, Clause 3 (*see pp. 12–13*) is very clear. Likewise, provisions such as the length of the term of a representative or a senator leave little room for disagreement.

But there are situations in which the framers of the Constitution worded phrases so that there could be a great deal of latitude in interpreting. For example: much controversy has arisen over the interpretation of the clause authorizing Congress "to lay and collect taxes, duties, imposts, and excises, to pay the debt and provide for the common defense and general welfare of the United States" (*see p. 20*). Countless words have been written and spoken about what the framers of the Constitution meant by the "general welfare." Another section allows Congress "to make all laws which shall be necessary and proper for carrying into execution the foregoing powers . . ." (*see p. 22*). Men who have been concerned with the nation's welfare have violently disagreed which laws are "necessary and proper."

Although wordings such as these have led to a great many arguments, the vagueness of the language has had one very important advantage: it has allowed each generation of Americans to apply these parts of the Constitution to its unique situation.

Controversy over the meaning of the Constitution began almost as soon as the document was ratified. One of the most long-lived of these disagreements has been titled "loose versus strict constructionism." Thomas Jefferson, mistrusting abuses of federal power and relying on the wisdom of state government, held a "strict constructionist" point of view; he felt that the Constitution allowed the federal government only those powers explicitly granted to it. Alexander Hamilton was a "loose constructionist." He argued that the federal government may do virtually anything that is not specifically forbidden by the Constitution. Hamilton's view, of course, allows the federal government a great many more powers than Jefferson's view does.

The Supreme Court has the final say in disagreements over the meaning of the Constitution, and it has at different times adopted strict and loose constructionist views. The history of the Supreme Court's decisions shows that at one time the court may have adopted a "strict" understanding of the wording of a phrase in the Constitution. But at another time, when the country faced a different situation, the Court was just as likely to understand the same phrase in much broader terms.

It is the language of the Constitution and the Supreme Court's willingness to change its mind about the meanings of words and phrases that has kept this document a usable framework of government. For example, one important phrase frequently argued before the Supreme Court is the commerce clause. The Constitution allows Congress "to regulate commerce with foreign nations, and among the several states, and with the Indian tribes."

Early in the nineteenth century the Supreme Court, under the leadership of the great Chief Justice John Marshall, in the celebrated case *Gibbons v. Ogden* (1824) upheld the right of Congress to regulate commerce between the states. The Court denied New York State the right to prevent any legally licensed vessel from entering its ports. This decision adhered closely to the simplest understanding of the commerce clause. In the nineteenth century many businesses began operations on a national scale. The federal government began to pass some laws to control the operations of larger enterprises. In 1890 Congress passed the Sherman Anti-Trust Act *(see pp. 183 – 184)* to curb big businesses, which many believed were destroying competition in the United States. Congress passed laws to regulate businesses that extended their operations into many states. Congress felt it had a right to pass these laws because the businesses were engaged in interstate commerce.

The first case to reach the Supreme Court under the Sherman Anti-Trust Act involved the sugar industry. In this case, *United States v. E. C. Knight Co.* (1895), the Supreme Court adhered to a "strict" construction of the commerce clause. The Supreme Court held that this business did not violate the anti-trust act because "Commerce succeeds to manufacturing and is not a part of it." The court ruled that although the sugar trust had a monopoly on the manufacture of sugar, which happened to be sold throughout the nation, they were engaged primarily in manufacturing. Manufacturing was not interstate commerce, so the sugar monopoly continued to operate because in the court's eyes Congress had no power to regulate manufacturing.

Ten years later, however, the Supreme Court adopted a slightly "looser" interpretation of the commerce clause. President Theodore Roosevelt believed that monopolies should be curbed or broken up, and the general public supported his view. In the case of *Swift and Co. v. United States* (1905), involving the meat-packing industry, the Supreme Court recognized that meat that was manufactured was also shipped throughout the country. In this case, therefore, the Supreme Court had changed its mind; manufacturing *was* involved in commerce. Thus the Court had given new meaning to the word *commerce*, for Congress now had the right to have some say in the activities of companies that shipped their goods from state to state. Congress was no longer limited to businesses whose main function was to transport goods.

A later illustration of "strict" construction of the commerce

7

clause was *Hammer v. Dagenhart* (1918) *(see pp. 187–188)*. In 1916 Congress passed a law designed to prohibit children under sixteen years of age from working in mines and quarries and to keep children under fourteen years of age from working in factories, mills, or canneries. Congress tried to prohibit companies employing children from shipping their products in interstate trade.

If this law had been upheld, it probably would have abolished most child labor in the United States because the great majority of companies employing children did sell their products outside the boundaries of their own states. The Court, in declaring the Child Labor Act unconstitutional, however, held "The Act in its effect does not regulate transportation among the States, but aims to standardize the ages at which children may be employed in mining and manufacturing within the States." And the Court concluded that the power to regulate or abolish child labor was a function of the individual states and not of the United States government. This case was decided by the narrow margin of five votes to four, but the Court had denied the federal government the right to regulate manufacturing policies not *directly* related to commerce.

Over two decades later, though, the Supreme Court adopted a much "looser" interpretation of the commerce clause. In 1938 Congress passed the Fair Labor Standards Act, which established a minimum wage of 25 cents an hour and the forty-four-hour work week. The law prohibited goods manufactured by children under sixteen years of age from being shipped in interstate commerce. In 1941, in the case of *United States v. Darby,* the Court declared that "While manufacture is not of itself interstate commerce the shipment of manufactured goods interstate is such commerce and the prohibition of such shipment by Congress is undoubtedly a 'regulation of commerce.'" The Court then dealt *Hammer v. Dagenhart* a death blow by holding "It should be and now is overruled."

Finally, in 1964, the Court, in upholding the Civil Rights Act of 1964, adopted what may be the loosest construction of the commerce clause to date. In two cases, *Heart of Atlanta Motel v. United States (see pp. 232–235)* and *Katzenbach v. McClung et al.,* the Supreme Court held that Congress has the right under the commerce clause to prevent racial segregation in a motel and in a restaurant, since they were both deemed sufficiently engaged in interstate commerce.

The power of Congress and the Supreme Court's understandings had changed in sixty-nine years. In 1895 the Court did not believe that the federal government under the Sherman Antitrust Act had the power to regulate a large business which sold sugar throughout the United States. But in 1964 the Court had expanded the commerce clause to allow Congress to prevent business which unquestionably had a sizable local trade from discriminating against Negroes.

The words of the Constitution, of course, have not changed since it was written in 1787 except for the few places affected by amendments, but the Supreme Court has interpreted words in the Constitution in such a way as to expand the nature of that document. There have been and always will be those who would wish that the Supreme Court had not reached a particular decision. But no document has created a government which has served so many people so well for so long a period of time as has the Constitution of the United States.

CONSTITUTION
OF THE UNITED STATES

Preamble

☆ WE THE PEOPLE OF THE UNITED STATES, in order to form a more perfect union, establish Justice, insure domestic tranquility, provide for the common defence, promote the general Welfare, and secure the Blessings of Liberty to ourselves and our Posterity, do ordain and establish this Constitution for the United States of America.

The Preamble is a statement of purpose. It does not establish the framework of the government. *We the people* makes clear that the framers felt this new government derived from the consent of the people and not state governments. This was a change from the Articles of Confederation, which formed a government founded on an agreement among state governments. The Constitution was founded on an agreement of the people.

Clearly, at the time of the writing of the Constitution, the states were dissatisfied with the "union" of the Articles and they desired "to form a more perfect union." The purposes of the new government stated in the Preamble are generally the purposes of the Articles of Confederation. But the framers hoped that the Constitution would better safeguard liberty and the general welfare than their previous government had done.

ARTICLE I

Article I, the longest article in the Constitution, describes the composition and powers of the legislature. This section is long partly because there was a great deal of disagreement in the convention about how the legislative branch of government should be constructed (*see pp. 3–4*). Many parts of this Article show the carefully constructed compromises that were part of the Philadelphia Convention. But the Article is long for another reason: the legislature is composed of two houses. The framers had to describe not only how Congress was to work in the whole framework of government but also how each branch of Congress was to work within the legislative framework.

The framers of the Constitution seemed to agree that no branch of government should have enough power to run the government without the help of the other two branches. The framers tried to balance the power of one branch against the power of another; this device has become known as "checks and balances." The power of the Congress is balanced against the power of the President; each has powers that check the powers of the other. As you read this article, see what powers the President is given to check the powers of Congress. See if there are any balances of power between the legislative branches.

Section 1

All legislative Powers herein granted shall be vested in a Congress of the United States, which shall consist of a Senate and House of Representatives.

Section 2

CLAUSE 1. The House of Representatives shall be composed of Members chosen every second Year by the People of the several States, and the Electors in each State shall have the Qualifications requisite for Electors of the most numerous Branch of the State Legislature.

Electors were the qualified voters. In 1787 voters were not all the adults in each state. In most states, only men who owned a certain amount of property were allowed to vote. Slaves and women had no chance to vote. Since 1787 the qualifications have been modified by Constitutional amendments, and changes in state laws have abolished property qualifications. The Fifteenth Amendment gave freed Negro men the right to vote, and the Nineteenth Amendment gave women the vote.

In some states the more numerous branch of the legislature elected the Senate, or upper house of their legislature. The qualifications for an elector for the members of the lower house were sometimes less than the qualifications for an elector for the members of the Senate. Membership in a state legislature meant often a person must have a certain amount of property. Thus the framers tried to extend the vote for the House of Representatives to as many people as possible; they stated that the electors for the House of Representatives must be the same as the electors for the more numerous branch of the state legislature.

CLAUSE 2. No Person shall be a Representative who shall not have attained to the Age of twenty-five Years, and been seven Years a Citizen of the United States, and who shall not, when elected, be an Inhabitant of that State in which he shall be chosen.

Only state laws can determine how long a person must live in a state to be considered an "inhabitant." Often around election time there will be a controversy over whether an official seeking election has lived long enough in the state. The framers included this requirement because an "inhabitant" of a state best knows the problems of the state whose interests he is elected to represent.

CLAUSE 3. Representatives and direct Taxes shall be apportioned among the several States which may be included within this Union, according to their respective Numbers, which shall be determined by adding to the whole Number of free Persons, including those bound to Service for a Term of Years, and excluding Indians not taxed, three fifths of all other Persons. The actual Enumeration shall be made within three Years after the first Meeting of the Congress of the United States, and within every subsequent Term of ten Years, in such Manner as they shall by Law direct. The Number of Representatives shall not exceed one for every thirty Thousand, but each State shall have at Least one Representative; and until such enumeration shall be made, the State of New Hampshire shall be entitled to chuse three, Massachusetts eight, Rhode-Island and Providence Plantations one, Connecticut five, New-York six, New Jersey four, Pennsylvania eight, Delaware one, Maryland six, Virginia ten, North Carolina five, South Carolina five, and Georgia three.

Those bound to service for a term of years refers to indentured servants, men and women who had promised to work, in most cases, for a term of seven years in return for passage from England and food, clothing, and lodging. After the term of service the servants were freemen; hence, they were counted as freemen for purposes of representation and taxation.

But slaves were a different matter; the Northern states wanted to count slaves for taxation whereas Southern states wanted to count them for representation (*see p. 3*). The compromise counted one slave as three fifths of a person. These sections of the Constitution are no longer in effect.

The stipulation that *the number of representatives shall not exceed one for every thirty thousand* also is no longer in effect because the population of the United States has grown too large. Congress limited the total number of members of the House of Representatives to 435 because the House was becoming too large to complete its work. Today the average representative represents about 400,000 people.

CLAUSE 4. When vacancies happen in the Representation from any State, the Executive Authority thereof shall issue Writs of Election to fill such Vacancies.

The *executive authority* is the governor of the state that has the vacancy in representation.

CLAUSE 5. The House of Representatives shall chuse their Speaker and other Officers; and shall have the sole Power of Impeachment.

Impeachment is a formal accusation against a public official for some crime. The crimes for which the House can impeach are listed in Article II, Section 4. Impeachment is different from conviction; it is a statement that the House of Representatives thinks a crime has been committed. The Senate must find the accused guilty before the official can be removed from office.

The framers chose the House of Representatives to take the first step in removing a public official to avoid impeachment for trivial reasons. A branch of Congress that represented so many different people could not easily agree on impeachment unless the causes were very important.

Section 3

CLAUSE 1. The Senate of the United States shall be composed of two Senators from each State, chosen by the Legislature thereof, for six Years; and each Senator shall have one Vote.

Wealth and public responsibility were very closely linked in colonial days; for example, in Virginia the wealthy planters were also the rulers of the colony. The framers were afraid to allow all the qualified voters a complete say in the government at a time when the wealthier colonists were the men most experienced in government.

The Senate was elected by state legislatures because membership in a state legislature required more property ownership than voting required. The voters for United States senator were wealthier than the people who had voted on the members of the state legislature. The framers thought an aristocratic Senate would balance and temper the desires of the more popularly elected House of Representatives.

State legislatures no longer elect senators. As more people

gained the right to vote, they proved that they were capable of making wise decisions about how to govern themselves. By the early part of the 1900's many people favored changing this part of the Constitution because they felt that the state legislatures that elected senators were influenced too much by big businessmen and too little by common men. Therefore, the Seventeenth Amendment was passed in 1913 in response to this demand.

CLAUSE 2. Immediately after they shall be assembled in Consequence of the first Election, they shall be divided as equally as may be into three Classes. The Seats of the Senators of the first Class shall be vacated at the Expiration of the second Year, of the second Class at the Expiration of the fourth Year, and of the third Class at the Expiration of the sixth Year, so that one-third may be chosen every second Year; and if Vacancies happen by Resignation, or otherwise, during the Recess of the Legislature of any State, the Executive thereof may make temporary Appointments until the next Meeting of the Legislature, which shall then fill such Vacancies.

The difference between the terms of senators and representatives reflects the framers' attitudes toward these branches of Congress. Representatives are elected every two years so that they will be responsive to the will of the people. Senators are elected every six years, and one-third of the Senate is new every two years. The senators, faced with less frequent elections, could be more reflective about their decisions. They could refuse to pass laws the representatives had passed in a burst of popular enthusiasm.

CLAUSE 3. No person shall be a Senator who shall not have attained to the Age of thirty Years, and been nine Years a Citizen of the United States, and who shall not, when elected, be an Inhabitant of that State for which he shall be chosen.

CLAUSE 4. The Vice President of the United States shall be President of the Senate, but shall have no Vote, unless they be equally divided.

The Constitution assigned the Vice President an inconspicuous role. But he was necessary in case the President died. While the Vice President is president of the Senate, he is rarely important. Within more recent times, however, Vice Presidents have been given important assignments by the Presidents they have served. They have attended cabinet meetings and have represented the President at important foreign and domestic functions.

14

CLAUSE 5. The Senate shall chuse their other Officers, and also a President pro tempore, in the Absence of the Vice President, or when he shall exercise the Office of President of the United States.

Pro tempore means "temporarily" or, more literally, "for the time being."

CLAUSE 6. The Senate shall have the sole Power to try all Impeachments. When sitting for that Purpose, they shall be on Oath or Affirmation. When the President of the United States is tried, the Chief Justice shall preside: And no Person shall be convicted without the Concurrence of two thirds of the Members present.

This section provides the remainder of the process by which a man may be removed from office. The Senate tries the official to determine his guilt. Because the Senate acts like a jury in trials of public officials, senators must take an oath. The requirement that the two houses are necessary to remove a man from office and the further requirement that the Senate needs two-thirds agreement, discourages removing officials. In fact, a President was impeached only once, and the Senate failed to muster the two-thirds vote required to remove him.

CLAUSE 7. Judgment in Cases of Impeachment shall not extend further than to removal from Office, and disqualification to hold and enjoy any Office of honor, Trust or Profit under the United States; but the Party convicted shall nevertheless be liable and subject to Indictment, Trial, Judgment and Punishment, according to Law.

Here the framers limited the powers of the Senate by permitting them only the right to remove officials from office. The second part of the clause makes clear that the Senate cannot take away the power to try in the courts or to judge the crime for which the official was removed.

Section 4

CLAUSE 1. The Times, Places and Manner of holding Elections for Senators and Representatives, shall be prescribed in each State by the Legislature thereof; but the Congress may at any time by Law make or alter such Regulations, except as to the Places of chusing Senators.

Except for the Reconstruction period following the Civil War, this part of the Constitution has not been controversial. The state legislatures have been fairly free to determine the manner of elections. Recently, the Civil Rights Act of 1964 and the Voting Rights Act of 1965 have led to bitter criticism that the federal government should not intervene in changing the "manner" of the elections established by state legislation, even though Congress is clearly authorized to do so by this section and by the Fifteenth Amendment.

CLAUSE 2. The Congress shall assemble at least once in every Year, and such Meeting shall be on the first Monday in December, unless they shall by Law appoint a different Day.

This section has been changed by the Twentieth Amendment, which was ratified in 1933. Congress now meets January 3. This law was changed to avoid a "lame duck" congress. When the Constitution was adopted, transportation and communication were very slow. The elections that took place in November would not be final for quite some time; it would take several months to complete the elections and notify all the winners. Meanwhile the country had to be governed; therefore, the Old Congress met in December. The November election would affect the Congress that met the following year. As communications improved, all the members of the December Congress knew whether or not they had been reelected in November. Those who still had a term to serve but had not been reelected were "lame ducks," politicians who had been "winged." These "lame ducks" then had no reason to try to please the people they represented, for they were soon to be replaced. The new amendment kept representatives and senators from serving in a session of Congress after they had failed to win reelection.

Section 5

CLAUSE 1. Each House shall be the Judge of the Elections, Returns and Qualifications of its own Members, and a Majority of each shall constitute a Quorum to do Business; but a smaller Number may adjourn from day to day, and may be authorized to compel the Attendance of absent Members, in such Manner, and under such Penalties as each House may provide.

A *quorum* is the number of members necessary for an organization to legally do business. A quorum may be fixed at almost any number, but as with Congress it is usually the majority. In the case of the Senate and House the Senate would need 51 members present and the House would need 218 members.

CLAUSE 2. Each House may determine the Rules of its

Proceedings, punish its Members for disorderly Behaviour, and, with the Concurrence of two thirds, expel a Member.

The framers allowed each house to determine the rules of its proceedings because they realized it was impossible to determine the rules that were necessary to meet changing situations. Both houses have a very elaborate set of rules which allow them to operate efficiently and fairly. One such rule allows unlimited debate in the Senate. And the Senate has a rule that permits cutting off debate on a vote of two thirds of the members. Unlike the Senate, the House has no such rule, since the large membership of that body would mean several members could continue unlimited debate through the whole session. In this case each house made different rules concerning its proceedings.

The "two-thirds" vote for expulsion allowed the houses the right to punish its members, but would keep them from using the rule except in serious circumstances.

CLAUSE 3. Each House shall keep a Journal of its Proceedings, and from time to time publish the same, excepting such Parts as may in their Judgment require Secrecy; and the Yeas and Nays of the Members of either House on any question shall, at the Desire of one fifth of those present, be entered on the Journal.

The *Congressional Record*, published since the first session of Congress during Washington's administration, is an invaluable record of the daily business of both houses. While it has had different names, the *Record* is kept primarily because the Constitution requires it to inform all members of what has been said and done. The *Record* contains a wealth of material: speeches of senators and representatives, members' votes on bills, messages from the President to Congress, periodical and newspaper articles members insert to bolster their particular position on some issue, summaries of bills introduced in Congress, and the texts of bills which become law. Most libraries have copies for anyone to read.

CLAUSE 4. Neither House, during the Session of Congress, shall, without the Consent of the other, adjourn for more than three days, nor to any other Place than that in which the two Houses shall be sitting.

Section 6

CLAUSE 1. The Senators and Representatives shall receive a Compensation for their Services, to be ascertained by Law, and paid out of the Treasury of the United States.

They shall in all Cases, except Treason, Felony and Breach of the Peace, be privileged from Arrest during their Attendance at the Session of their respective Houses, and in going to and returning from the same, and for any Speech or Debate in either House, they shall not be questioned in any other Place.

If a member of either house could be charged with libel for statements made during debate in Congress, such a ruling would seriously limit the freest possible debate in Congress. In a heated debate over an important issue a member of Congress might make an intemperate statement about another person. Under ordinary circumstances the statement would be a basis for a libel suit. But the framers of the Constitution believed it was better to allow lawmakers the freest kind of speech even if they abused the privilege. For only if all members of Congress were unafraid of airing their feelings on an issue would they have the best chance of arriving at a wise decision.

CLAUSE 2. No Senator or Representative shall, during the Time for which he was elected, be appointed to any civil Office under the Authority of the United States, which shall have been created, or the Emoluments whereof shall have been encreased during such time; and no Person holding any Office under the United States, shall be a Member of either House during his Continuance in Office.

The framers wanted to keep the branches of government separate so each could balance out the powers of the others. This provision of the Constitution prohibits a member of Congress from simultaneously holding an office in the executive or judiciary branch of government.

Section 7

CLAUSE 1. All Bills for raising Revenue shall originate in the House of Representatives; but the Senate may propose or concur with Amendments as on other Bills.

The framers of the Constitution did not like the idea of taxation any more than people do today. But they knew that the government had to have the power to tax. Therefore, they compromised and stated that taxes should originate only in the branch of government closest to the people. Thus if members of the House voted too many oppressive taxes, the people could vote them out of office every two years.

CLAUSE 2. Every Bill which shall have passed the House

of Representatives and the Senate, shall, before it becomes a Law, be presented to the President of the United States; If he approves he shall sign it, but if not he shall return it, with his Objections to that House in which it shall have originated, who shall enter the Objections at large on their Journal, and proceed to reconsider it. If after such Reconsideration two thirds of that House shall agree to pass the Bill, it shall be sent, together with the Objections, to the other House, by which it shall likewise be reconsidered, and if approved by two thirds of that House, it shall become a Law. But in all such Cases the votes of both Houses shall be determined by Yeas and Nays, and the Names of the Persons voting for and against the Bill shall be entered on the Journal of each house respectively. If any Bill shall not be returned by the President within ten Days (Sundays excepted) after it shall have been presented to him, the Same shall be a Law, in like Manner as if he had signed it, unless the Congress by their Adjournment prevent its Return, in which Case it shall not be a Law.

The section of the Constitution that explains the President's power to disapprove acts of Congress is under the article that describes the powers of the legislature. The framers saw the President's veto as related to Congress' power: the veto was an attempt to check immoderate congressional power.

Note that a bill can become law in two ways: the President may sign it into law, or if he fails to sign it within ten days it automatically becomes a law. These alternatives give the President a chance to show his approval or disapproval of the bill.

The President has two ways of vetoing a bill. He can veto it during the normal course of a session of Congress or in the last few days of a congressional session he can exercise what is known as a "pocket veto." Toward the end of a congressional session Congress tries to hurry with its business and a lot of bills are passed. In this case if the President fails to sign a bill and there are fewer than ten days left in the legislative session, the bill is vetoed.

Voting by *yeas and nays* means that the vote of each member of the Senate and House is recorded in the *Congressional Record*. This allows anyone who is interested, including senators and representatives, to find out how a certain member of Congress voted. Occasionally, bills are passed or rejected by voice vote, in which case no names are recorded. But the overriding of a veto is so important that the framers wanted everyone to know how the congressmen voted.

CLAUSE 3. Every Order, Resolution, or Vote to which the Concurrence of the Senate and House of Representatives may be necessary (except on a question of Adjournment) shall be presented to the President of the United States; and before the Same shall take Effect, shall be approved by him, or being disapproved by him, shall be repassed by two thirds of the Senate and House of Representatives, according to the Rules and Limitations prescribed in the Case of a Bill.

Section 8

Section 8 contains the heart of the powers granted to Congress. These powers are perhaps the most important difference between the Congress under the Constitution and the Congress of the Confederation. The powers granted to Congress in this section are the powers that helped make the constitutional government a successful one. But Congress has had to be sure that it passed laws only within the limits of the powers granted to it. And congressmen and Supreme Court justices have often disagreed about the exact nature of the powers.

CLAUSE 1. The Congress shall have Power To lay and collect Taxes, Duties, Imposts and Excises, to pay the Debts and provide for the common Defence and general Welfare of the United States; but all Duties, Imposts and Excises shall be uniform throughout the United States;

Most of this section is very specific about Congress' power to tax, but the words *general welfare* were vague enough to allow for considerable disagreement. Some people have interpreted this clause to mean that Congress can pass laws for the specific purposes mentioned and for the general welfare, but not for the specific purpose of merely providing for the general welfare. More recently, though, the courts have permitted such laws as the Social Security Act of 1935 (*see pp. 209–210*), a law designed solely for the general welfare. Chapters 7 and 8 have some of the courts' decisions on this issue.

CLAUSE 2. To borrow Money on the credit of the United States;
CLAUSE 3. To regulate Commerce with foreign Nations, and among the several States, and with the Indian Tribes;

This section, often referred to as the "interstate commerce" clause, is an example of the framers' failure to make statements that left no room for doubt. The framers thought of interstate commerce in the very limited sense of goods such as wheat from Pennsylvania that were transported to other colonies. The colonists had a lively trade, though certainly not as complicated as it is today. In the past 175 years the words "interstate commerce" have come to apply to many other things than manufactured and agricultural goods. Things such as telephone service, radio and television broadcasts, telegrams, large trucking companies, and railroads are a kind of commerce between states. Congress has acquired the right to regulate these things because the Supreme Court has included them under the term "interstate commerce." As one would expect, there has been disagreement over the term (*see pp. 6–8*). Since 1964 public accommodations have been regulated by Congress as part of interstate commerce. (*See Heart of Atlanta Motel* v. *United States, pp. 232–235.*)

CLAUSE 4. To establish an uniform Rule of Naturalization, and uniform Laws on the subject of Bankruptcies throughout the United States;

CLAUSE 5. To coin Money, regulate the Value thereof, and of foreign Coin, and fix the Standard of Weights and Measures;

CLAUSE 6. To provide for the Punishment of counterfeiting the Securities and current Coin of the United States;

CLAUSE 7. To establish Post Offices and post Roads;

CLAUSE 8. To promote the Progress of Science and useful Arts, by securing for limited Times to Authors and Inventors the exclusive Right to their respective Writings and Discoveries;

These rights are copyrights and patents.

CLAUSE 9. To constitute Tribunals inferior to the supreme Court;

CLAUSE 10. To define and punish Piracies and Felonies committed on the high Seas, and Offences against the Law of Nations;

CLAUSE 11. To declare War, grant Letters of Marque and Reprisal, and make Rules concerning Captures on Land and Water;

While only Congress can declare war, the power of the Commander-in-Chief of the army and navy gives to the President an opportunity to use armed forces in conflicts without a formal declaration of war. In these cases, however, Congress approves the use of armed forces either by voting funds or by voting a joint resolution approving the policy. Thus Congress also can express disapproval of his actions.

Letters of marque and reprisal were commissions allowing privately owned vessels to engage in warfare against foreign ships. Usually when a private ship attacked the ship of another nation, its act was considered piracy. In times of war or hostility the government would permit private ships to act as a kind of navy—to attack enemy ships without being prosecuted for piracy.

CLAUSE 12. To raise and support Armies, but no Appropriation of Money to that Use shall be for a longer Term than two Years;

The colonials did not have a standing army, but when necessary a farmer would put down his plow and pick up his rifle to defend his home. Many of the battles of the Revolutionary War were fought with a small volunteer army supplemented by farmer-patriots from the surrounding area who joined the battle to protect their homes.

The only standing army the colonists knew was the oppressive British army the colonists had come to fear in their fight for independence. Therefore, the framers made clear that the new United States was not going to have an army powerful enough to influence the policies of the nation.

CLAUSE 13. To provide and maintain a Navy;

CLAUSE 14. To make Rules for the Government and Regulation of the land and naval Forces;

CLAUSE 15. To provide for calling forth the Militia to execute the Laws of the Union, suppress Insurrections and repel Invasions;

CLAUSE 16. To provide for organizing, arming, and disciplining the Militia, and for governing such Part of them as may be employed in the Service of the United States, reserving to the States respectively, the Appointment of the Officers, and the Authority of training the Militia according to the discipline prescribed by Congress;

CLAUSE 17. To exercise exclusive Legislation in all Cases whatsoever, over such District (not exceeding ten Miles square) as may, by Cession of particular States, and the Acceptance of Congress, become the Seat of the Government of the United States, and to exercise like Authority over all Places purchased by the Consent of the Legislature of the State in which the Same shall be, for the Erection of Forts, Magazines, Arsenals, dock-Yards, and other needful Buildings;—And

CLAUSE 18. To make all Laws which shall be necessary and proper for carrying into Execution the foregoing Powers, and all other Powers vested by this Constitution in the Government of the United States, or in any Department or Officer thereof.

This clause, sometimes called the "elastic" clause, has been controversial, since the exact meaning of *necessary and proper* is subject to

debate. Some people have argued that the "necessary laws" were those that carefully followed the powers listed in the previous seventeen clauses. They were quite strict about limiting the powers of Congress. But others placed a looser meaning on the words "necessary and proper," and they would permit any law that was implied or sug- gested by the listed powers. Thus this clause was interpreted in different ways by loose and strict constructionists to support their understandings of the Constitution.

Section 9

CLAUSE 1. The Migration or Importation of such Persons as any of the States now existing shall think proper to admit, shall not be prohibited by the Congress prior to the Year one thousand eight hundred and eight, but a Tax or duty may be imposed on such Importation, not exceeding ten dollars for each Person.

This clause, which prohibits Congress from banning the slave trade before 1808, was a compromise measure. Southern delegates to the Philadelphia Convention wanted a two-thirds majority in Congress required for approval of trade and navigation acts, since they felt many of these acts would aid Northern interests (*see p. 4*) and damage their agricultural exports. But in place of the two-thirds majority they wanted, Southerners were persuaded to accept this clause. The slave trade could not be prohibited until 1808.

CLAUSE 2. The Privilege of the Writ of Habeas Corpus shall not be suspended, unless when in Cases of Rebellion or Invasion the public Safety may require it.

The literal translation of the Latin phrase *habeas corpus* is "you should have the body." A writ of habeas corpus is an order by a judge to the sheriff, peace officer, or jailer to produce the subject named in the writ in court. Habeas corpus today generally means that a person has a right to demand that the sheriff bring him before a judge to see if he has been rightfully accused of a crime. There are several different kinds of habeas corpus, though all demand that the imprisoned individual be brought before a judge.

CLAUSE 3. No Bill of Attainder or ex post facto Law shall be passed.

A *bill of attainder* is an act of a legislature that punishes an individual without benefit of a trial; this method of punishment was used by the English parliament against its citizens. An *ex post facto law* is defined by the Supreme Court as a law that "makes an action done before the passing of the law, and which was innocent when done, criminal, and punishes such action." However, laws dealing with civil matters may be retroactive, since these matters do not punish an individual for an innocent act. For example, Congress could grant a pay raise to federal employees in September and say it took effect as of the previous March.

CLAUSE 4. No Capitation, or other direct, tax shall be laid, unless in Proportion to the Census or Enumeration herein before directed to be taken.

No *capitation* (head) tax or other direct tax could be collected by the federal government unless it was uniformly levied on the population. The government could not directly tax one person $1 and another person $2. In George Washington's time the federal government gained its revenue chiefly from tariff duties, excise taxes, and land sales. Times changed, and the government needed new sources of revenue. This provision of the Constitution was changed in 1913 by the Sixteenth Amendment to allow for the federal income tax.

CLAUSE 5. No Tax or Duty shall be laid on Articles exported from any State.

CLAUSE 6. No Preference shall be given by any Regulation of Commerce or Revenue to the Ports of one State over those of another: nor shall Vessels bound to, or from, one State, be obliged to enter, clear, or pay Duties in another.

CLAUSE 7. No Money shall be drawn from the Treasury, but in Consequence of Appropriations made by Law; and a regular Statement and Account of the Receipts and Expenditures of all public Money shall be published from time to time.

CLAUSE 8. No Title of Nobility shall be granted by the United States: And no Person holding any Office of Profit or Trust under them, shall, without the Consent of the Congress, accept of any present, Emolument, Office, or Title, of any kind whatever, from any King, Prince, or foreign State.

Section 10

Section 10 is designed to make sure the states do not try to take over the powers the Consitution has specifically granted to the Congress or to do certain things denied to the federal government.

CLAUSE 1. No State shall enter into any Treaty, Alliance, or Confederation; grant Letters of Marque and Reprisal; coin Money; emit Bills of Credit; make any Thing but gold and silver Coin a Tender in Payment of Debts; pass any Bill of Attainder, ex post facto Law, or Law impairing the Obligation of Contracts, or grant any Title of Nobility.

CLAUSE 2. No State shall, without the Consent of the Congress, lay any Imposts or Duties on Imports or Exports, except what may be absolutely necessary for executing its inspection Laws: and the net Produce of all Duties and Imposts, laid by any State on Imports or Exports, shall be for the Use of the Treasury of the United States; and all such Laws shall be subject to the Revision and Controul of the Congress.

CLAUSE 3. No State shall, without the Consent of Congress, lay any Duty of Tonnage, keep Troops, or Ships of War in time of Peace, enter into any Agreement or Compact with another State, or with a foreign Power, or engage in War, unless actually invaded, or in such imminent Danger as will not admit of delay.

ARTICLE II

Section 1

CLAUSE 1. The Executive Power shall be vested in a President of the United States of America. He shall hold his Office during the Term of four Years, and, together with the Vice President, chosen for the same Term, be elected, as follows

CLAUSE 2. Each State shall appoint, in such Manner as the Legislature thereof may direct, a Number of Electors, equal to the whole Number of Senators and Representatives to which the State may be entitled in the Congress; but no Senator or Representative, or Person holding an Office of Trust or Profit under the United States, shall be appointed an Elector.

The framers had difficulty deciding how the President should be elected, since they felt most voters might not choose wisely. Yet if Congress or state legislators elected the President, the legislative and executive branches would not be kept separate. This separation was necessary to keep the checks and balances of power in order.

Therefore, the framers settled on an alternative known as the "electoral college." State legislators would choose the electors, who in turn would vote for the President. And ideally the electoral college would exercise its independent judgment. Thus the President would be neither the direct voice of the people nor a pawn of any legislature.

CLAUSE 3. The Electors shall meet in their respective States, and vote by ballot for two Persons, of whom one at least shall not be an Inhabitant of the same State with themselves. And they shall make a List of all the Persons voted for, and of the Number of Votes for each; which List they shall sign and certify, and transmit sealed to the Seat of the Government of the United States, directed to the President of the Senate. The President of the Senate shall, in the Presence of the Senate and House of Representatives, open all the Certificates, and the Votes shall then be counted. The Person having the greatest Number of Votes shall be the President, if such Number be a Majority of the whole Number of Electors appointed; and if there be more than one who have such Majority, and have an equal Number of Votes, then the House of Representatives shall immediately chuse by Ballot one of them for President; and if no Person have a Majority, then from the five highest on the List the said House shall in like Manner chuse the President. But in chusing the President, the Votes shall be taken by States, the Representation from each State having one Vote; A quorum for this Purpose shall consist of a Member or Members from two thirds of the States, and a Majority of all the States shall be necessary to a Choice. In every Case, after the Choice of the President, the Person having the greatest Number of Votes of the Electors shall be the Vice President. But if there should remain two or more who have equal Votes, the Senate shall chuse from them by Ballot the Vice President.

In writing this section of the Constitution, the framers assumed that the electors from each state would vote for their "favorite son," an important man from their state. The framers foresaw most elections being settled in the House of Representatives. Actually, though, the House has chosen the President only twice, in 1800 and 1824.

This portion of the Constitution was changed in 1804 after the 1800 election, in which Thomas Jefferson and Aaron Burr tied in votes for the presidency. This tie took place because the framers had not anticipated the rise of political parties.

All the Republicans cast their votes for Jefferson and Burr, although Jefferson was their choice for President and Burr for Vice President. To avoid this tie between the presidential and vice presidential candidates from the same party, the Twelfth Amendment was adopted.

Nowadays the political parties choose their candidates in a convention that meets the summer before the November presidential election; the electoral college does not exercise the free choice the framers intended it to. In fact, the electoral college has so little say in the outcome of a presidential election that many people feel that an amendment is necessary to end it. These people feel that the President should be elected by the majority of the popular vote, since in practice that is the way he is usually elected anyway.

CLAUSE 4. The Congress may determine the Time of chusing the Electors, and the Day on which they shall give their Votes; which Day shall be the same throughout the United States.

CLAUSE 5. No Person except a natural born Citizen, or a Citizen of the United States, at the time of the Adoption of this Constitution, shall be eligible to the Office of President; neither shall any Person be eligible to that Office who shall not have attained to the Age of thirty five Years, and been fourteen Years a Resident within the United States.

CLAUSE 6. In Case of the Removal of the President from Office, or of his Death, Resignation or Inability to discharge the Powers and Duties of the said Office, the same shall devolve on the Vice President, and the Congress may by Law provide for the Case of Removal, Death, Resignation or Inability, both of the President and Vice President, declaring what Officer shall then act as President, and such Officer shall act accordingly, until the Disability be removed, or a President shall be elected.

In 1947 the Presidential Succession Act provided that in event of the death of both the President and Vice President, the Speaker of the House of Representatives is next in line for the presidency. If the Speaker of the House cannot serve, the presidency would pass to the president pro tempore of the Senate, and from him to the Secretary of State, and by specified order down the list of Cabinet members.

Amendment XXV *(see pp. 49–51)* will provide for the continuous operation of the office of the presidency in the event of a presidential disability. Several times a President has been ill and there has been some question as to whether or not he should have been relieved of his duties.

CLAUSE 7. The President shall, at stated times, receive for his Services, a Compensation, which shall neither be encreased nor diminished during the Period for which he shall have been elected, and he shall not receive within that Period any other Emolument from the United States, or any of them.

In some American colonies the governor who was appointed by the king was paid by the legislative body. When the colonists were dissatisfied with the governor's actions, they could not remove him from office but they could refuse to pay him. Usually this was an effective means of getting a governor to resign. The framers did not want Congress to control the President in such a way.

CLAUSE 8. Before he enter on the Execution of his Office, he shall take the following Oath or Affirmation: – "I do solemnly swear (or affirm) that I will faithfully execute the Office of President of the United States, and will to the best of my Ability, preserve, protect and defend the Constitution of the United States."

Section 2

CLAUSE 1. The President shall be Commander in Chief of the Army and Navy of the United States, and of the Militia of the several States, when called into the actual Service of the United States; he may require the Opinion, in writing, of the principal Officer in each of the executive Departments, upon any Subject relating to the Duties of their respective Offices, and he shall have power to grant Reprieves and pardons for Offences against the United States, except in Cases of Impeachment.

In Article I, Section 8, Clause 12, the power of Congress to limit appropriations for the army is stated, and this clause too reflects a mistrust of a standing army. In this case the framers made sure that the army had little power to affect political affairs by making the President commander-in-chief, hence, the man who made final decisions.

Also, this clause is the closest the Constitution comes to recognizing the President's need for advisors. George Washington initiated what has become known as the President's Cabinet, by asking "the principal officers in each of the executive departments" to meet with him.

CLAUSE 2. He shall have Power, by and with the Advice and Consent of the Senate, to make Treaties, provided two thirds of the Senators present concur and he shall nominate, and by and with the Advice and Consent of the Senate, shall appoint Ambassadors, other public Ministers and Consuls, Judges of the supreme Court, and all other Officers of the United States, whose Appointments are not herein otherwise provided for, and which shall be established by Law: but the Congress may by Law vest the Appointment of such inferior Officers, as they think proper, in the President alone, in the Courts of Law, or in the Heads of Departments.

The Constitution provides that treaties are the supreme law of the land (*see Article VI, Section 2*). That is to say, a law that violates a treaty is null and void. Because treaties are given such importance, the framers wanted to place a safeguard or a check on the President's power to make treaties. Thus the President is required to get the advice and consent of two thirds of the Senate before a treaty is ratified. In a way the Senate's consent on treaties is similar to the President's veto power: each was designed to limit the power of the other.

CLAUSE 3. The President shall have Power to fill up all Vacancies that may happen during the Recess of the Senate, by granting Commissions which shall expire at the End of their next Session.

Section 3

He shall from time to time give to the Congress Information of the State of the Union, and recommend to their Consideration such Measures as he shall judge necessary and expedient; he may, on extraordinary Occasions, convene both Houses, or either of them, and, in Case of Disagreement between them, with Respect to the Time of Adjournment, he may adjourn them to such Time as he shall think proper; he shall receive Ambassadors and other public Ministers; he shall take Care that the Laws be faithfully executed, and shall Commission all the Officers of the United States.

The President gives the *State of the Union message,* sometimes referred to as his annual message, to Congress early each year.

The President's power to receive ambassadors has important consequences. The President can recognize a new government by receiving an ambassador; recognizing a government means that our government admits that the present government in a country is the legal one we wish to do business with. This kind of recognition is very important in international affairs. Likewise, the President can request a country to recall its ambassador, which is the equivalent of breaking diplomatic relations, an important break that sometimes precedes war.

Section 4

The President, Vice President and all civil Officers of the United States, shall be removed from Office on Impeachment for, and Conviction of, Treason, Bribery, or other high Crimes and Misdemeanors.

ARTICLE III

Just as the framers of the Constitution kept the legislative and executive branches of the government separate by refusing to let Congress elect the President, likewise the framers were concerned with keeping the judiciary free. This separation was designed to permit the courts to decide the merits of a case on the evidence within the case itself and without interference from other branches of the government.

Section 1

The judicial Power of the United States, shall be vested in one supreme Court, and in such inferior Courts as the Congress may from time to time ordain and establish. The Judges, both of the supreme and inferior Courts, shall hold their Offices during good Behaviour, and shall, at stated Times, receive for their Services, a Compensation, which shall not be diminished during their Continuance in Office.

One way the framers kept the courts separate from the other branches of government was to permit a judge to hold office *during good behavior,* which meant for life unless his behavior gave cause for his removal. This was an important judicial principle that the English courts had had to fight to establish. Early English kings had felt that a judge should hold his office as long as the judge's rulings pleased the king. Until about one hundred years before the writing of our Constitution, English judges had been subject to dismissal by the king at his pleasure. Thus the framers wanted to make sure that the judges were free from coercion by assuring a judge his job for life.

Section 2

CLAUSE 1. The judicial Power shall extend to all Cases, in Law and Equity, arising under this Constitution, the Laws of the United States, and Treaties made, or which shall be made, under their Authority;—to all Cases affect-

30

ing Ambassadors, other public Ministers and Consuls; — to all Cases of admiralty and maritime Jurisdiction; — to Controversies to which the United States shall be a Party; — to Controversies between two or more States; — between a State and Citizens of another State; — between Citizens of different States; — between Citizens of the same State claiming Lands under Grants of different States, and between a State, or the Citizens thereof, and foreign States, Citizens or Subjects.

In England common law was developed over a long period by court decisions. Some people felt they had been wronged but could find no remedy under the common law since the situation was not covered. Therefore, the king established a set of courts that became known as the equity courts. They were supposed to overcome the complexities of common law and the absence of laws. The practice of common law and equity courts was used in Colonial America. Thus it was natural that this clause of the Constitution should refer to them. However, very few states today have equity courts, since legislatures attempt to cover all possible injustices that could occur in our regular courts. Federal courts, however, act in equity — that is, act or rule in order to be equitable, or fair. A court can issue an injunction in equity to restrain a person from an act that may harm others.

The provision *between a state and citizen of another state* has since been changed by the Eleventh Amendment *(see p. 40).*

CLAUSE 2. In all Cases affecting Ambassadors, other public Ministers and Consuls, and those in which a State shall be Party, the supreme Court shall have original Jurisdiction. In all other Cases before mentioned, the supreme Court shall have appellate Jurisdiction, both as to Law and Fact, with such Exceptions, and under such Regulations as the Congress shall make.

The framers of the Constitution listed the most important kinds of cases they thought should be considered by the Supreme Court. The court was given *original jurisdiction;* that is, the Supreme Court was to rule on the case without having lower courts rule first.

CLAUSE 3. The Trial of all Crimes, except in Cases of Impeachment, shall be by Jury; and such Trial shall be held in the State where the said Crimes shall have been committed; but when not committed within any State, the Trial shall be at such Place or Places as the Congress may by Law have directed.

The provisions for jury trial came from English common law, which had established that a twelve-man jury must come to a unanimous verdict on each case it tries.

Section 3

CLAUSE 1. Treason against the United States, shall consist only in levying War against them, or in adhering to their Enemies, giving them Aid and Comfort. No Person shall be convicted of Treason unless on the Testimony of two Witnesses to the same overt Act, or on Confession in open Court.

The treason laws here are very specific because English kings had punished their enemies for treason when the person's crime really was opposing the policies of the king. However, English law slowly tried to clarify the laws surrounding treason, and one provision they had established for the welfare of the prisoners was that two witnesses were necessary for conviction. Thus the framers of the Constitution incorporated this provision in their law to avoid abuses of the law.

CLAUSE 2. The Congress shall have Power to declare the Punishment of Treason, but no Attainder of Treason shall work Corruption of Blood, or Forfeiture except during the Life of the Person attainted.

In England, when a person was convicted of treason, the king could take away the person's property and deny his heirs the right to inherit. Thus the person and his family were punished for treason. The Constitution specifies that the punishment for treason is to extend to the life of the person who committed the act, and is not to extend to his relatives.

ARTICLE IV

Section 1

Full Faith and Credit shall be given in each State to the public Acts, Records, and judicial Proceedings of every other State. And the Congress may by general Laws prescribe the Manner in which such Acts, Records and Proceedings shall be proved, and the Effect thereof.

Documents such as mortgages, wills, deeds, contracts, judicial decisions, and other legal papers that are valid in one state must be accepted at face value by all the other states. The Supreme Court has ruled, however, that one state does not have to enforce the criminal laws of another.

Section 2

CLAUSE 1. The Citizens of each State shall be entitled to all Privileges and Immunities of Citizens in the several States.

Examples of these *privileges and immunities* would be the right to travel, live, and do business in any state without undue restrictions such as passports. There are limitations to these privileges in such areas as the licenses needed to practice medicine, law, and dentistry. In these cases the citizen of another state must meet each state's requirements in order to be licensed in that particular state.

CLAUSE 2. A person charged in any State with Treason, Felony, or other Crime, who shall flee from Justice, and be found in another State, shall on Demand of the executive Authority of the State from which he fled, be delivered up, to be removed to the State having Jurisdiction of the Crime.

This Constitutional provision whereby a fugitive from justice is returned to the state in which he committed his crime is called rendition. Although the clause reads "shall . . . be delivered up," the Supreme Court has held that the provision is morally but not legally binding. Therefore the governor of a state may refuse to return a fugitive; he may decide the prisoner has not had a fair trial or the other state's laws are too harsh. However, usually the governor does permit rendition, or extradition.

CLAUSE 3. No Person held to Service or Labour in one State, under the Laws thereof, escaping into another, shall, in Consequence of any Law or Regulation therein, be discharged from such Service or Labour, but shall be delivered up on Claim of the Party to whom such Service or Labour may be due.

Before slavery and indenture ended in this country, this law meant that an escaped slave or servant had to be returned to his owner or master—that even when a slave escaped into a state that forbade slavery, the slave still had to be returned, since he was a slave under the laws of the state from which he fled. This clause is no longer in effect.

Section 3

CLAUSE 1. New States may be admitted by the Congress into this Union; but no new State shall be formed or

33

erected within the Jurisdiction of any other State; nor any State be formed by the Junction of two or more States, or Parts of States, without the Consent of the Legislatures of the States concerned as well as of the Congress.

Five states which had been parts of other states were admitted under this clause with consent of Congress. These were Vermont from New York, Kentucky from Virginia, Tennessee from North Carolina, Maine from Massachusetts, and West Virginia from Virginia.

CLAUSE 2. The Congress shall have Power to dispose of and make all needful Rules and Regulations respecting the Territory or other Property belonging to the United States; and nothing in this Constitution shall be so construed as to Prejudice any Claims of the United States, or of any particular State.

Section 4

The United States shall guarantee to every State in this Union a Republican Form of Government, and shall protect each of them against Invasion; and on Application of the Legislature, or of the Executive (when the Legislature cannot be convened) against domestic Violence.

The Constitution does not define the term *republican form of government*. James Madison, one of the framers, defined a republic as one "which derives all its powers directly or indirectly from the great body of the people, and is administered by persons holding offices during pleasure, for a limited period, or during good behavior." Except for a period following the Civil War in the South, the federal government has not imposed its will on state governments under this clause.

ARTICLE V

The Congress, whenever two thirds of both houses shall deem it necessary, shall propose Amendments to this Constitution, or, on the Application of the Legislatures of two thirds of the several States, shall call a Convention for proposing Amendments, which, in either Case, shall be valid to all Intents and Purposes, as Part of this Constitution, when ratified by the Legislatures of three fourths of the several States, or by Conventions in three fourths

34

thereof, as the one or the other Mode of Ratification may be proposed by the Congress; Provided that no Amendment which may be made prior to the Year One thousand eight hundred and eight shall in any Manner affect the first and fourth Clauses in the Ninth Section of the first Article; and that no State, without its Consent, shall be deprived of its equal Suffrage in the Senate.

ARTICLE VI

Section 1

All Debts contracted and Engagements entered into, before the Adoption of this Constitution, shall be as valid against the United States under this Constitution, as under the Confederation.

Section 2

This Constitution, and the Laws of the United States which shall be made in Pursuance thereof; and all Treaties made, or which shall be made, under the Authority of the United States, shall be the supreme Law of the Land; and the Judges in every State shall be bound thereby, any Thing in the Constitution or Laws of any State to the Contrary notwithstanding.

Without this section the Constitution would have had little authority. If the framers had not made clear that the Constitution was to be the "supreme" law and that there was no higher law, the dispute between laws of state and federal governments could have torn the new government apart because there would have been no way of deciding whether state or federal law was supreme.

Section 3

The Senators and Representatives before mentioned, and the Members of the several State Legislatures, and all executive and judicial Officers, both of the United States and of the several States, shall be bound by Oath or Affirmation, to support this Constitution; but no religious Test shall ever be required as a Qualification to any Office or public Trust under the United States.

ARTICLE VII

The Ratification of the Convention of nine States, shall be sufficient for the Establishment of this Constitution between the States so ratifying the Same.

DONE in Convention by the Unanimous Consent of the States present the Seventeenth Day of September in the Year of our Lord one thousand seven hundred and Eighty seven and of the Independence of the United States of America the Twelfth. IN WITNESS whereof We have hereunto subscribed our Names.

G°. Washington
Presid^t and deputy from Virginia

The Articles of Confederation had required unanimous consent for changes. The men at the Philadelphia convention knew that if they required ratification by thirteen states for the Constitution, the new government would never become operative. Therefore the framers provided that only nine states need ratify. They hoped that after nine states had ratified, the other four would be forced to join in their own self-interest.

Amendments

The Constitution is concerned mainly with describing the nature of a new government and describing the extent and limits of its power. Many people objected to the Constitution because they felt that there were few guarantees that the government would not violate the rights of the individual. Although the Constitution did guarantee the right to a writ of habeas corpus, it did not safeguard such rights as free speech and the freedom of assembly.

Nevertheless, this shortcoming was soon overcome when the Bill of Rights, or the first ten amendments, was adopted. These ten amendments to the Constitution are given a particular name because they are distinct from the Constitution and the other amendments. These amendments were designed to safeguard those individual rights that Thomas Jefferson had called "certain unalienable rights" in the Declaration of Independence.

AMENDMENT I

Congress shall make no law respecting an establishment of religion, or prohibiting the free exercise thereof; or abridging the freedom of speech, or of the press; or the right of the people peaceably to assemble, and to petition the Government for a redress of grievances.

One purpose of this amendment was to prevent the creation of an officially supported church in the United States. The question has arisen as to the degree to which the federal government may support any religious group. Most Supreme Court decisions have ruled in favor of a strict separation. For example, the court ruled that public funds could be used to bus children to public and parochial schools but that prayers written by state officials may not be used in the public schools.

The right to free speech is one that the citizens have jealously guarded. However, the Supreme Court had upheld federal legislation limiting free speech in times of war when the speech would present a "clear and present danger" to the safety of the nation.

AMENDMENT II

A well regulated Militia, being necessary to the security of a free State, the right of the people to keep and bear Arms, shall not be infringed.

In a frontier life firearms were necessary. Frontier settlers used arms to secure food and to defend themselves. This is one reason the Bill of Rights secures this privilege. However, the right to keep and bear arms does not mean that states are not permitted to regulate firearms. A state may require a permit for carrying a gun.

AMENDMENT III

No Soldier shall, in time of peace, be quartered in any house, without the consent of the Owner, nor in time of war, but in a manner to be prescribed by law.

This article was designed to prevent the government from following the British practice before the Revolution of quartering troops in private homes. There was a strong reaction in Colonial times against this practice.

AMENDMENT IV

The right of the people to be secure in their persons, houses, papers, and effects, against unreasonable searches and seizures, shall not be violated and no Warrants shall issue but upon probable cause supported by Oath or

Affirmation, and particularly describing the place to be searched, and the persons or things to be seized.

This article assured citizens they would not be subjected to arbitrary interference by government agents in their private affairs. This does not mean that agents can never search one's property; it means they must show cause why they think a search is justified and then a judge will issue a warrant permitting them to search.

AMENDMENT V

No person shall be held to answer for a capital, or otherwise infamous crime, unless on a presentment or indictment of a Grand Jury, except in cases arising in the land or naval forces, or in the Militia, when in actual service in time of War or public danger; nor shall any person be subject for the same offence to be twice put in jeopardy of life or limb; nor shall be compelled in any Criminal Case to be a witness against himself, nor be deprived of life, liberty, or property, without due process of law; nor shall private property be taken for public use, without just compensation.

The *grand jury* determines whether there is enough evidence to bring a person to trial for the crimes the state has set forth.

Some people do not like the provision that a person does not have to testify against himself; he may remain silent and answer no questions. Although the Constitution does not intend this, some people feel that when a person refuses to answer questions he is guilty and is hiding something. Actually, when a person refuses to testify against himself, he is invoking a right that has a long history in English and American law.

The *due process of law* clause has been a source of controversy because the Supreme Court has voided

social legislation based on this clause. The federal government attempted to set a minimum wage for women and children working in the District of Columbia. But the Supreme Court voided the law because the minimum-wage law violated the due-process clause by depriving the women, children, and employer of their liberty to agree to lower wages if they desired.

Governments have the right of *eminent domain* – the right to take private property when it is in the public interest. This amendment, however, safeguards abuses of this right by assuring the individual he will receive "just compensation" for his property.

AMENDMENT VI

In all criminal prosecutions, the accused shall enjoy the right to a speedy and public trial, by an impartial jury of the State and district wherein the crime shall have been committed, which district shall have been previously ascertained by law, and to be informed of the nature and cause of the accusation; to be confronted with the witnesses against him; to have compulsory process for obtaining Witnesses in his favor, and to have the Assistance of Counsel for his defence.

AMENDMENT VII

In suits at common law, where the value in controversy shall exceed twenty dollars, the right of trial by jury shall be preserved, and no fact tried by a jury shall be otherwise re-examined in any Court of the United States, than according to the rules of the common law.

AMENDMENT VIII

Excessive bail shall not be required, nor excessive fines imposed, nor cruel and unusual punishments inflicted.

AMENDMENT IX

The enumeration in the Constitution, of certain rights, shall not be construed to deny or disparage others retained by the people.

The absence of mention of an individual right in the Constitution does not necessarily mean that the individual does not have that right. And one is not to assume that the unspecified rights are not still retained by the individual.

AMENDMENT X

The powers not delegated to the United States by the Constitution, nor prohibited by it to the States, are reserved to the States respectively, or to the people.

The purpose of this amendment was to clarify the federal government-state government relationship. But there has been bitter controversy over the meaning of the amendment. Many people who feel that the federal government has an extraordinary amount of power interpret this clause to mean that only those powers specifically spelled out in the Constitution belong to the federal government. All other powers belong to the states. Many people who jealously guard the power of the state governments feel that the "delegated powers" of the federal government are quite limited.

AMENDMENT XI

The Judicial power of the United States shall not be construed to extend to any suit in law or equity, commenced or prosecuted against one of the United States by Citizens of another State, or by Citizens or Subjects of any Foreign State.

This amendment changed Article III, Section 2, Clause 1.

AMENDMENT XII

The Electors shall meet in their respective states, and vote by ballot for President and Vice-President, one of whom, at least, shall not be an inhabitant of the same state with themselves; they shall name in their ballots the person voted for as President, and in distinct ballots the person voted for as Vice-President; and they shall make distinct lists of all Persons voted for as President, and of all persons voted for as Vice-President and of the number of votes for each, which lists they shall sign and certify, and transmit sealed to the seat of the Government of the United States, directed to the President of the Senate;—The President of the Senate shall, in the presence of the Senate and House of Representatives, open all the certificates and the votes shall then be counted;—The person having the greatest number of votes for President, shall be the President, if such number be a majority of the whole number of Electors appointed; and if no person have such majority, then from the persons having the highest numbers not exceeding three on the list of those voted for as President, the House of Representatives shall choose immediately, by ballot, the President. But in choosing the President, the votes shall be taken by states, the representation from each state having one vote; a quorum for this purpose shall consist of a member or members from two-thirds of the states, and a majority of all the states shall be necessary to a choice. And if the

House of Representatives shall not choose a President whenever the right of choice shall devolve upon them, before the fourth day of March next following, then the Vice-President shall act as President, as in the case of the death or other constitutional disability of the President. The person having the greatest number of votes as Vice-President, shall be the Vice-President, if such number be a majority of the whole number of Electors appointed, and if no person have a majority, then from the two highest numbers on the list, the Senate shall choose the Vice-President; a quorum for the purpose shall consist of two-thirds of the whole number of Senators, and a majority of the whole number shall be necessary to a choice. But no person constitutionally ineligible to the office of President shall be eligible to that of the Vice-President of the United States.

Although this amendment avoids a tie between the presidential and vice presidential candidates of the same party (*see pp.* 26–27), many people feel that the amendment did not do enough to solve the problems of the electoral college. Presidents have been elected when they polled fewer popular votes than their opponents; Samuel J. Tilden and Grover Cleveland polled more popular votes than Rutherford B. Hayes and Benjamin Harrison, who were elected to the presidency by the electoral college. Also, unless a state requires members of the electoral college to vote for the names on the ballot, theoretically a member of the electoral college is free to vote as he chooses. While this rarely happens, it is still a legal possibility.

AMENDMENT XIII

Section 1

Neither slavery nor involuntary servitude, except as a punishment for crime whereof the party shall have been duly convicted, shall exist within the United States, or any place subject to their jurisdiction.

Section 2

Congress shall have power to enforce this article by appropriate legislation.

This amendment and the following one were ratified shortly after the Civil War to free the slaves.

41

AMENDMENT XIV

Section 1

All persons born or naturalized in the United States, and subject to the jurisdiction thereof, are citizens of the United States and of the State wherein they reside. No State shall make or enforce any law which shall abridge the privileges or immunities of citizens of the United States; nor shall any State deprive any person of life, liberty, or property, without due process of law; nor deny to any person within its jurisdiction the equal protection of the laws.

This amendment was designed to give the freed Negro the rights of full citizenship by preventing states from passing laws which might establish slavery again. Despite the provisions of Section 1, Southern states made laws that did not violate the wording of the amendment but which did enforce segregation of the Negro population. Recently, however, the federal government has passed laws attempting to uphold the intention of the Fourteenth Amendment.

Section 2

Representatives shall be apportioned among the several States according to their respective numbers, counting the whole number of persons in each State, excluding Indians not taxed. But when the right to vote at any election for the choice of electors for President and Vice President of the United States, Representatives in Congress, the Executive and Judicial officers of a State, or the members of the Legislature thereof, is denied to any of the male inhabitants of such State, being twenty-one years of age, and citizens of the United States, or in any way abridged, except for participation in rebellion, or other crime, the basis of representation therein shall be reduced in the proportion which the number of such male citizens shall bear to the whole number of male citizens twenty-one years of age in such State.

This section, and the two that follow, were designed to punish those who had aided the Southern cause during the Civil War.

Section 3

No person shall be a Senator or Representative in Congress, or elector of President and Vice President, or hold any office, civil or military, under the United States, or under any State, who, having previously taken an oath, as a member of Congress, or as an officer of the United States, or as a member of any State legislature, or as an executive or judicial officer of any State, to support the Constitution of the United States, shall have engaged in insurrection or rebellion against the same, or given aid or comfort to the enemies thereof. But Congress may by a vote of two-thirds of each House, remove such disability.

Section 4

The validity of the public debt of the United States, authorized by law, including debts incurred for payment of pensions and bounties for services in suppressing insurrection or rebellion, shall not be questioned. But neither the United States nor any State shall assume or pay any debt or obligation incurred in aid of insurrection or rebellion against the United States, or any claim for the loss or emancipation of any slave; but all such debts, obligations and claims shall be held illegal and void.

Section 5

The Congress shall have power to enforce, by appropriate legislation, the provisions of this article.

AMENDMENT XV

Section 1

The right of citizens of the United States to vote shall not be denied or abridged by the United States or by any State on account of race, color, or previous condition of servitude.

Section 2

The Congress shall have power to enforce this article by appropriate legislation.

This amendment attempted to assure freed Negroes the right to vote. However, it was circumvented in some states by poll taxes, by literacy tests, and by other practices. The Voting Rights Act of 1965 was an effort to implement Section 2 of this amendment.

AMENDMENT XVI

The Congress shall have power to lay and collect taxes on incomes, from whatever source derived, without apportionment among the several states, and without regard to any census or enumeration.

In 1895 the Supreme Court invalidated an income tax law that had been passed the year before. But this amendment was adopted in 1913 to meet the public's demand for this form of taxation.

AMENDMENT XVII

CLAUSE 1. The Senate of the United States shall be composed of two senators from each State, elected by the people thereof, for six years; and each Senator shall have one vote. The electors in each State shall have the qualifications requisite for electors of the most numerous branch of the State legislature.

CLAUSE 2. When vacancies happen in the representation of any State in the Senate, the executive authority of such State shall issue writs of election to fill such vacancies: PROVIDED, That the legislature of any State may empower the executive thereof to make temporary appointments until the people fill the vacancies by election as the legislature may direct.

CLAUSE 3. This amendment shall not be so construed as to affect the election or term of any senator chosen before it becomes valid as part of the Constitution.

In the early twentieth century there was a great desire for reform. (*See Chapter* 7.) Many people felt that senators were elected by state legislatures that in turn were controlled by a few important businessmen. This mistrust, coupled with popular demand, brought about this amendment in 1913.

AMENDMENT XVIII

Section 1

After one year from the ratification of this article, the manufacture, sale, or transportation of intoxicating liquors within, the importation thereof into, or the exportation thereof from the United States and all territory subject to the jurisdiction thereof for beverage purposes is hereby prohibited.

Section 2

The Congress and the several States shall have concurrent power to enforce this article by appropriate legislation.

Section 3

This article shall be inoperative unless it shall have been ratified as an amendment to the Constitution by the legislatures of the several States, as provided in the Constitution, within seven years from the date of the submission hereof to the States by the Congress.

This amendment was repealed by the Twenty-first Amendment.

AMENDMENT XIX

CLAUSE 1. The right of citizens of the United States to vote shall not be denied or abridged by the United States or by any State on account of sex.
CLAUSE 2. The Congress shall have power, by appropriate legislation, to enforce the provisions of this article.

The women's rights movement, dating from the early part of the last century, worked toward a number of reforms to give women more economic and legal rights. This amendment was a great step forward in their fight for equal rights. (*See Chapter 7 of the text, pp. 158–165.*)

AMENDMENT XX

Section 1

The terms of the President and Vice-President shall end at noon on the twentieth day of January, and the terms of Senators and Representatives at noon on the third day of January, of the years in which such terms would have ended if this article had not been ratified; and the terms of their successors shall then begin.

Section 2

The Congress shall assemble at least once in every year, and such meeting shall begin at noon on the third day of January, unless they shall by law appoint a different day.

Section 3

If, at the time fixed for the beginning of the term of the President, the President-elect shall have died, the Vice-President-elect shall become President. If a President shall not have been chosen before the time fixed for the beginning of his term, or if the President-elect shall have failed to qualify, then the Vice-President-elect shall act as President until a President shall have qualified; and the Congress may by law provide for the case wherein neither a President-elect nor a Vice-President-elect shall have qualified, declaring who shall then act as President, or the manner in which one who is to act shall be selected, and such person shall act accordingly until a President or Vice-President shall have qualified.

Section 4

The Congress may by law provide for the case of the death of any of the persons from whom the House of Representatives may choose a President whenever the right of choice shall have devolved upon them, and for the case of the death of any of the persons from whom the Senate may choose a Vice-President whenever the right of choice shall have devolved upon them.

Section 5

Sections 1 and 2 shall take effect on the 15th day of October following the ratification of this article.

Section 6

This article shall be inoperative unless it shall have been ratified as an amendment to the Constitution by the legislatures of three-fourths of the several States within seven years from the date of its submission.

This amendment was necessary to adjust the provisions of the old Constitutional date for Congress and the inauguration of the President to a society in which transportation and communication had rapidly advanced. For a discussion of these changes see Article 1, Section 4, Clause 2 on page 16.

AMENDMENT XXI

Section 1

The eighteenth article of amendment to the Constitution of the United States is hereby repealed.

Section 2

The transportation or importation into any State, Territory or possession of the United States for delivery or use therein of intoxicating liquors, in violation of the laws thereof, is hereby prohibited.

Section 3

This article shall be inoperative unless it shall have been ratified as an amendment to the Constitution by convention in the several States, as provided in the Constitution, within seven years from the date of the submission hereof to the States by the Congress.

AMENDMENT XXII

Section 1

No person shall be elected to the office of the President more than twice, and no person who has held the office of President, or acted as President, for more than two years of a term to which some other person was elected President shall be elected to the office of the President more than once. But this Article shall not apply to any person holding the office of President when this Article was proposed by the Congress, and shall not prevent any person who may be holding the office of President, or acting as President, during the term within which this

Article becomes operative from holding the office of President or acting as President during the remainder of such term.

Section 2

This article shall be inoperative unless it shall have been ratified as an amendment to the Constitution by the legislatures of three fourths of the several States within seven years from the date of its submission to the States by the Congress.

This amendment has been controversial. The amendment was partially inspired by the fact that Franklin D. Roosevelt had been elected to an unprecedented four terms. Many people feel that this provision is harmful because it makes the President a "lame duck" in his second term, since he cannot succeed himself. Others feel that in a time of crisis such as a war it might be unwise to change leaders just because a President had already served two terms.

AMENDMENT XXIII

Section 1

The District constituting the seat of Government of the United States shall appoint in such manner as the Congress may direct:

A number of electors of President and Vice President equal to the whole number of Senators and Representatives in Congress to which the District would be entitled if it were a State, but in no event more than the least populous State; they shall be in addition to those appointed by the States, but they shall be considered, for the purposes of the election of President and Vice President, to be electors appointed by a State; and they shall meet in the District and perform such duties as provided by the twelfth article of amendment.

Section 2

The Congress shall have power to enforce this article by appropriate legislation.

This amendment allows residents of the District of Columbia to vote in presidential elections.

48

AMENDMENT XXIV

Section 1

The right of citizens of the United States to vote in any primary or other election for President or Vice President, for electors for President or Vice President, or for Senator or Representative in Congress, shall not be denied or abridged by the United States or any State by reason of failure to pay any poll tax or other tax.

Section 2

The Congress shall have the power to enforce this article by appropriate legislation.

This amendment is another step in the history of the amendments that have attempted to expand and secure the right to vote.

AMENDMENT XXV

At the time of President Kennedy's assassination the country took a close look at the constitutional provisions for succession to the Presidency. When Vice President Johnson became President, the office of Vice President became vacant for the remainder of his term. It was obvious that an amendment was needed to allow appointment of a new Vice President and to clarify the complicated question of succession.

At another time it might be possible that the President would be alive but disabled, mentally or physically. At that time the Vice President should assume his duties as Acting President. Both President Eisenhower and President Johnson have undergone surgery while in office, each appointing his Vice President to replace him if necessary. Luckily, it never became necessary for the Vice President to exercise his power. But if it had been necessary and this solution had been challenged, the Supreme Court might not have found it acceptable!

In December, 1963, an amendment was introduced providing the conditions under which the Vice President may assume the Presidency. After many debates and conferences, the Twenty-fifth Amendment was approved and sent in July, 1965, to the states for ratification. Finally, with several state legislatures competing to be the thirty-eighth to ratify, the Twenty-fifth Amendment received ratification by the necessary three fourths of the states and became law. Thus, on February 10, 1967, after almost 200 years, the conditions for the succession of the Vice President to the Presidency were clearly defined.

Section 1

In case of the removal of the President from office or of his death or resignation, the Vice President shall become President.

Section 2

Whenever there is a vacancy in the office of the Vice President, the President shall nominate a Vice President who shall take the office upon confirmation by a majority vote of both Houses of Congress.

This section would apply whenever the Vice President became President, as happened in 1963, or whenever the Vice President died in office.

Section 3

Whenever the President transmits to the President pro tempore of the Senate and the Speaker of the House of Representatives his written declaration that he is unable to discharge the powers and duties of his office, and until he transmits to them a written declaration to the contrary, such powers and duties shall be discharged by the Vice President as Acting President.

This section would be applied at times when the President must undergo surgery, as happened with Presidents Eisenhower and Johnson, or when the President felt himself too ill to carry out the duties of his office.

Section 4

CLAUSE 1. Whenever the Vice President and a majority of either the principal officers of the executive departments or of such other body as Congress may by law provide, transmit to the President pro tempore of the Senate and the Speaker of the House of Representatives their written declaration that the President is unable to discharge the powers and duties of his office, the Vice President shall immediately assume the powers and duties of the office as Acting President.

CLAUSE 2. Thereafter, when the President transmits to the President pro tempore of the Senate and the Speaker of the House of Representatives his written declaration that no inability exists, he shall resume the powers and duties of his office unless the Vice President and a majority of either the principal officers of the executive department or of such other body as Congress may by law provide, transmit within four days to the President pro tempore of the Senate and the Speaker of the House of Representatives their written declaration that the President is unable to discharge the powers and duties of his office. Thereupon Congress shall decide the issue, assembling within forty-eight hours for that purpose if not in session. If the Congress, within twenty-one days after receipt of the latter written declaration, or, if Congress is not in session, within twenty-one days after Congress is required to assemble, determines by two-thirds vote of both houses that the President is unable to discharge the powers and duties of his office, the Vice President shall continue to discharge the same as Acting President; otherwise the President shall resume the powers and duties of his office.

This section would be applied when the President felt that he was entirely capable of carrying out his duties, but the Vice President and a majority of either the Cabinet or a group appointed by Congress disagreed with him. It also would apply if the President were for some reason unable to notify Congress himself; for instance, if he were extremely ill.

II
What Ideas in the Constitution Came from England?

Divine Right of Kings 1609

The United States does not have a monarchy, but the early founders of our country came from the England that was ruled by James I, a king who believed his absolute power to govern came from God. To those who did not agree with him, James I appeared a tyrannical ruler. The Pilgrims that settled Plymouth in 1620 left England for Holland in 1609 because they disliked some of James' laws, particularly laws governing religion.

When our country's founders tried to establish a government that would unite the colonies, they looked to past forms of government as guides. Some founders saw monarchy as a possible form of government, but knew most colonists would not like the idea of a king. Most men greatly feared the power of a king and thought the government should specifically forbid a monarchy.

When James I made his statement about the divine right of kings, the Europeans of 1609 were accustomed to monarchy as their only form of government. Most people would have agreed that the king was the highest authority in the land and that his authority had God's blessing.

King James I (1603–1625) had more difficulties than many of his contemporary monarchs, partly because he had an unwavering faith in the rightness of his actions; also he had to deal with Parliament, a legislative body that for its time had strong ideas about its own power and the king's power. James clashed with Parliament as early as 1604 over his right to change laws concerning religion. Parliament abruptly informed him that "Your Majesty would be misinformed if any man should deliver [declare] that the kings of England have any absolute power in themselves either to alter religion, or make any laws concerning the same, otherwise than as in temporal cases by consent of Parliament."

James I and Parliament held opposing views that were never really reconciled. Parliament thought the king should rule only with Parliament's consent. James I made his point of view quite clear in this speech to Parliament in March of 1609.

As you read this statement by King James I, try to answer the following questions: Why was a king who had the divine right as James defines it in a stronger position than a king without that right? Why might the founders of our country fear a king who believed in the "divine right of kings"? Why might a government that did not have a monarch want to claim that God had given his blessing to that government?

(1) The State of Monarchy is the supremest thing upon earth: For Kings are not only Gods Lieutenants upon earth, and sit upon Gods throne, but even by God himself they are called Gods. There be three principal similitudes that illustrates the state of Monarchy: One taken out of the word of God; and the two other out of the grounds of Policy and Philosophy. In the Scriptures Kings are called Gods, and so their power after a certain relation compared to the Divine power. Kings are also compared to Fathers of families: for a King is truly *parens patriae* [father of his country] the politic father of his people. And lastly, Kings are compared to the head of this microcosm of the body of man.

Kings are justly called Gods, for that they exercise a manner of resemblance of Divine power upon earth: For if you will consider the Attributes to God, you shall see how they agree in the person of a King. God hath power to create, to destroy, make, or unmake at his pleasure, to give life, or send death, to judge all, and to be judged nor accountable to none: To raise low things, and to make high things low at his pleasure, and to God are both soul and body due. And the like power have Kings: they make and unmake their subjects: they have the power of raising, and casting down: of life, and of death: Judges over all their subjects, and in all causes, and yet accountable to none but God only. They have power to exalt low things, and abase high things, and make of their subjects like men at the Chess; A pawn to take a Bishop or a Knight, and to cry up, or down any of their subjects, as they do their money. And to the king is due both the affection of the soul, and the service of the body of his subjects. . . . so is it sedition in Subjects to dispute what a King may do in the height of his power: But just Kings will ever be

53

willing to declare what they will do, if they will not incur the curse of God. I will not be content that my power be disputed upon: but I shall ever be willing to make the reason appear of all my doings, and rule my actions according to my Laws.

☆   ☆   ☆

SIMILITUDES . . . MONARCHY A similitude is a comparison drawn between two things. Thus a comparison is to be drawn between the state of the monarchy and three other ideas that are to follow.

MICROCOSM . . . MAN A microcosm is a smaller unit that resembles or represents a larger unit. The king, then, is the head of the unit that stands for the body of all men; that is, the king is the head, the highest ranking man, among all men.

MAKE . . . CHESS Men here refers to chessmen, the figures with which the game is played. The king says he can make his subjects act like chessmen.

TO MAKE . . . DOINGS The king promises to explain the reasons for his actions.

Protest to King James I 1621

Although many of the members of Parliament accepted the theory of divine right of kings, they still jealously guarded what they considered their specific rights and privileges. Often the king and Parliament clashed over the issue of taxation; the king needed money that Parliament would refuse to grant. But sometimes they clashed over individual rights.

In 1621 Parliament petitioned James to go to war with Spain and to make a Protestant marriage for his son Charles. England, at that time, was a Protestant nation, and the Catholic marriage James hoped to make would have been deeply resented. James refused the petition and refused to permit any more discussion on the issue. In answer, Parliament issued the following petition asserting its right to freedom of speech. James was so angered by this statement that he sent for the journals of the House and tore out the pages on which it was recorded.

But the protest was made for what Parliament considered one of its most basic rights—a right it had cherished for centuries. It is not surprising then that Englishmen who emigrated to the New World fiercely guarded the right to free speech and made sure it was one of the principles of their new government.

(2) Sir Thomas Roe presented the draft of a Petition for Liberty of speech agreed upon by the Subcommittee. That whereas the House of Commons had ever enjoyed free liberty of speech in making laws and presenting grievances either public or private, and if breach of duty or modesty should be committed by any member of that House in words dishonorable to his Majesty or against his royal crown and dignity such offenders were only subject to the censure of the said house. . . .

☆　　☆　　☆

Petition of Right 1628

James I died in 1625 without decisively resolving his quarrel with Parliament over the nature of his authority. He was succeeded by his son Charles, who believed more strongly than his father in the divine right of kings. Like his father, Charles I believed that the king had the right to make and administer the laws of the land.

Charles I (1625–1649) had even less success in dealing with Parliament than his father had. At odds with that body over religious and political issues, Charles dissolved Parliament in 1626 and resorted to the quartering of troops upon the English people and the use of forced loans to raise funds. Constantly in need of revenue, Charles again called Parliament into session in 1628. The House of Commons used the occasion to adopt the Petition of Right, which Charles was forced to sign. Charles continued to violate the Petition; this action and other conflicts with Parliament led to a civil war. Parliament was taken over by Puritan leaders and the king was beheaded.

Although the Petition of Right was not observed by Charles after he signed it, it is still a very important document in the history of English law. This document prohibits the king and Parliament from imprisoning an individual unless he has broken a law. This agreement limits a king's power to punish his subjects at will. It also makes the responsibilities of subjects clear.

Compared with our Constitution's Bill of Rights, the Petition of Right seems a quite reasonable and restrained document. But the Bill of Rights of the Constitution was written over 150 years after the Petition of Right and was the product of English law and of more than one hundred fifty years of colonial experience. The Petition of Right was one of the ideas early colonists brought to America; it was an idea that Americans used, expanded, and developed.

As you read, note those rights that are also in the Bill of Rights in the Constitution (*see pp. 36–40*). How have these rights changed? What new rights are included in the Bill of Rights?

55

(3) Humbly show unto our sovereign lord the king, the Lords spiritual and temporal, and Commons in parliament assembled, that whereas it is declared and enacted by a statute made in the time of the reign of King Edward the First (1272–1307) . . . that no tallage [tax or toll] or aid shall be laid or levied by the king or his heirs in this realm, without the good will and assent of the archbishops, bishops, earls, barons, knights, burgesses, and other the freemen of the commonality of this realm.

And where also by the statute called The Great Charter of the Liberties of England [*Magna Carta*] it is declared and enacted, that no freeman may be taken or imprisoned or be disseised [deprived] of his freehold or liberties or his free customs, or be outlawed or exiled or in any other manner destroyed, but by the lawful judgment of his peers, or by the law of the land.

They do therefore humbly pray your most excellent Majesty, that no man hereafter be compelled to make or yield any gift, benevolence, tax, or such like charge, without common consent by act of parliament; and that none be called to make answer or to take such oath or to give attendance or to be confined or otherwise molested or disquieted concerning same, or for refusal thereof; and that no freeman, in any such manner as is before mentioned, be imprisoned or detained; and that your Majesty will be pleased to remove the said soldiers and mariners, and that your people may not be so burdened in time to come; and that the foresaid commissions for proceeding by martial law may be revoked and annulled; and that hereafter no commissions of like nature may issue forth to any person or persons whatsoever, to be executed as aforesaid, lest by colour of them any of your Majesty's subjects be destroyed or put to death, contrary to the laws and franchises of the land.

All which they most humbly pray of your most excellent Majesty, as their rights and liberties and according to the laws and statutes of this realm; and that your Majesty should also vouchsafe to declare that the awards, doings, and proceedings to the prejudice of your people, in any of the premises, shall not be drawn hereafter into consequence or example; and that your Majesty should be also graciously pleased, for the further comfort and surety of your people, to declare your royal will and pleasure that in the things aforesaid all your officers and ministers shall serve you according to the laws and statutes of the realm, as they tender the honour of your Majesty and the prosperity of this kingdom.

☆　　☆　　☆

TALLAGE OR AID   A tallage is a tax or a customs duty levied by a king or lord upon his subjects. Aid is a money grant in aid to the king.

ARCHBISHOPS . . . COMMONALITY All the people listed are members of Parliament. Thus no tax can be levied without the consent of Parliament.

FREEHOLD This term refers to an estate, office, or other holding that is given to a person for the length of his life.

FREE CUSTOMS These are rights that have the force of law through habitual use. Thus a family that has used a spring to water animals for several generations has the right to defend its use of the spring under law.

BENEVOLENCE This is a gift or an act of charity. But in English history a benevolence also could mean, as it does here, a tax disguised as a gift levied by the king without the consent of Parliament.

COLOUR OF THEM Colour refers to the outward appearance or showing of an object. "Colour of them" refers here to the showing or presenting of a commission that upholds martial law.

DECLARE . . . EXAMPLE A prejudice is an injury. The premises are the previously mentioned grievances in the Petition of Right. Thus Parliament requests the king to stop the actions that are harming the people—those actions that have been spelled out in the Petition. The king is requested to stop any proceedings that are now going on before the proceedings achieve their final outcome or before any subject is made an example of through these proceedings.

TENDER To wait upon or serve.

The Poor in England 1649

In England a great deal of land belonged to a few people in high positions. But many poor people lived in England; and while many survived by paying for the right to farm the land of the large landowners, many begged for food. The grievances of England's poor farmers in 1649, the year Charles I was executed, are recounted in the following selection from the pen of Gerrard Winstanley. Winstanley led a group of landless farmers who tried to take possession of some common land and grow crops on it. The Digger movement, as it was called, was quickly suppressed.

The writings of Gerrard Winstanley are interesting because they contain an idea that we accept as basic to our form of government: "All men are created equal" with equal rights under the law. Winstanley lays the basis for this kind of understanding of the rights of individual men by declaring that the poor have as much God-given right to use the earth for their livelihood as the rich. Equality of opportunity, regardless of accident of birth, underlies our Bill of Rights (*see pp. 36 – 40*).

DOCUMENT

(4) We whose names are subscribed, do in the name of all the poor oppressed people in *England*, declare unto you, that call yourselves Lords of Manors . . . [that] our Maker, hath enlightened our hearts so far, as to see, That the earth was not made purposely for you, to be Lords of it, and we to be your slaves, Servants, and Beggars; but it was made to be common Livelihood to all, without respect of persons. . . .

For though you and your Ancestors got your Propriety by murder and theft, and you keep it by the same power from us, that have an equal right to the Land with you, by the righteous Law of Creation, yet we shall have no occasion of quarreling (as you do) about that disturbing devil, called *Particular Propriety*. . . .

And to prevent all your scrupulous Objections, know this, That we must neither buy nor sell; Money must not any longer (after our work of the Earths community is advanced) be the great god, that hedges in some, and hedges out others; for Money is but part of the Earth: And surely, the Righteous Creator . . . did never ordain, That unless some of Mankind, do bring that mineral (Silver and Gold) in their hands, to others of their own kind, that they should neither be fed, nor be clothed. . . .

And seeing and finding ourselves poor, wanting Food to feed upon, while we labor the Earth, to cast in Seed, and to wait till the first Crop comes up; and wanting Ploughs, Carts, Corn, and such materials to plant the Commons withal, we are willing to declare our condition to you. . . .

We hear and see, that some of you, that have been Lords of Manors, do cause the trees and Woods that grow upon the Commons, which you pretend a Royalty unto, to be cut down and sold, for your own private use, whereby the Common Land, which your own mouths do say belongs to the poor, is impoverished and the poor oppressed people robbed of their Rights. . . .

Therefore we are resolved to be cheated no longer, nor be held under the slavish fear of you no longer, seeing the Earth was made for us, as well as for you; And if the Common Land belongs to us who are the poor oppressed, surely the woods that grow upon the Commons belong to us likewise; therefore we are resolved to try the uttermost in the light of reason, to know whether we shall be free men, or slaves. If we lie still, and let you steal away our birthrights, we perish; and if we Petition we perish also, though we have paid taxes, given free quarter, and ventured our lives to preserve the Nation's freedom as much as you, and therefore by the law of contract with you, freedom in the land is our portion as well as yours, equal with you; And if we strive for freedom and your murdering, governing Laws destroy us, we can but perish.

Therefore we require, and we resolve to take both Common Lands, and Common woods to be a livelihood for us, and look upon you as equal with us, not above us, knowing very well, that *England*, the land of our Nativity, is to be a common Treasury of livelihood to all, without respect of persons.

☆　　☆　　☆

COMMONS   The common grazing lands given by the lord of the manor to the people who farm the land and to be used by all for the raising of their cattle. Many towns on the east coast of the United States that were founded by Englishmen today have parks in the center of the town called "Commons." This land was once the common grazing land.

PARTICULAR PROPRIETY   An individual's property, the family lands, was called particular propriety.

Habeas Corpus Act 1679

Monarchy was restored in England in 1660 after twenty years of Puritan government, when Charles I's son, Charles II, became king. Charles II had less strong views than his father about the authority of a king. When Parliament passed the Habeas Corpus Act in 1679, Charles II was willing to sign the bill. Charles II was aware of his father's fate, and perhaps the king felt that if he fell from power, his supporters might gain some protection from this law.

The law itself has a long history. For several hundred years Parliament had been trying to assure men the right to request a judge to issue a writ of habeas corpus (see p. 23). This kind of writ protects an individual from being imprisoned for a non-criminal act or without knowledge of the reason for his imprisonment.

Because this act so clearly spells out a man's right to demand that he be imprisoned for only just causes he is aware of, it has become a landmark in English history. Much of English law was the basis for the Constitution, and the writ of habeas corpus was no exception to this. Reread the section of the Constitution that assures this right (see p. 23). Why are there certain times that the right to demand a writ of habeas corpus can be suspended? Why might this suspension be a good or bad idea?

(5) Whereas great delays have been used by sheriffs, gaolers, and other officers, to whose custody any of the king's subjects have been committed for criminal or supposed criminal matters, in making returns of writs of *Habeas Corpus* to them directed, by standing out an *Alias* and *Pluries Habeas Corpus*, and sometimes more, and by other shifts to avoid their yielding obedience to such writs, contrary to their duty and the known laws of the land, whereby many of the king's subjects have been and hereafter may be long detained in prison, in such cases where by law they are bailable, to their great charges and vexation:

II. For the prevention whereof, and the more speedy relief of all persons imprisoned for any criminal or supposed criminal matters; be it enacted . . ., that whensoever any person or persons shall bring any Habeas Corpus directed unto any sheriff or sheriffs, gaoler, minister, or other person whatsoever, for any person in his or their custody, and the said writ shall be served upon the said officer, or left at the gaol or prison . . ., that the said officer or officers, his or their under-officers, under-keepers or deputies, shall within three days after the service thereof as aforesaid (unless the commitment aforesaid were for treason or felony, plainly and specially expressed in the warrant of commitment) upon payment or tender of the charges of bringing the said prisoner, to be ascertained by the judge or court that awarded the same, and endorsed upon the said writ, not exceeding twelve pence per mile, and upon security given by his own bond to pay the charges of carrying back the prisoner, if he shall be remanded by the court or judge to which he shall be brought according to the true intent of this present act, and that he will not make any escape by the way, make return of such writ; and bring or cause to be brought the body of the party so committed or restrained, unto or before the Lord Chancellor, or Lord Keeper of the great seal of England for the time being, or the judges or barons of the said court from whence the said writ shall issue, or unto and before such other person or persons before whom the said writ is made returnable, according to the command thereof; and shall then likewise certify the true causes of his detainer or imprisonment, unless the commitment of the said party be in any place beyond the distance of twenty miles from the place or places where such court or person is or shall be residing; and if beyond the distance of twenty miles, and not above one hundred miles, then within the space of ten days, and if beyond the distance of one hundred miles, then within the space of twenty days, after such delivery aforesaid, and not longer.

III. And to the intent that no sheriff, gaoler or other officer may pretend ignorance of the import of any such writ; be it enacted by the authority aforesaid, that all such writs shall be marked . . . and shall be signed by the person that awards the same; and if any person or persons shall be or stand committed or detained as aforesaid, for any crime, unless for felony or treason plainly expessed in the warrant of commitment, in the vacation-time, and out of term, it shall and may be lawful to and for the person or persons so committed or detained (other than persons convict or in execution by legal process) or any one on his or their behalf, to appeal or complain to the Lord Chancellor or Lord Keeper, or any one of his Majesty's justices, either of the one bench or of the other, or the barons of the exchequer of the degree of the coif; and the said Lord Chancellor, Lord Keeper, justices or barons or any of them, upon view of the copy or copies of the warrant or warrants of commitment and detainer, or otherwise upon oath made that such copy or copies were denied to be given by such person or persons in whose custody the prisoner or prisoners is or are detained, are hereby authorized, and required, upon request made in writing by such person or persons or any on his, her or their behalf, attested and subscribed by two witnesses who were present at the delivery of the same, to award and grant an *Habeas Corpus* under the seal of such court whereof he shall then be one of the judges to be directed to the officer or officers in whose custody the party so committed or detained shall be, returnable immediate before the said Lord Chancellor or Lord Keeper, or such justice, baron or any other justice or baron of the degree of the coif of any of the said courts; and upon service thereof as aforesaid, the officer or officers, his or their under-officer or under-officers, under-keeper or under-keepers, or their deputy, in whose custody the party is so committed or detained, shall within the times respectively before limited, bring such prisoner or prisoners before the said Lord Chancellor or Lord Keeper, or such justices, barons or one of them, before whom the said writ is made returnable, and in case of his absence before any of them, with the return of such writ, and the true causes of the commitment and detainer; and thereupon within two days after the party shall be brought before them, the said Lord Chancellor or Lord Keeper, or such justice or baron before whom the prisoner shall be brought as aforesaid, shall discharge the said prisoner from his imprisonment, taking his or their recognizance, with one or more surety or sureties, in any sum according to their discretions, having regard to the quality of the prisoner and nature of the offence. . . .

☆   ☆   ☆

IN MAKING . . . DIRECTED [The sheriffs have delayed] in returning the prisoners and the writs to the judges as they were directed.

BY STANDING . . . *CORPUS* [The sheriffs have delayed] by waiting out the other writs of habeas corpus that were sent after the first ones were ignored.

IN VACATION – TIME . . . TERM   Those times when the judges are on vacation or the court is not in session.

English Bill of Rights 1689

Seventeenth-century England was in a state of religious as well as political upheaval. There were three major religious divisions: the Anglican Church, or the Church of England, which was the official religion; Puritanism, which accused the Anglican Church of leaning too heavily on Roman Catholicism; and Roman Catholicism, which considered the Anglican Church heretical because of its Protestant teachings. Religion was one of the emotional issues of the time. The religion of the monarch was an even more emotionally charged issue. Since Charles II's mother was Roman Catholic, there had been a great deal of fear that he would seek to restore the Roman Catholic Church in England. Charles II managed to keep religious questions from becoming major issues.

But Charles's brother, James II, who became king when Charles II died in 1685, was much less moderate than his brother. James II antagonized many Anglicans and Puritans by openly avowing his Roman Catholicism. Secondly, James II had not learned that Parliament must be handled gently. Besides appointing Roman Catholics to high places in his army, the king also suspended penal laws against Roman Catholics and other dissenters without permission of Parliament. Parliament sent a letter to William of Orange, a possible successor to the throne, inviting him to come to England. James II fled to France. This change in monarchs was called the Glorious Revolution.

Before Parliament would allow William and his wife Mary to ascend the throne as joint sovereigns, Parliament asked them to sign the following Bill of Rights. The signing of this Bill of Rights marked the end of the contest between Parliament and the king over the right to rule; William and Mary accepted the Bill of Rights without being coerced. The Bill first makes clear that Parliament feels that James II committed illegal acts as king. As you read, note those statements that seem to be directed against James II. How many of these accusations are justified and how many are the result of the anger Parliament felt after James's actions? Other parts of the Bill of Rights are rights that had been demanded before. List these "old rights" and the sources of these rights. Finally, how many of these rights can you find in our Bill of Rights?

(6) Whereas the said late King James II having abdicated the government, and the throne being thereby vacant, his Highness the prince of Orange (whom it hath pleased Almighty God to make the glorious instrument of delivering this kingdom from popery and arbitrary power) did (by advice of the lords spiritual and temporal, and diverse principal persons of the Commons) cause letters to be written to the lords spiritual and temporal, being Protestants, and other letters to the several counties, cities, universities, boroughs, and Cinque Ports, for the choosing of such persons to represent them, as were of right to be sent to parliament, to meet and sit at Westminster upon the two-and-twentieth day of January, in this year 1689, in order to such an establishment as that their religion, laws, and liberties might not again be in danger of being subverted; upon which letters elections have been accordingly made.

And thereupon the said lords spiritual and temporal and Commons, pursuant to the respective letters and elections, being now assembled in a full and free representation of this nation, taking into their most serious consideration the best means for attaining the ends aforesaid, do in the first place (as their ancestors in like case have usually done), for the vindicating and asserting their ancient rights and liberties, declare:

1. That the pretended power of suspending laws, or the execution of laws, by regal authority, without consent of parliament, is illegal.

2. That the pretended power of dispensing with laws, or the execution of laws, by regal authority, as it hath been assumed and exercised of late, is illegal.

3. That the commission for erecting the late court of commissioners for ecclesiastical causes, and all other commissions and courts of like nature, are illegal and pernicious.

4. That levying money for or to the use of the crown by pretense of prerogative, without grant of parliament, for longer time or in other manner than the same is or shall be granted, is illegal.

5. That it is the right of the subjects to petition the king, and all commitments and prosecutions for such petitioning are illegal.

6. That the raising or keeping a standing army within the kingdom in time of peace, unless it be with consent of parliament, is against law.

7. That the subjects which are Protestants may have arms for their defense suitable to their conditions, and as allowed by law.

8. That election of members of parliament ought to be free.

9. That the freedom of speech, and debates or proceedings in parliament, ought not to be impeached or questioned in any court or place out of parliament.

10. That excessive bail ought not to be required, nor excessive fines imposed, nor cruel and unusual punishments inflicted.

11. That jurors ought to be duly impaneled and returned, and jurors which pass upon men in trials for high treason ought to be freeholders.

12. That all grants and promises of fines and forfeitures of particular persons before conviction are illegal and void.

13. And that for redress of all grievances, and for the amending, strengthening, and preserving of the laws, parliament ought to be held frequently.

☆   ☆   ☆

CINQUE PORTS *Cinque* means "five," and the ports were seaports in England that had special trading privileges; the original "five" ports referred to were Hastings, Sandwich, Dover, Romney, and Hithe. By 1689, though, Rye and Winchelsea were included in the title, too.

IN DANGER . . . SUBVERTED In danger of being overthrown.

COURT . . . ECCLESIASTICAL CAUSES Special commissioners administered portions of the funds of the Church of England. Also the court administered English law and the discipline of the Church of England.

John Locke on Representation and Democracy 1689

The Glorious Revolution of 1688 was not without its critics; since James II was Roman Catholic, Catholic countries such as France and Spain were hardly willing to call the revolution "glorious." Most of Europe was governed by kings who asserted their divine right to govern; these monarchs and their followers found the idea of a Parliament replacing one king, who had tried to exercise absolute authority, with another king, who in writing agreed that he had no right to supersede Parliament, a disquieting one.

The Glorious Revolution, which gave England its Bill of Rights and a limited form of monarchy, needed a good publicist. John Locke, an English philosopher, was just such a man. His views on individual rights and government helped justify the more limited form of monarchy that came into being with the ascension of William and Mary.

When James I stated the divine right of kings (*see pp.* 52–54), he began his argument by stating that "monarchy is the supremest thing upon earth," but Locke began his statement by looking at the other extreme—those natural rights he felt belonged to all men. Since these men began at different places, it is not surprising that they came to widely different conclusions. For Locke, after stating the natural rights that belong to each man, concluded that man becomes a part of a political body or community by willingly obeying the laws of that community. Governments then have the right to govern because the governed have given their consent to the government for the good of the community. The corollary then would also hold: a government has a right to govern only as long as the governed continue to give their consent.

See how many of the ideas in this selection are repeated in the introduction to the Declaration of Independence. For John Locke not only became the publicist for the Glorious Revolution, but he also became the inspiration for the American Revolution.

(see pp. 52–54)

DOCUMENT

(7) Men being, as has been said, by Nature all free, equal, and independent, no one can be put out of this Estate, and subjected to the political Power of another, without his own Consent. The only Way whereby anyone divests himself of his natural Liberty . . . is by agreeing with other Men to join and unite into a Community, for their comfortable, safe, and peaceful living one amongst another, in a secure Enjoyment of their Properties, and a greater Security against any that are not of it. This any Number of Men may do, because it injures not the freedom of the rest; they are left as they were in the Liberty of the State of Nature. When any number of Men have so *consented to make one Community or Government*, they are thereby presently incorporated, and make *one Body Politic* wherein the *Majority* have a Right to act and conclude the rest.

For when any Number of Men have, by the Consent of every Individual, made a Community, they have thereby made that *Community* one Body, with a Power to act as one Body, which is only by the Will and Determination of the Majority. . . .

The great End of Men's entering into Society, being the Enjoyment of their Properties in Peace and Safety, and the great Instrument and means of that being the Laws established in that Society; the *first and fundamental positive Law* of all Commonwealths, is the *establishing the Legislative* Power. . . .

These are the *Bounds* which the trust that is put in them by the Society, and the Law of God and Nature have *set to the Legislative* Power of every Commonwealth, in all Forms of Government.

First, They are to govern by *promulgated established Laws,* not to be varied in particular Cases, but to have one Rule for Rich and Poor, for the Favourite at Court, and the Country-Man at Plough.

Secondly, These Laws also ought to be designed *for* no other End ultimately, but the *Good of the People.*

Thirdly, They must *not raise Taxes* on the *Property of the People, without the Consent of the People,* given by themselves or their Deputies. And this properly concerns only such Governments where the *Legislative* is always in being, or at least where the People have not reserved any Part of the Legislative to Deputies, to be from Time to Time chosen by themselves.

Fourthly, The *Legislative* neither must *nor can transfer the Power of making Laws* to any Body else, or place it anywhere, but where the People have.

★　　★　　★

II. Footnotes

[1]Charles Howard McIlwain, ed., *The Political Works of James I* (Harvard University Press, Cambridge, Mass., 1918) 307–310.

[2]Wallace Notestein, Frances Helen Relf, and Hartley Simpson, eds., *Commons Debates, 1621* (Yale University Press, New Haven, Conn., 1935) IV 37.

[3]Edward P. Cheyney, ed., *Readings in English History Drawn from the Original Sources* (Ginn and Co., Boston, Mass., 1908) 458–459.

[4]George H. Sabine, ed., *The Works of Gerrard Winstanley* (Cornell University Press, Ithaca, N.Y., 1941) 269–274. Copyright, 1941, by Cornell University. Used by permission of Cornell University Press.

[5]William Stubbs, ed., *Select Charters and Other Illustrations of English Constitutional History From the Earliest Times to the Reign of Edward the First,* 8th edition (Oxford, at the Clarendon Press, 1900) 517–519.

[6]Cheyney, *Readings in English History,* 545–546.

[7]John Locke, *The Works of John Locke, Esq.,* 3rd edition (Arthur Bettesworth, John Pemberton, and Edward Symon, London, England, 1727) II, 185, 195, and 198.

III
How Did Colonial Experience Shape the Constitution?

The Mayflower Compact 1620

Some of the Protestants in England in the early 1600's felt that the Anglican Church had not gone far enough in its reformation. These people, called Puritans, were not free to worship as they pleased. One group of Puritans finally left England for Holland in 1609. However, it wasn't long before this group, the people we know as Pilgrims, decided that to preserve their faith they would be wise to leave Holland and settle in the northern part of Virginia. The ocean voyage was rough and the colonists landed instead on Cape Cod.

The Pilgrims knew that the authority of the Virginia Company did not extend so far north. Since everyone on this famous voyage of the *Mayflower* was not a Pilgrim, some of the leaders worried that these "strangers" would refuse to obey the leaders of the colony.

The Pilgrim leaders drew up the Mayflower Compact to form a temporary government and maintain law and order. This agreement made no specific laws and did not establish one particular kind of government. But everyone that signed the document (most of the adult males), agreed to abide by the Compact.

It is surprising that these Pilgrim leaders, who came from a land that had a monarchy, particularly as it was practiced under James I, could have made such an agreement. But the Pilgrims also came from a land that had a Parliament which demanded a say in the way James was going to govern. The Pilgrim leaders' compact was unique for its time because the leaders agreed among themselves to rule for the common good. The leaders did not agree to follow the laws of the Virginia colony nor the laws of the towns from which they came. Instead they mutually agreed to make and obey the laws that were necessary for the general good.

As you read think how King James I would have felt about this Compact if the colony had been a town in England.

(1) In the name of God, Amen. We whose names are underwritten, the loyal subjects of our dread sovereign Lord, King James, by the grace of God, of Great Britain, France, & Ireland king, defender of the faith, etc., having undertaken, for the glory of God, and advancement of the Christian faith, and honour of our king and country, a voyage to plant the first colony in the Northern parts of Virginia, do by these presents solemnly and mutually in the presence of God, and one of another, covenant and combine ourselves together into a civil body politic, for our better ordering and preservation and furtherance of the ends aforesaid; and by virtue hereof to enact, constitute, and frame such just and equal laws, ordinances, acts, constitutions, and offices, from time to time, as shall be thought most meet and convenient for the general good of the Colony: under which we promise all due submission and obedience. In witness whereof we have here subscribed our names at Cape Cod the eleventh of November, in the year of the reign of our sovereign lord, King James, of England, France & Ireland the eighteenth, and of Scotland the fifty-fourth. Anno: Dom. 1620.

☆   ☆   ☆

Representative Government in Virginia 1621

By the time the Virginia colony had achieved a measure of representative government in 1619, the colony had gone through many changes. The first permanent English settlement on the east coast of North America had been financed by a company of stockholders called the London Company. The early colony did not prosper. Men died from malaria, and the corn crop they grew barely kept them alive. Many were indentured servants, people who had promised a number of years of service to the London Company in return for their passage over. These men lived under the rigid discipline of the leaders.

But by 1619 the colony had changed. Most of the indentured servants had served their terms and had become independent farmers. John Rolfe had discovered a crop for the colonists to grow for export to England—tobacco. The London Company then ordered the new governor, George Yeardley, to introduce English common law and gather a representative assembly, which first met in 1619.

An ordinance of the London Company, enacted at a meeting held in England in 1621, made clear the exact rights of the Virginia settlers to govern themselves. Parts of this ordinance are quoted below:

DOCUMENT

(2) Know ye that we, the . . . Company . . . intending . . . to settle such a Form of Government . . . [in Virginia], as may be to the greatest Benefit and Comfort of the People . . . have thought fit to make our Entrance by ordering and establishing such Supreme Councils. . . .

II. We therefore, the said Treasurer, Council, and Company, by Authority directed to us from his Majesty . . . do hereby order and declare, that, from hence forward, there shall be Two Supreme Councils in *Virginia*, for the better government of the said Colony aforesaid.

III. The one of which Councils, to be called THE COUNCIL OF STATE (and whose Office shall chiefly be assisting, with their Care, Advice, and Circumspection, to the said Governor) shall be chosen, nominated, placed, and displaced, from time to time, by us, the said Treasurer, Council, and Company. . . .

IV. The other Council, more generally to be called by the Governor once yearly . . . shall consist . . . of the said Council of State and two burgesses of every Town, Hundred, or other particular Plantation, to be respectively chosen by the inhabitants: Which Council shall be called THE GENERAL ASSEMBLY, wherein (as also in the said Council of State) all Matters shall be decided, determined, and ordered, by the greater Part of the Voices then present; reserving to the Governor always a Negative Voice. And this General Assembly shall have free Power to . . . enact such general Laws and Orders, for the Behoof [benefit] of the said Colony, and the good Government thereof, as shall, from time to time, appear necessary or requisite. . . .

☆ ☆ ☆

Church and State 1636–1644

During the seventeenth century very few Protestants or Catholics believed in the separation of church and state as we know it today in the United States. Most thought that the ideal state was a theocracy, in which the church was superior to the civil government, much as the soul of man is superior to his physical body. Many of the European governments were church-dominated, but the best example of a theocratic state was the Massachusetts Bay Colony as it existed during most of the seventeenth century. John Cotton, one of the leading Puritan theologians during the early days of Massachusetts, expressed his ideas on the relation between church and state in a letter written in 1636:

(3) It is better that the commonwealth be fashioned to the setting forth of God's house, which is his church: than to accommodate the church frame to the civil state. Democracy, I do not conceive that ever God did ordain as a fit government either for church or commonwealth. If the people be governors, who shall be governed? As for monarchy, and aristocracy, they are both of them clearly approved, and directed in scripture, yet so as referreth the sovereignty to himself, and setteth up Theocracy in both, as the best forms of government in the commonwealth, as well as in the church.

☆   ☆   ☆

Cotton Mather, the leading Puritan minister during the latter part of the seventeenth and early part of the eighteenth century, and a staunch supporter of the supremacy of the Church, wrote approvingly of the efforts of John Cotton to establish theocratic rule in Massachusetts. In what way is the government Cotton Mather describes similar to a government headed by a monarch who believes in the divine right of kings? In what ways is this theocracy different from a monarchy? Why might a theocracy not be entirely opposed to a democracy?

(4) . . . Upon his [John Cotton's] arrival . . . He found the whole country in a perplexed and a divided estate, as to their *civil* constitution. . . . It was then required [requested] of Mr. *Cotton*, that he would, from the laws wherewith God governed his ancient people, form an *abstract* of such as were of a moral and a lasting equity: which he performed as acceptably as judiciously. But inasmuch as very much of an *Athenian democracy* was in the mould of the *government*, by the *royal charter* . . . Mr. Cotton effectually recommended it unto them, that none should be *electors*, nor *elected*

70

therein, except such as were *visible subjects* of our Lord Jesus Christ, personally *confederated* in our churches. In these, and many other ways, he propounded unto them, an endeavor after a *theocracy*, as near as might be, to that which was the glory of *Israel*, the *peculiar people*.

☆   ☆   ☆

FROM THE . . . ANCIENT PEOPLE The laws are the laws recorded mostly in the first five books of the Old Testament.

AN ABSTRACT A summary.

VISIBLE SUBJECTS . . . . IN OUR CHURCHES The electors of the government were those men who were church members. They were "visible" because it was customary for a man who desired church membership to make a public (visible) confession. He would state that he knew Christ was his savior and that he was among the elect who would share the kingdom of heaven.

ENDEAVOR . . . ISRAEL The Puritans should try to establish a theocracy as similar as possible to the theocracy that glorified ancient Israel.

Although John Cotton and Cotton Mather expressed the prevailing sentiment in New England, there were a few persons who believed that neither church nor state should dominate the affairs of the other. Roger Williams, who had left England to seek a greater degree of freedom in America, advocated the separation of church and state much as we know it today. For a while he remained in Massachusetts, but he was driven from that colony for expressing heretical beliefs. He sought refuge in Plymouth, but even the kindly William Bradford considered him a man "very unsettled in judgment" and a person "to be pitied and prayed for."

Finding no peace or safety in any of the established villages in New England, Roger Williams fled to the shores of Narragansett Bay and founded a small settlement which eventually became the Rhode Island colony. The following selection from Williams' writing indicates his beliefs regarding the proper relationship between church and state:

DOCUMENT

(5) It is the will and command of *God*, that . . . a *permission* of the most *Paganish, Jewish, Turkish,* or *Antichristian consciences* and *worships,* be granted to *all* men in all *Nations* and *Countries:* and they are only to be *fought* against with that *Sword*

which is only *(in Soul matters) able* to *conquer,* to wit, the *Sword of Gods Spirit,* the *Word* of *God.* . . .

God requireth not an *uniformity* of *Religion* to be *enacted* and *enforced* in any *civil state;* which enforced *uniformity* (sooner or later) is the greatest occasion of *civil War, ravishing* of *conscience, persecution* of *Christ Jesus* in his servants, and of the *hypocrisy* and destruction of millions of souls. . . .

True *civility* and *Christianity* may both flourish in a *state* or *Kingdom,* notwithstanding the *permission* of divers and contrary *consciences,* either of *Jew* or *Gentile.*

☆   ☆   ☆

AND THEY ARE . . . WORD OF GOD The pagans are to be fought against with the only effective sword, the word of God. Williams argues that people who profess religions other than the Christian one can be conquered not by suppression but by converting them by preaching the word of God to them.

Maryland Toleration Act 1649

The Catholics in England were in no higher favor than the dissenting Puritans. But George Calvert, the first Lord Baltimore, was a friend of Charles I; and although he was a Roman Catholic in a Protestant country, he was granted the right to settle the colony of Maryland. Calvert hoped the colony would be a haven for Catholics, but Protestants were allowed to settle as well. In fact, more Protestants settled in Maryland than Catholics.

In 1649, after the death of Charles I, the Puritans gained control in England. Lord Baltimore, perhaps realizing that his situation was precarious, replaced his Catholic governor with a Protestant one. At the same time he proposed the passage of the famous Act of Toleration. When the act was passed, it protected the right to worship for those who believed in Jesus Christ. Lord Baltimore was concerned that the Catholics would be subject to religious persecution if the Protestant Puritans gained control. The Puritans did repeal the Act in 1654, but it was restored in 1658, when Maryland was returned to the Calvert family.

Although religious toleration was not extended to all people by this act, it is a landmark toward religious toleration. The Act of Toleration, and the creation of the colony of Maryland itself, suggested that religious differences could exist within a colony without causing total disorder in the government. Also, the act begins to suggest that religious worship is a private matter of conscience that should not be interfered with by the government.

(6) And whereas the enforcing of the conscience in matters of Religion has frequently fallen out [proved] to be of dangerous Consequence in those commonwealths where it hath been practiced, And for the more quiet and peaceable government of this Province, and the better to preserve mutual Love and amity among the Inhabitants thereof. Be it therefore . . . enacted . . . that no person or persons whatsoever within this Province . . . professing to believe in Jesus Christ, shall from henceforth be any way troubled, Molested, or discountenanced [discouraged] for or in respect of his or her religion nor in the free exercise thereof within this Province or the Islands thereunto belonging nor any way compelled to the belief or exercise of any other Religion against his or her consent, so as they be not unfaithful to the Lord Proprietary, or molest or conspire against the civil Government established or to be established in the Province under him or his heirs. And that all and every person and persons that shall presume Contrary to this act and the true intent and meaning thereof directly or indirectly either in person or estate willfully to wrong disturb trouble or molest any person whatsoever within this Province professing to believe in Jesus Christ for or in respect of his or her religion or the free exercise thereof . . . that such person or persons so offending, shall be compelled to pay treble [triple] damages to the party so wronged . . . and for every such offence shall also forfeit 20 [shillings] sterling in money or the value thereof, half thereof for the use of the Lord Proprietary, and his heirs . . . and the other half for the use of the party so wronged or molested as aforesaid, Or if the party so offending as aforesaid shall refuse or be unable to recompense the party so wronged, or to satisfy such fine or forfeiture, then such Offender shall be severely punished by public whipping and imprisonment during the pleasure of the Lord Proprietary . . . for the time being without bail . . .

☆   ☆   ☆

The Zenger Case 1735

John Peter Zenger emigrated to America in 1710 and began publishing the *New York Weekly Journal* in 1733, the second newspaper published in that colony. A serious controversy developed between Governor Cosby's supporters and many of the long-time residents of New York who disliked the governor's methods of administration. Zenger published articles by the governor's enemies in the columns of his newspaper. These articles were not complimentary. Governor Cosby ordered certain articles from that journal burned and then brought Zenger to trial for libel. Zenger, a relatively poor man, was defended by a lawyer employed by the governor's foes. This lawyer, Andrew Hamilton of Philadelphia, was one of the most distinguished lawyers in the colonies.

The position taken by the court, in accordance with then existing law, was that defaming a person, whether the statement was true or false, constituted libel. Attorney Hamilton argued that truth should be a defense against the charge of libel. The jury freed Zenger. Although this case did not change New York law, this definition of libel freed newspapers from the tyranny of government.

The following account was written a hundred years after the case by a New York historian who used some accounts by eyewitnesses to the events. As you read, find out what "libelous" truths Zenger printed in his newspaper. Find statements that suggest the document was written a hundred years after the case. How would freedom of the press have been affected if the jury had decided Zenger was guilty?

DOCUMENT

(7) I will here give a note, made by Chancellor Kent:

"Report of the case of Peter Zenger, printer of the New York weekly journal. . . . On the 17th of November, 1734, Zenger was arrested and imprisoned by the order of the council, for printing and publishing seditious libels. He was then brought before the chief justice, on habeas corpus, ... and was re-committed. On 28th January, 1735, the grand jury having found no bill against him, the attorney-general filed an *information* against him, for a false, scandalous, malicious and seditious libel. . . . He pleaded not guilty to the information. The court, on motion, ordered a *struck jury*. The trial came on in the supreme court. . . .

"The printing and publishing were confessed, and Mr. Hamilton, of Philadelphia, the counsel for the prisoner, . . . insisted in his defence, on the truth of the facts charged as libellous. The chief justice told the counsel for defendant, that he could not be admitted to give the truth of the libel in evidence. Mr. Hamilton insisted that the jury were judges of both law and the fact. Verdict, not guilty. . . ."

The trial of John Peter Zenger makes so important a feature in the picture of New York in 1734 and 1735, that I will, before closing this chapter, dwell at length upon the subject.

Dr. John W. Francis tells us . . . that the late Gouverneur Morris told him that "the trial of Zenger, in 1735, was the germ of American freedom — the morning star of that liberty which subsequently revolutionized America."

74

It throws light upon the state of the province, the feelings of the people, their opposition to the mode of government fastened upon them by England, and consequently upon their conduct thirty and forty years after. It proves the prevailing opinion entertained of Governour Cosby, his council, and his judges; and it exhibits the character and talents of Andrew Hamilton. . . .

I have given the brief and luminous note of Mr. Kent; but as the trial, published at the time, by Zenger, and republished in Lancaster by W. Dunlap, in 1756, is scarce, and the state trials rarely consulted, I will, for the above reasons, make extracts from it, and endeavour by comment, to elucidate it.

The words charged to be a false, scandalous, malicious, and seditious libel, are these; "Your appearance in print at last, gives a pleasure to many, though most wish you had come fairly into the open field, and not appeared behind retrenchments made of the supposed laws against libelling: these retrenchments, gentlemen, may soon be shewn to you and all men to be very weak, and to have neither law nor reason for their foundation, so cannot long stand you in stead; therefore, you had much better as yet leave them, and come to what the people of this city and province think are the points in question. They think as matters now stand, that their liberties and properties are precarious, and that slavery is like to be entailed on them and their posterity, if some past things be not amended, and this they collect from many past proceedings." "One of our neighbours of New Jersey being in company, observing the strangers of New York full of complaints, endeavoured to persuade them to remove into Jersey. . . ."

When the trial came on, Mr. Hamilton avowed the printing and publishing as being the truth. . . .

Hamilton confessed the printing and publishing. Bradley observed that "the jury *must* find a verdict for the king." "Not so, Mr. Attorney," said Hamilton, "there are two words in that bargain; I hope it is not our bare printing and publishing a paper that will make it a libel: you will have something more to do, before you make my client a libeller; for the words themselves must be libellous, that is, false, scandalous and seditious, or else we are not guilty." Bradley gave the usual definition of a libel: he asserted, "that whether the person defamed is a private man or magistrate, whether living or dead, whether the libel is true or false, or if the party against whom it is made is of good or evil fame, it is nevertheless a libel: for in a settled state of government, the party grieved, ought to complain for every injury done him, in the ordinary course of the law. And as to its publication, the law had taken so great care of men's reputations, that if one maliciously repeats it, or signs it, in the presence of another, or delivers the libel or a copy of it over, to scandalize the party, he is to be punished as a publisher of a libel. . . . He then insisted that it was clear . . . that Mr. Zenger had offended in a most notorious and gross manner, in scandalizing his excellency, our governour, who is the king's immediate represent- ative, and the supreme magistrate of this province. . . . Hamilton . . . insisted, that the just complaint of a number of men suffering under the bad administration of a government, was no libel. He said, that Bradley, by reading and expounding the *information,* had shown that the prosecution had been directed by the governour and council; and by the appearance of the crowded court, it was apparent that people think there is a great deal more at stake than appears on the surface of this business; and, therefore, he should be both plain and particular in what he had to say. He pointed out, that the authorities Bradley had cited, were from that terrible and long exploded court, the star-chamber. . . .

Bradley, the attorney-general, interrupted the barrister, and insisted that the confession of publication, was a confession that Zenger was guilty of what was charged in the information, as scan- dalous and leading to sedition.

Hamilton observed, that Mr. Attorney now omitted the word *false.* "We are charged," he said, "with printing and publishing a certain false, malicious, seditious and scandalous libel. This word *false,* must have some meaning, or else how came it there? I hope Mr. Attorney will not say, he put it there by chance, and I am of the opinion his information would not be good without it. But to show that it is the principal thing which, in my opinion, makes a libel, I put the case, if the information had been for printing and publish- ing a certain *true* libel, would that be the same thing? Or could Mr. Attorney support such an information by any precedent in the English law? No; the falsehood makes the scandal, and both make the libel.

☆   ☆   ☆

INFORMATION A statement of the charges given to a magis- trate in order to start criminal proceedings against the defendant. An information was used in this case to sidestep the grand jury which had decided not to charge Peter Zenger. The attorney gen- eral could file the information against Zenger solely on the basis of his oath of office. Zenger's lawyer made it clear later that many colonists found the practice distasteful.

STRUCK JURY The "struck" refers to the method of selecting the jury. A number of people are called and each side gets to strike a number of jurors until the jury size is the correct one under the law.

TO BE ENTAILED To happen as the logical outcome.

CONSIDERABLE MEN   Men of high position and stature in the community.

MEN OF KNOWN . . . ANY LAW   To vote, a man had to own property; however, the government now was denying men who fulfilled this qualification the right to vote. This action was contrary to all practices up to that time.

STAR–CHAMBER   A court, developed from early English kings' advisors, that dealt with criminal matters. Parliament dissolved it in 1661 because there had been many abuses of its power under Charles I and James I. The term became associated with an arbitrary and tyrannical court.

The Albany Plan of Union 1754

The Albany Plan of Union was drafted in 1754 to help the colonies better defend themselves against the French, who had built forts in the Ohio valley west of the Appalachian Mountains. Some of the colonial leaders saw danger in the situation, since the Iroquois Indians, who had been friendly with the English, were showing signs of siding with the French. To meet this threat, representatives from the northern colonies met in Albany. The result of the meeting was the Albany Plan, written largely by Ben Franklin.

The document provides for a government, headed by a president-general, that would have the power to tax, to raise an army, and to deal with Indian affairs. While the plan was a good one for meeting the threat that faced the colonies, not one colonial legislature ratified it. The colonists at this time did not see the French and Indian threats as serious enough to merit their giving up to a central government any of their rights to govern themselves. But the Albany meeting was important in the rush for independence that was to follow in twenty years. As you read, think of the possibilities and difficulties of forming a government that would unite the diverse colonies.

DOCUMENT

(8) It is proposed that humble application be made for an act of Parliament of Great Britain, by virtue of which one general government may be formed in America, including all the said colonies, within and under which government each colony may retain its present constitution, except in the particulars wherein a change may be directed by the said act, as hereafter follows.

1. That the said general government be administered by a President-General, to be appointed and supported by the crown;

and a Grand Council, to be chosen by the representatives of the people of the several Colonies met in their respective assemblies.

2. That within ——— months after the passing such act, the House of Representatives that happen to be sitting within that time, or that shall be especially for that purpose convened, may and shall choose members for the Grand Council. . . .

4. That there shall be a new election of the members of the Grand Council every three years. . . .

5. That after the first three years, when the proportion of money arising out of each Colony to the general treasury can be known, the number of members to be chosen for each Colony shall, from time to time, in all ensuing elections, be regulated by that proportion, yet so as that the number to be chosen by any one Province be not more than seven, nor less than two.

6. That the Grand Council shall meet once in every year, and oftener if occasion require, at such time and place as they shall adjourn to at the last preceding meeting, or as they shall be called to meet at by the President-General on any emergency; he having first obtained in writing the consent of seven of the members to such call, and sent duly and timely notice to the whole.

7. That the Grand Council have power to choose their speaker; and shall neither be dissolved, prorogued, nor continued sitting longer than six weeks at one time, without their own consent or the special command of the crown. . . .

9. That the assent of the President-General be requisite to all acts of the Grand Council, and that it be his office and duty to cause them to be carried into execution.

10. That the President-General, with the advice of the Grand Council, hold or direct all Indian treaties, in which the general interest of the Colonies may be concerned; and make peace or declare war with Indian nations.

11. That they make such laws as they judge necessary for regulating all Indian trade.

12. That they make all purchases from Indians, for the crown, of lands not now within the bounds of particular Colonies, or that shall not be within their bounds when some of them are reduced to more convenient dimensions.

13. That they make new settlements on such purchases, by granting lands in the King's name, reserving a quitrent to the crown for the use of the general treasury.

14. That they make laws for regulating and governing such new settlements, till the crown shall think fit to form them into particular governments.

15. That they raise and pay soldiers and build forts for the defence of any of the Colonies, and equip vessels of force to guard

the coasts and protect the trade on the ocean, lakes, or great rivers; but they shall not impress men in any Colony, without the consent of the Legislature.

16. That for these purposes they have power to make laws, and lay and levy such general duties, imposts, or taxes, as to them shall appear most equal and just (considering the ability and other circumstances of the inhabitants in the several Colonies), and such as may be collected with the least inconvenience to the people; rather discouraging luxury, than loading industry with unnecessary burdens.

17. That they may appoint a General Treasurer and Particular Treasurer in each government when necessary; and, from time to time, may order the sums in the treasuries of each government into the general treasury; or draw on them for special payments, as they find most convenient.

18. Yet no money to issue but by joint orders of the President-General and Grand Council; except where sums have been appropriated to particular purposes, and the President-General is previously empowered by an act to draw such sums. . . .

21. That the laws made by them for the purposes aforesaid shall not be repugnant, but, as near as may be, agreeable to the laws of England, and shall be transmitted to the King in Council for approbation, as soon as may be after their passing; and if not disapproved within three years after presentation, to remain in force. . . .

25. That the particular military as well as civil establishments in each Colony remain in their present state, the general constitution notwithstanding; and that on sudden emergencies any Colony may defend itself, and lay the accounts of expense then arising before the President-General and General Council, who may allow and order payment of the same, as far as they judge such accounts just and reasonable.   ☆   ☆   ☆

WITHIN THEIR BOUNDS . . . DIMENSIONS When grants of land were given to the earliest proprietors, no one had a realistic understanding of how big the New World was. Because the wordings of land grants were vague and overly general, colonies such as Virginia had claim to many thousands of square miles they could not use, defend properly, or govern efficiently. By 1754 colonies were beginning to define more realistically their boundaries. This statement then means that the proposed government will purchase Indian lands that are now part of the colony but will not be when the new boundaries of the colony are set.

QUITRENT In England farmers who rented land from a large landowner paid rent by working in the landowner's fields. Sometimes, in place of work, the renter would pay a quitrent.

Letters from a Farmer
in Pennsylvania 1767

The American colonies had many close ties with England; they spoke the same language, English laws were used in colonial government, and many of the English ideas about individual rights had been transplanted to the colonies. Despite these ties, the colonies broke from England. The reasons historians give for such a break are many; some feel that the American colonies had grown too big and prosperous to be colonies, some feel George III was an oppressive monarch and held to a poor colonial policy, others argue that after the end of the French and Indian War in 1763 the colonists no longer had to rely on England for protection from the French colonies to the north, and finally many say the colonies resented taxation without representation in the English Parliament. All of these views are part of the answer.

Whatever the final reason, the decision to make the break with England was a long and agonizing one for most of the colonists. A few of the more belligerent patriots like Sam Adams felt that the only answer in the colonies' tax disputes with England was to declare independence. A man like John Dickinson, later one of the framers of the Constitution, represented the more moderate position prior to the Revolution. Dickinson opposed the British policy of taxation that had caused so much resentment. Parliament had finally agreed to repeal the Stamp Act shortly after it was passed in 1764 after the colonies protested. But in 1767 Parliament passed the Townshend Act, a revenue act that imposed import duties in the colonies. Shortly after, Dickinson wrote "Letters from a Farmer in Pennsylvania" in protest. In these pamphlets he urged moderation on the part of the colonists. He had a very clear view of the responsibility of the governors and the governed. Compare his view of responsibility with Locke's view (see pp. 64 – 66) and with the opening statements in the Declaration of Independence (see pp. 91 – 95).

(9) My dear Countrymen, I rejoice to find that my two former letters to you have been generally received with so much favour. . . .

The meaning of [these letters] is, to convince the people of these colonies, that they are at this moment exposed to the most imminent dangers; and to persuade them immediately, vigorously, and unanimously, to exert themselves, in the most firm, but most peaceable manner, for obtaining relief.

The cause of *liberty* is a cause of too much dignity, to be sullied by turbulence and tumult. It ought to be maintained in a manner suitable to her nature. Those who engage in it, should breathe a sedate, yet fervent spirit, animating them to actions of prudence, justice, modesty, bravery, humanity, and magnanimity. . . .

Every government at some time or other falls into wrong measures. These may proceed from mistake or passion. But every such measure does not dissolve the obligation between the governors and the governed. The mistake may be corrected; the passion may subside. It is the duty of the governed to endeavour to rectify the mistake, and to appease the passion. They have not at first any other right, than to represent their grievances, and to pray for redress . . . If their applications are disregarded, then that kind of *opposition* becomes justifiable, which can be made without breaking the laws, or disturbing the public peace. This consists in the *prevention of the oppressors reaping advantage from their oppressions*, and not in their punishment. For experience may teach them, what reason did not and harsh methods cannot be proper, till milder ones have failed.

If at length it becomes UNDOUBTED that an inveterate [long-standing] resolution is formed to annihilate the liberties of the governed, the *English* history affords frequent examples of resistance by force. What particular circumstances will in any future case justify such resistance, can never be ascertained, till they happen. Perhaps it may be allowable to say generally, that it never can be justifiable, until the people are FULLY CONVINCED, that any further submission will be destructive to their happiness. . . .

It . . . ought forever to be remembered, that resistance, in the case of colonies against their mother country, is extremely different from the resistance of a people against their prince. A nation may change their king, or race of kings, and, retaining their ancient form of government, be gainers by changing . . . But if once *we* are separated from our mother country, what new form of government shall we adopt, or where shall we find another *Britain,* to supply our loss? Torn from the body to which we are united by religion, liberty, laws, affections, relation, language and commerce, we must bleed at every vein.

In truth—the prosperity of these provinces is founded in their dependence on *Great-Britain;* and when she returns to her "old good humour, and her old good nature" . . . I hope they will always think it their duty and interest, as it most certainly will be, to promote her welfare by all the means in their power. . . .

If, however, it shall happen, by an unfortunate course of affairs, that our applications to his Majesty and the Parliament for redress, prove ineffectual, let us THEN take *another step,* by withholding from *Great-Britain* all the advantages she has been used to receive from us. THEN let us try, if our ingenuity, industry, and frugality, will not give weight to our remonstrances. Let us all be united with one spirit, in one cause. Let us invent—let us work—let us save—let us, continually, keep up our claim, and incessantly repeat our complaints—But, above all, let us implore the protection of that infinitely good and gracious being, "by whom kings reign, and princes decree justice."

☆   ☆   ☆

The Intolerable Acts 1774

The Townshend Act imposed a duty on English paint, lead, paper, and tea. Parliament reacted to the adverse response in the colonies to this new act by repealing all but the duty on tea in 1770. Another issue was raised when the East India Company was granted a monopoly to sell tea at less than the current cost in the colonies. Many colonial merchants resented the granting of a monopoly to a company that could put independent merchants out of business. Some colonies refused to let the tea be unloaded; others refused to sell the tea. Boston, encouraged by Sam Adams, staged its famous Boston Tea Party and flavored the harbor with the cargo from three tea ships. In response to the "tea party" Parliament passed the following "Intolerable Acts."

(10) *The Boston Port Act,* March 31, 1774

Whereas dangerous commotions and insurrections have been fomented and raised in the town of Boston . . . *in which commotions and insurrections certain valuable cargoes of teas* . . . *were seized and destroyed: And whereas, in the present condition of the said town and harbour, the commerce of his Majesty's subjects cannot be safely carried on there* . . . *be it enacted* . . . That from and after the first day of June, one thousand seven hundred and seventy-four, it shall not be lawful for any person . . . to lade, put, or cause to procure to be laden or put, off or from any quay, wharf, or other place, within the said town of *Boston* . . . into any ship . . . any goods, wares or merchandise whatsoever, to be transported or carried into any other country, province, or place . . . or to . . . discharge . . . on land . . . any goods, wares or merchandise whatsoever, to be brought in from any other country.

[These provisions to continue] until it shall sufficiently appear to his Majesty that full satisfaction hath been made by . . . the inhabitants . . . of Boston to the united company of merchants of *England* trading to the *East Indies,* for the damage sustained . . . by the destruction of their goods . . .

☆　　☆　　☆

DOCUMENT

(11) *Massachusetts Government Act,* May 20, 1774

Be it . . . enacted . . ., that from and after the first day of *August,* one thousand seven hundred and seventy-four, so much of the charter, granted by their majesties King *William* and Queen *Mary* to the inhabitants of the said province of the Massachusetts Bay . . . be revoked . . . And that from and after the said first day of *August,* one thousand seven hundred and seventy-four, the council, or court of assistants of the said province for the time being, shall be composed of such of the inhabitants or proprietors of lands within the same as shall be thereunto nominated and appointed by his Majesty. . . .

And it is hereby further enacted, That the said assistants or counsellors . . . shall hold their offices respectively, for and during the pleasure of his Majesty. . . .

And be it further enacted . . ., That from and after the first day of *July,* one thousand seven hundred and seventy-four, it shall be . . . lawful for his Majesty's governor . . . to nominate and appoint . . . and also to remove, without the consent of the council, all judges of the inferior courts of common pleas, commissioners of *Oyer* and *Terminer,* the attorney general, provosts, marshals, justices of the peace, and other officers to the council or courts of justice . . .

☆　　☆　　☆

DOCUMENT

(12) *Administration of Justice Act,* May 20, 1774

Whereas in his Majesty's province of Massachusetts Bay, in New England, an *attempt hath lately been made to throw off the authority of the Parliament of* Great Britain . . . *and* an actual and avowed *resistance, by open force, to the execution of certain acts of Parliament, hath been suffered to take place . . . and whereas, in the present disordered state of the said province, it is of the utmost importance . . . that neither the magistrates acting in support of the laws, nor any of his Majesty's subjects aiding and assisting therein . . . should be discouraged from the proper discharge of their*

83

duty . . .: in order therefore to remove every such discouragement from the minds of his Majesty's subjects, and to induce them, upon all proper occasions, to exert themselves in support of the public peace of the province, and of the authority of the King and Parliament of Great Britain *over the same;* be it enacted . . ., That if any . . . indictment shall be found . . . for murder, or other capital offence, in the province of the *Massachusetts Bay,* and it shall appear, by information given upon oath to the governor . . . that the fact was committed by the person . . . either in the execution of his duty as a magistrate, for the suppression of riots, or in the support of the laws of revenue, . . . and if it shall also appear, to the satisfaction of the said governor . . . that an indifferent trial cannot be had within the said province, in that case, it shall and may be lawful for the governor . . . to direct . . . that the . . . indictment . . . shall be tried in some other of his Majesty's colonies, or in *Great Britain . . .*

☆   ☆   ☆

First Continental Congress 1774

The British policy of punishing Massachusetts for the Boston Tea Party by the passage of the Intolerable Acts electrified America. Radicals and moderates alike gathered at Carpenter's Hall in Philadelphia on September 5, 1774, to discuss the crisis confronting all the colonies. This meeting, which included representatives from all the colonies except Georgia, was the First Continental Congress.

In the fall of 1774 Americans were greatly concerned over British policies. As yet, few people openly advocated independence from Great Britain. All wanted liberty but hoped that Britain would moderate her stand and return to old policies. This desire for liberty without a break with England is reflected in the letter the Continental Congress sent to General Gage, the commander of the British troops in Boston and the governor of Massachusetts.

The request that General Gage keep his soldiers from violating people's rights and that he try to keep the situation from becoming too tense was mildly stated. But grievances were there—grievances that appear often in the next fifteen years of the nation's history. The anger so quietly expressed in this document underlies the section of the Declaration of Independence that lists King George III's violations of colonists' rights. Also the patriots remembered the actions of General Gage's soldiers when they were at last free to form their own government. After reading this section, find the section in the Constitution you think may reflect the grievances in this document.

84

(13) Sir,

The inhabitants of the town of Boston have informed us, the representatives of his Majesty's faithful subjects in all the colonies from Nova Scotia to Georgia, that the fortifications erecting within that town, the frequent invasion of private property, and the repeated insults they receive from the soldiery, have given them great reason to suspect a plan is formed very destructive to them, and tending to overthrow the liberties of America.

Your excellency cannot be a stranger to the sentiments of America with respect to the acts of Parliament, under the execution of which, those unhappy people are oppressed, the approbation universally expressed of their conduct, and the determined resolution of the colonies, for the preservation of their common rights, to unite in their opposition to those acts. In consequence of these sentiments, they have appointed us the guardians of their rights and liberties, and we are under the deepest concern, that whilst we are pursuing every dutiful and peaceful measure to procure a cordial and effectual reconciliation between Great Britain and the colonies, your excellency should proceed in a manner that bears so hostile an appearance, and which even those oppressive acts do not warrant.

We entreat your excellency to consider what a tendency this conduct must have to irritate and force a free people, however well disposed to peaceful measures, into hostilities, which may prevent the endeavours of this Congress to restore a good understanding with our parent state, and may involve us in the horrors of a civil war.

☆　　☆　　☆

Rights of British Americans 1774

Not all responses to the Intolerable Acts were as moderate as those of the Continental Congress in their letter to General Gage. In the wave of indignation that swept the colonies into the Continental Congress, Thomas Jefferson composed a series of resolutions for the Virginia delegation to that Congress. A majority of the delegation considered his criticisms of British policy too severe and did not adopt the resolution. But these ideas were made public when they were published as a pamphlet entitled "A Summary View of the Rights of British America."

This selection represents the feelings of many Americans in 1774. This first published writing of Jefferson's clearly states the feeling of unjustified oppression and yet the desire to remain a part of the British Empire.

Many of the ideas Jefferson uses were ideas that resulted from an English heritage. When Jefferson protests that Americans' rights to freedom are a "law of nature," he sounds like Gerrard Winstanley asserting that the poor in England have rights that the rich must recognize. And Jefferson's statement that "kings are servants, not proprietors of the people" reminds us of Locke's theory that government derives from the consent of the governed.

When Jefferson refers to the rights of British Americans, he looks to the future because the grievances reappear in the Declaration of Independence. But the ideas that Jefferson states in this document will appear in a much fuller form after Jefferson has had two more years to think about how governments should operate.

(14) That . . . thro' the reigns which preceded his majesty's, . . . the violations of our right were less alarming, because repeated at more distant intervals, than that rapid and bold succession of injuries which is likely to distinguish the present from all other periods of American history. Scarcely have our minds been able to emerge from the astonishment into which one stroke of parliamentary thunder has involved us, before another more heavy and more alarming is fallen on us. Single acts of tyranny may be ascribed to the accidental opinion of a day; but a series of oppressions, begun at a distinguished period, and pursued unalterably thro' every change of ministers, too plainly prove a deliberate, systematical plan of reducing us to slavery.

That the act passed in the 4th year of his majesty's reign entitled "An act for granting certain duties in the British colonies and plantations in America, etc." [Stamp Act] . . . .

And one other act passed in the 7th year of his reign entitled "An act for granting duties on paper, tea, etc." [Townshend Duties] form that connected chain of parliamentary usurpation which has already been the subject of frequent applications to his majesty and the houses of Lords and Commons of Great Britain; and, no answers having yet been condescended to any of these, we shall not trouble his majesty with a repetition of the matters they contained.

But the one other act passed in the same 7th year of his reign, having been a peculiar attempt, must ever require peculiar mention. It is entitled "An act for suspending the legislature of New York."

One free and independent legislature hereby takes upon itself to suspend the powers of another, free and independent as itself, thus exhibiting a phenomenon, unknown in nature, the creator and creature of its own power. Not only the principles of common sense, but the common feelings of human nature must be surrendered up, before his majesty's subjects here can be persuaded to believe that they hold their political existence at the will of a British Parliament. Shall these governments be dissolved, their property annihilated, and their people reduced to a state of nature, at the imperious breath of a body of men whom they never saw, in whom they never confided, and over whom they have no powers of punishment or removal, let their crimes against the American public be ever so great? Can any one reason be assigned why 160,000 electors in the island of Great Britain should give law to four millions in the states of America, every individual of whom is equal to every individual of them in virtue, in understanding, and in bodily strength? Were this to be admitted, instead of being a free people, as we have hitherto supposed, and mean to continue, ourselves, we should suddenly be found the slaves, not of one, but of 160,000 tyrants distinguished too from all others by this singular circumstance that they are removed from the reach of fear, the only restraining motive which may hold the hand of a tyrant. . . .

That these are our grievances which we have thus laid before his majesty with that freedom of language and sentiment which becomes a free people, claiming their rights as derived from the laws of nature, and not as the gift of their chief magistrate. . . . Open your breast, Sire, to liberal and expanded thought. Let not the name of George the third be a blot in the page of history. You are surrounded by British counsellors, but remember that they are parties. You have no ministers for American affairs, because you have none taken from among us, nor amenable to the laws on which they are to give you advice. It behooves you therefore to think and to act for yourself and your people . . . It is neither our wish nor our interest to separate from [Great Britain]. We are willing on our part to sacrifice everything which reason can ask to the restoration of that tranquility for which all must wish. On their part let them be ready to establish union on a generous plan. Let them name their terms, but let them be just. Accept of every commercial preference it is in our power to give for such things as we can raise for their use, or they make for ours. But let them not think to exclude us from going to other markets, to dispose of those commodities which they cannot use, nor to supply those wants which they cannot supply. Still less let it be proposed that our properties within our own territories shall be taxed or regulated by any power on earth but our own. The God who gave us life, gave us liberty at the same time: the hand of force may destroy, but cannot disjoin them. This, Sire, is our last, our determined resolution: and that you will be pleased to interpose with that efficacy which your earnest endeavors may insure to procure redress of these our great grievances, to quiet the minds of your subjects in British America against any apprehensions of future encroachment, to establish fraternal love and harmony thro' the whole empire, and that that may continue to the latest ages of time, is the fervent prayer of all British America.

☆　　☆　　☆

EXHIBITING A PHENOMENON . . . POWER In Jefferson's day most men saw the world as a very orderly place; each creature had its own position in the order. God, the Creator, was the highest in the scale, and the lowest creatures were at the bottom. Thus it is impossible for a man in Jefferson's day to imagine a creator and a creature as equals. Jefferson objects to Parliament's action because he sees Parliament and the New York legislature as equal creatures. He argues that Parliament is trying to make itself a creator (by suspending New York's legislature) at the same time it is a creature (an equal of that legislature).

THE GOD . . . DISJOIN THEM God gave men the gift of life and liberty. An act of force can destroy life and liberty (by killing the man), but that force cannot separate the two things.

The Virginia Bill of Rights 1776

In June of 1776 Virginia patriots adopted a constitution to provide their colony with a government. The Virginia constitution began with a Bill of Rights that was to serve as a model for other states' Bills of Rights and for the Constitution's Bill of Rights. Thomas Jefferson relied on some of its ideas in writing the Declaration of Independence, for the Virginia Bill of Rights expressed the idea that all men are free and independent and that government exists for the benefit of the people. This document and John Locke's writing (see pp. 64–66) were important in shaping Jefferson's thoughts on government and independence. See how often wordings in this document are repeated in the Declaration of Independence (see pp. 91–95).

The document was to become important much later in the nation's history as well. Since it was the basis of many state constitutions, it is not surprising that many of the ideas contained in the Virginia Bill of Rights were widespread. As you read, see how many provisions of this document are incorporated in the Constitution. See how many of the "rights" listed here are also listed in the first ten amendments to the Constitution.

(15) A declaration of rights made by the representatives of the good people of Virginia, assembled in full and free convention; which rights do pertain to them and their posterity, as the basis and foundation of government.

Section 1. That all men are by nature equally free and independent, and have certain inherent rights, of which, when they enter into a state of society, they cannot, by any compact, deprive or divest their posterity; namely, the enjoyment of life and liberty, with the means of acquiring and possessing property, and pursuing and obtaining happiness and safety.

Section 2. That all power is vested in, and consequently derived from, the people; that magistrates are their trustees and servants, and at all times amenable to them.

Section 3. That government is, or ought to be, instituted for the common benefit, protection, and security of the people, nation, or community; of all the various modes and forms of government, that is best which is capable of producing the greatest degree of happiness and safety, and is most effectually secured against the danger of maladministration; and that, when any government shall be found inadequate or contrary to these purposes, a majority of the community hath an indubitable, inalienable, and indefeasible right to reform, alter, or abolish it, in such manner as shall be judged most conducive to the public weal.

Section 4. That no man, or set of men, are entitled to exclusive or separate emoluments or privileges from the community, but in consideration of public services; which, not being descendible, neither ought the offices of magistrate, legislator, or judge to be hereditary.

Section 5. That the legislative and executive powers of the State should be separate and distinct from the judiciary; and that the members of the two first may be restrained from oppression, by feeling and participating the burdens of the people, they should, at fixed periods, be reduced to a private station, return into the body from which they were originally taken, and the vacancies be supplied by frequent, certain, and regular elections, in which all, or any part of the former members, to be again eligible, or ineligible, as the laws shall direct.

Section 6. That elections of members to serve as representatives of the people, in assembly, ought to be free; and that all men, having sufficient evidence of permanent common interest with, and attachment to, the community, have the right of suffrage, and cannot be taxed or deprived of their property for public uses, without their own consent, or that of their representatives so elected, nor bound by any law to which they have not, in like manner, assembled, for the public good.

Section 7. That all power of suspending laws, or the execution of laws, by any authority, without consent of the representatives of the people, is injurious to their rights, and ought not to be exercised.

Section 8. That in all capital or criminal prosecutions a man hath a right to demand the cause and nature of his accusation, to be confronted with the accusers and witnesses, to call for evidence in his favor, and to a speedy trial by an impartial jury of twelve men of his vicinage, without whose unanimous consent he cannot be found guilty; nor can he be compelled to give evidence against himself; that no man be deprived of his liberty, except by the law of the land or the judgment of his peers.

Section 9. That excessive bail ought not to be required, nor excessive fines imposed, nor cruel and unusual punishments inflicted.

Section 10. That general warrants, whereby an officer or messenger may be commanded to search suspected places without evidence of a fact committed, or to seize any person or persons not named, or whose offence is not particularly described and supported by evidence, are grievous and oppressive, and ought not to be granted.

Section 11. That in controversies respecting property, and in suits between man and man, the ancient trial by jury is preferable to any other, and ought to be held sacred.

Section 12. That the freedom of the press is one of the great bulwarks of liberty, and can never be restrained but by despotic governments.

Section 13. That a well-regulated militia, composed of the body of the people, trained to arms, is the proper, natural, and safe defence of a free State; that standing armies, in time of peace, should be avoided, as dangerous to liberty; and that in all cases the military should be under strict subordination to, and governed by, the civil power.

Section 14. That the people have a right to uniform government; and, therefore, that no government separate from, or independent of the government of Virginia, ought to be erected or established within the limits thereof.

Section 15. That no free government, or the blessings of liberty, can be preserved to any people, but by a firm adherence to justice, moderation, temperance, frugality, and virtue, and by frequent recurrence to fundamental principles.

Section 16. That religion, or the duty which we owe to our Creator, and the manner of discharging it, can be directed only by reason and conviction, not by force or violence; and therefore all men are equally entitled to the free exercise of religion, according to the dictates of conscience; and that it is the mutual duty of all to practise Christian forbearance, love, and charity towards each other.

☆   ☆   ☆

VICINAGE   Landholdings that were close together. Thus a man was to be judged by men who lived in his neighborhood.

The Declaration of Independence 1776

The decision by the American colonists to proclaim their independence was no hasty or ill-considered action. The colonists had been fighting British troops for well over a year before the Continental Congress decided to sever their bonds with the British crown. The decision was based on their faith in the righteousness of their cause, the obvious impossibility of a reconciliation with the London government, and their confidence in their capacity to succeed in the struggle and to govern themselves.

This historic document, written almost entirely by Thomas Jefferson, contains the classic statement that "all men are created equal," which was the moral justification of revolution. The longest part of the document lists the injuries the colonists felt they had sustained at the hands of King George III. Although Parliament had passed the Intolerable Acts signed by the king, Jefferson and his associates chose to aim their barbs at the British monarchy, believing that, as their sovereign, he was ultimately responsible for their troubles.

The Declaration ends with a vow to "pledge to each other our Lives, our Fortunes and our sacred Honor." This was not mere rhetoric. No one understood better than the men who signed the Declaration what their fate would be should they fail. They were not only risking their lives in fighting the British, but if these men survived an unsuccessful revolution their fate at the hands of an angry British government would hardly have been a happy one.

In retrospect few historians would agree with the signers of the Declaration of Independence that George III was as evil as they depict him to be. As you read, select phrases that suggest that Jef-

91

ferson's attitude toward George III was not entirely objective. Compare these grievances with the Constitution to see how many were guarded against in the new government.

(16) When in the Course of human events, it becomes necessary for one people to dissolve the political bands which have connected them with another, and to assume among the Powers of the earth, the separate and equal station to which the Laws of Nature and of Nature's God entitle them, a decent respect to the opinions of mankind requires that they should declare the causes which impel them to the separation.

We hold these truths to be self-evident, that all men are created equal, that they are endowed by their Creator with certain unalienable Rights, that among these are Life, Liberty and the pursuit of Happiness. That to secure these rights, Governments are instituted among Men, deriving their just powers from the consent of the governed, That whenever any Form of Government becomes destructive of these ends, it is the Right of the People to alter or to abolish it, and to institute new Government, laying its foundation on such principles and organizing its powers in such form, as to them shall seem most likely to effect their Safety and Happiness. Prudence, indeed, will dictate that Governments long established should not be changed for light and transient causes; and accordingly all experience hath shown, that mankind are more disposed to suffer, while evils are sufferable, than to right themselves by abolishing the forms to which they are accustomed. But when a long train of abuses and usurpations, pursuing invariably the same Object evinces a design to reduce them under absolute Despotism, it is their right, it is their duty, to throw off such Government, and to provide new Guards for their future security. — Such has been the patient sufferance of these Colonies; and such is now the necessity which constrains them to alter their former Systems of Government. The history of the present King of Great Britain is a history of repeated injuries and usurpations, all having in direct object the establishment of an absolute Tyranny over these States. To prove this, let Facts be submitted to a candid world.

He has refused his Assent to Laws, the most wholesome and necessary for the public good.

He has forbidden his Governors to pass Laws of immediate and pressing importance, unless suspended in their operation till his Assent should be obtained; and when so suspended, he has utterly neglected to attend to them.

He has refused to pass other Laws for the accommodation of large districts of people, unless those people would relinquish the right of Representation in the Legislature, a right inestimable to them and formidable to tyrants only.

He has called together legislative bodies at places unusual, uncomfortable, and distant from the depository of their Public Records, for the sole purpose of fatiguing them into compliance with his measures.

He has dissolved Representative Houses repeatedly, for opposing with manly firmness his invasions on the rights of the people.

He has refused for a long time, after such dissolutions, to cause others to be elected; whereby the Legislative Powers, incapable of Annihilation, have returned to the People at large for their exercise; the State remaining in the mean time exposed to all the dangers of invasion from without, and convulsions within.

He has endeavoured to prevent the population of these States; for that purpose obstructing the Laws for Naturalization of Foreigners; refusing to pass others to encourage their migration hither, and raising the conditions of new Appropriations of Lands.

He has obstructed the Administration of Justice, by refusing his Assent to Laws for establishing Judiciary Powers.

He has made Judges dependent on his Will alone, for the tenure of their offices, and the amount and payment of their salaries.

He has erected a multitude of New Offices, and sent hither swarms of Officers to harass our People, and eat out their substance.

He has kept among us, in times of peace, Standing Armies without the Consent of our legislature.

He has affected to render the Military independent of and superior to the Civil Power.

He has combined with others to subject us to a jurisdiction foreign to our constitution, and unacknowledged by our laws; giving his Assent to their Acts of pretended Legislation:

For quartering large bodies of armed troops among us:

For protecting them, by a mock Trial, from Punishment for any Murders which they should commit on the Inhabitants of these States:

For cutting off our Trade with all parts of the world:

For imposing taxes on us without our Consent:

For depriving us in many cases, of the benefits of Trial by Jury:

For transporting us beyond Seas to be tried for pretended offences:

For abolishing the free System of English Laws in a neighbouring Province, establishing therein an Arbitrary government, and enlarging its Boundaries so as to render it at once an example and fit instrument for introducing the same absolute rule into these Colonies:

For taking away our Charters, abolishing our most valuable Laws, and altering fundamentally the Forms of our Governments:

For suspending our own Legislatures, and declaring themselves invested with Power to legislate for us in all cases whatsoever.

He has abdicated Government here, by declaring us out of his Protection and waging War against us.

He has plundered our seas, ravaged our Coasts, burnt our Towns, and destroyed the lives of our people.

He is at this time transporting large armies of foreign mercenaries to compleat the works of death, desolation and tyranny, already begun with circumstances of Cruelty & perfidy scarcely paralleled in the most barbarous ages, and totally unworthy the Head of a civilized nation.

He has constrained our fellow Citizens taken Captive on the high Seas to bear Arms against their Country, to become the executioners of their friends and Brethren, or to fall themselves by their Hands.

He has excited domestic insurrections amongst us, and has endeavoured to bring on the inhabitants of our frontiers, the merciless Indian Savages, whose known rule of warfare, is an undistinguished destruction of all ages, sexes and conditions.

In every stage of these Oppressions We have Petitioned for Redress in the most humble terms: Our repeated Petitions have been answered only by repeated injury. A Prince, whose character is thus marked by every act which may define a Tyrant, is unfit to be the ruler of a free People.

Nor have We been wanting in attention to our Brittish brethren. We have warned them from time to time of attempts by their legislature to extend an unwarrantable jurisdiction over us. We have reminded them of the circumstances of our emigration and settlement here. We have appealed to their native justice and magnanimity, and we have conjured them by the ties of our common kindred to disavow these usurpations, which, would inevitably interrupt our connections and correspondence. They too have been deaf to the voice of justice and of consanguinity. We must, therefore, acquiesce in the necessity, which denounces our Separation, and hold them, as we hold the rest of mankind, Enemies in War, in Peace Friends.

We, therefore, the Representatives of the United States of America, in General Congress, Assembled, appealing to the Supreme Judge of the world for the rectitude of our intentions, do, in the Name, and by Authority of the good People of these Colonies, solemnly publish and declare, That these United Colonies are, and of Right ought to be Free and Independent States; and that they are Absolved from all Allegiance to the British Crown, and that all political connection between them and the State of Great Britain, is and ought to be totally dissolved; and that as Free and Independent States, they have full Power to levy War, conclude Peace, contract Alliances, establish Commerce, and to do all other Acts and Things which Independent States may of right do. And for the support of this Declaration, with a firm reliance on the Protection of Divine Providence, we mutually pledge to each other our Lives, our Fortunes and our sacred Honor.

☆ ☆ ☆

III. Footnotes

[1] William MacDonald, ed., *Select Charters and Other Documents Illustrative of American History, 1606–1775* (Macmillan Co., New York, 1899) 33–34.

[2] Francis Newton Thorpe, ed., *The Federal and State Constitutions, Colonial Charters, and Other Organic Laws of the States, Territories, and Colonies Now or Heretofore Forming the United States of America*, VII (Government Printing Office, Washington, D.C., 1909) 3810–3811.

[3] Thomas Hutchinson, *The History of the Colony and Province of Massachusetts Bay*, Lawrence Shaw Mayo, ed. (Harvard University Press, Cambridge, Mass., 1936) I, 415.

[4] Cotton Mather, *Magnalia Christi Americana* (Silas Andrus, Hartford, Conn., 1820) I, 243.

[5] Roger Williams, *The Bloudy Tenant of Persecution* (Narragansett Edition, Providence, R.I., 1867) 3–4.

[6] MacDonald, ed., *Select Charters and Other Documents*, 105–106.

[7] William Dunlap, *History of the New Netherlands Province of New York and State of New York to the Adoption of the Federal Constitution* (Carter and Thorp, New York, 1839) I, 300–305.

[8] Albert Henry Smyth, ed., *The Writings of Benjamin Franklin* (Macmillan Co., New York, 1905) III, 207–226.

[9] John Dickinson, *Letters from a Farmer in Pennsylvania to the Inhabitants of the British Colonies* (Edds and Gill, Boston, Mass., 1768) 15–19.

[10, 11, 12] MacDonald, ed., *Select Charters and Other Documents*, 337–355.

[13] *Journals of the Continental Congress, 1774–1789* (Government Printing Office, Washington, D.C., 1904) I, 60–61.

[14] Reprinted by permission of the Princeton University Press. Julian P. Boyd, ed., *The Papers of Thomas Jefferson* (Princeton University Press, Princeton, N.J., 1950) I, 125–126, 134–135.

[15] Thorpe, ed., *The Federal and State Constitutions*, 3812–3814.

[16] Perley Poore Ben, comp., *The Federal and State Constitutions, Colonial Charters, and other Organic Acts of the United States*, Part I, 2nd edition (Government Printing Office, Washington, D.C., 1878) 3, 4, 5.

95

IV

What Were the Problems
of the Early Government?

Articles of Confederation 1777

Even before the Declaration of Independence was announced, the Continental Congress set up a committee to draft a framework for a new government. Late in 1777 the Articles of Confederation were quickly approved by the Congress. The Articles formally went into effect in 1781 after ratification by the last state, Maryland.

The new Congress had few new powers that the Continental Congress did not have; most of the governmental power rested with each state. This framework of government developed from earlier governments that had operated in the colonies. While under British rule each colony had to pay taxes to the king, most had a great deal of latitude in governing themselves. Therefore, when the colonies found themselves independent, their first government was one that left things much as they were.

The Articles of Confederation were weak. The new Congress was empowered to do only those things the states could not successfully do themselves: settle boundary disputes, keep an army and a navy, conduct foreign affairs, and coin money. The Congress did not have the power to tax the states; the government was supported solely by the tax money the state legislatures were willing to grant to it. The government had no way of demanding the money.

The Articles of Confederation had a direct bearing on the Constitution. Their failure led to a new government. In attempting to live under such a loose form of government, the new states learned that a Congress that had no power to tax had no power at all. Americans soon realized that their new country was not just an extension of the old independent colonies; to survive, they needed a new government that would mold them into a nation.

The Articles of Confederation also served as a guidepost for the men who framed the Constitution. Some of the provisions of the Articles became, with little change, parts of the Constitution. Compare the two documents to find out why the provisions that are similar worked well in both systems of government. Notice the articles which differ from the later Constitution.

(1) ARTICLE I. The stile [title] of this confederacy shall be "The United States of America."

ARTICLE II. Each State retains its sovereignty, freedom and independence, and every power, jurisdiction and right, which is not by this confederation expressly delegated to the United States, in Congress assembled.

ARTICLE III. The said States hereby severally enter into a firm league of friendship with each other, for their common defence, the security of their liberties, and their mutual and general welfare, binding themselves to assist each other, against all force offered to, or attacks made upon them, or any of them, on account of religion, sovereignty, trade, or any other pretence whatever.

ARTICLE IV. The better to secure and perpetuate mutual friendship and intercourse among the people of the different States in this Union, the free inhabitants of each of these States, paupers, vagabonds and fugitives from justice excepted, shall be entitled to all privileges and immunities of free citizens in the several States; and the people of each State shall have free ingress and regress to and from any other State, and shall enjoy therein all the privileges of trade and commerce, subject to the same duties, impositions and restrictions as the inhabitants thereof respectively, provided that such restrictions shall not extend so far as to prevent the removal of property imported into any State, to any other State of which the owner is an inhabitant; provided also that no imposition, duties or restriction shall be laid by any State, on the property of the United States, or either of them.

If any person guilty of, or charged with treason, felony, or other high misdemeanor in any State, shall flee from justice, and be found in any of the United States, he shall upon demand of the Governor or Executive power, of the State from which he fled, be delivered up and removed from the State having jurisdiction of his offence. Full faith and credit shall be given in each of these States to the records, acts and judicial proceedings of the courts and magistrates of every other State.

ARTICLE V. Freedom of speech and debate in Congress shall not be impeached or questioned in any court, or place out of

Congress, and the members of Congress shall be protected in their persons from arrests and imprisonments, during the time of their going to and from, and attendance on Congress, except for treason, felony, or breach of the peace.

ARTICLE VI. No State without the consent of the United States in Congress assembled, shall send any embassy to, or receive any embassy from, or enter into any conferrence, agreement, alliance or treaty with any king, prince or state; nor shall any person holding any office of profit or trust under the United States, or any of them, accept of any present, emolument, office or title of any kind whatever from any king, prince or foreign state; nor shall the United States in Congress assembled, or any of them, grant any title of nobility.

No two or more States shall enter into any treaty, confederation or alliance whatever between them, without the consent of the United States in Congress assembled, specifying accurately the purposes for which the same is to be entered into, and how long it shall continue.

No State shall lay any imposts or duties, which may interfere with any stipulations in treaties, entered into by the United States in Congress assembled, with any king, prince or state, in pursuance of any treaties already proposed by Congress, to the courts of France and Spain.

No vessels of war shall be kept up in time of peace by any State, except such number only, as shall be deemed by the United States, in Congress assembled, for the defence of such State, or its trade; nor shall any body of forces be kept up by any State, in time of peace, except such number only, as in the judgment of the United States, in Congress assembled, shall be deemed requisite to garrison the forts necessary for the defence of such State; but every State shall always keep up a well regulated and disciplined militia, sufficiently armed and accoutred, and shall provide and constantly have ready for use, in public stores, a due number of field pieces and tents, and a proper quantity of arms, ammunition and camp equipage. . . . .

ARTICLE VIII. All charges of war, and all other expenses that shall be incurred for the common defence or general welfare, and allowed by the United States in Congress assembled, shall be defrayed out of a common treasury, which shall be supplied by the several States . . . .

. . . The taxes for paying that proportion shall be laid and levied by the authority and direction of the Legislatures of the several States within the time agreed upon by the United States in Congress assembled.

ARTICLE IX. The United States in Congress assembled, shall have the sole and exclusive right and power of determining on peace and war, except in the cases mentioned in the sixth article—of sending and receiving ambassadors—entering into treaties and alliances, provided that no treaty of commerce shall be made whereby the legislative power of the respective States shall be restrained from imposing such imposts and duties on foreigners, as their own people are subjected to, or from prohibiting the exportation or importation of any species of goods or commodities whatsoever—of establishing rules for deciding in all cases, what captures on land or water shall be legal, and in what manner prizes taken by land or naval forces in the service of the United States shall be divided or appropriated—of granting letters of marque and reprisal in times of peace—appointing courts for the trial of piracies and felonies committed on the high seas and establishing courts for receiving and determining finally appeals in all cases of captures, provided that no member of Congress shall be appointed a judge of any of the said courts.

The United States in Congress assembled shall also be the last resort on appeal in all disputes and differences now subsisting or that hereafter may arise between two or more States concerning boundary, jurisdiction or any other cause whatever;

. . . . All controversies concerning the private right of soil claimed under different grants of two or more States, whose jurisdiction as they may respect such lands, and the States which passed such grants are adjusted, the said grants or either of them being at the same time claimed to have originated antecedent to such settlement or jurisdiction, shall on the petition of either party to the Congress of the United States, be finally determined as near as may be in the same manner as is before prescribed for deciding disputes respecting territorial jurisdiction between different States.

The United States in Congress assembled shall also have the sole and exclusive right and power of regulating the alloy and value of coin struck by their own authority, or by that of the respective States.—fixing the standard of weights and measures throughout the United States.—regulating the trade and managing all affairs with the Indians, not members of any of the States, provided that the legislative right of any State within its own limits be not infringed or violated—establishing and regulating post-offices from one State to another, throughout all the United States, and exacting such postage on the papers passing thro' the same as may be requisite to defray the expenses of the said office—appointing all officers of the land forces, in the service of the United States, excepting regimental officers—appointing all the officers of the naval forces, and commissioning all officers whatever in the service of the United States—making rules for the government and regulation of the said land and naval forces, and directing their operations.

ARTICLE XIII. Every state shall abide by the determinations of the United States in Congress assembled, on all questions which by this confederation are submitted to them. And the articles of this confederation shall be inviolably observed by every State, and the Union shall be perpetual; nor shall any alteration at any time hereafter be made in any of them; unless such alteration be agreed to in a Congress of the United States, and be afterwards confirmed by the Legislatures of every State.

And whereas it has pleased the Great Governor of the world to incline the hearts of the Legislatures we respectively represent in Congress, to approve of, and to authorize us to ratify the said articles of confederation and perpetual union. Know ye that we the undersigned delegates, by virtue of the power and authority to us given for that purpose, do by these presents, in the name and in behalf of our respective constituents, fully and entirely ratify and confirm each and every of the said articles of confederation and perpetual union, and all and singular the matters and things therein contained. . . .

☆   ☆   ☆

RESTRICTIONS SHALL NOT . . . . . EITHER OF THEM
When inhabitants of any state move to another state, they will have to abide by the taxes and restrictions of the new state with two exceptions: 1. the new state may not restrict the individual's right to move his property. 2. the state may not tax or limit property of the United States.

LETTERS OF MARQUE AND REPRISAL   See page 21.

Northwest Ordinance 1787

Possibly the most important single act of the Congress of the Confederation was the adoption of the Northwest Ordinance. The major issue was whether territories belonging to the United States would be organized with the intent of bringing new states into the Union with the same rights and privileges as the original thirteen. Some argued that new states should not have a status equal with that of the states which had fought and suffered through the revolution. There was historical precedent for this approach. The usual practice of nations and empires had been to govern new territories without allowing the peoples living there the same privileges as citizens living in the parent nation. However, a majority of the Congress of the Confederation voted to organize territories which would eventually be admitted as states; these states were to have all the rights of the original thirteen. This early decision allowed for a peaceable and flexible means for the country to grow. It also eliminated the possibility of conflicts between the new and the original states over unequal rights.

The first articles of the Northwest Ordinance are interesting for another reason – they deal with such individual rights as the freedom to worship and the right to a writ of habeas corpus. The Articles of Confederation have no such lengthy guarantee of individual rights: the Congress of the Confederation had so little power that individual rights were not endangered by it. Most states guaranteed individual rights in their state constitutions, but in 1787 the Northwest Territory did not have such constitutional provisions. Congress' concern with the guaranteeing of individual rights is interesting in light of the events that soon followed when the major criticism of the new Constitution that replaced the Articles of Confederation was the absence of a Bill of Rights to protect individuals against oppression by the new federal government.

DOCUMENT

(2) ARTICLE I. No person, demeaning himself in a peaceable and orderly manner, shall ever be molested on account of his mode of worship, or religious sentiments, in the said territory.

ARTICLE II. The inhabitants of the said territory shall always be entitled to the benefits of the writs of *habeas corpus,* and of the trial by jury; of a proportionate representation of the people in the legislature, and of judicial proceedings according to the course of the common law. All persons shall be bailable, unless for capital offences, where the proof shall be evident, or the presumption great. All fines shall be moderate; and no cruel or unusual punishments shall be inflicted. No man shall be deprived of his liberty or property, but by the judgment of his peers, or the law of the land, and should the public exigencies make it necessary, for the common preservation, to take any person's property, or to demand his particular services, full compensation shall be made for the same. And, in the just preservation of rights and property, it is understood and declared, that no law ought ever to be made or have force in the said territory, that shall, in any manner whatever, interfere with or affect private contracts, or engagements, *bona fide,* and without fraud previously formed.

ARTICLE III. Religion, morality, and knowledge being necessary to good government and the happiness of mankind, schools and the means of education shall forever be encouraged. The utmost good faith shall always be observed towards the Indians; their lands and property shall never be taken from them without their consent; and in their property, rights and liberty they never shall be invaded or disturbed, unless in just and lawful wars authorized by Congress; but laws founded in justice and humanity shall, from time to time, be made, for preventing wrongs being done to them, and for preserving peace and friendship with them. . . .

ARTICLE V. There shall be formed in the said territory not less than three nor more than five States; and the boundaries of the States, as soon as Virginia shall alter her act of cession and consent to the same, shall become fixed and established. . . .

And whenever any of the said States shall have sixty thousand free inhabitants therein, such State shall be admitted, by its delegates, into the Congress of the United States, on an equal footing with the original States, in all respects whatever; and shall be at liberty to form a permanent constitution and State government: *Provided,* The constitution and government, so to be formed, shall be republican, and in conformity to the principles contained in these articles, and, so far as it can be consistent with the general interest of the confederacy, such admission shall be allowed at an earlier period, and when there may be a less number of free inhabitants in the State than sixty thousand.

☆   ☆   ☆

WRITS OF *HABEAS CORPUS.* See page 23.

CAPITAL OFFENCES   Crimes punishable by death.

BONA FIDE   In good faith.

Shays' Rebellion 1786

Following the Revolutionary War the states had war debts they wanted to pay. States could pay debts by collecting taxes, but these taxes usually were head taxes that fell most heavily on the small farmers who already were in debt for their land. Some states issued paper money that made the paying of debts easier for the farmers. But the people to whom the debts were owed felt they had been cheated by cheap money. In Massachusetts the legislature was controlled by wealthy merchants; since they held the notes the farmers owed, they refused to issue paper money to help farmers pay debts and they continued to tax farmers heavily.

Soon farmers were being taken to court for their debts. The situation became very tense. Daniel Shays reluctantly became the leader of a group of farmers that tried to keep a county court from sitting and bringing any more debtors into court. The rebellion was finally put down by a state militia but not without a great deal of difficulty.

Shays' Rebellion was a state problem, but it achieved national importance because it showed the weaknesses of the Confederation. Massachusetts appealed to the Confederation at first for help, but the Confederation had no money and no troops. The new nation now realized its inability to keep order. The people were sufficiently aroused by the rebellion to realize that their present federal government was not adequate.

George Washington wrote to Benjamin Lincoln, the leader of state troops, inquiring about the rebellion. Washington asked, "Are your people getting mad?" The document that follows is Lincoln's reply to Washington's letter. As you read this document, find the statements that suggest Lincoln is not in sympathy with the rebellion.

DOCUMENT

(3) . . . Although I cannot pretend to give a full and complete answer to them, yet I will make some observations which shall involve in them the best answers to the several questions in my power to give. . . .

"Are we to have the goodly fabric, that eight years were spent in rearing, pulled over our heads?" There is great danger that it will be so, I think, unless the tottering system shall be supported by arms, and even then a government which has no other basis than the point of the bayonet, should one be suspended thereon, is so totally different from the one established, at least in idea, by the different States that if we must have recourse to the sad experiment of arms it can hardly be said that we have supported "the goodly fabric." In this view of the matter, it may be "pulled over our heads." This probably will be the case, for there doth not appear to be virtue enough among the people to preserve a perfect republican government.

"What is the cause of all these commotions?" The causes are too many and too various for me to pretend to trace and point them out. I shall therefore only mention some of those which appear to be the principal ones. Among those I may rank the ease with which property was acquired, with which credit was obtained, and debts were discharged in the time of the war. Hence people were diverted from their usual industry and economy. A luxuriant mode of living crept into vogue, and soon that income, by which the expenses of all should as much as possible be limited, was no longer considered as having any thing to do with the question at which expense families ought to live, or rather which they ought not to have exceeded. The moment the day arrived when all discovered that things were fast returning back into their original channels, that the in-

dustrious were to reap the fruits of their industry, and that the
indolent and improvident would soon experience the evils of their
idleness and sloth, very many startled at the idea, and instead of
attempting to subject themselves to such a line of conduct, which
duty to the public and a regard to their own happiness evidently
pointed out, they contemplated how they should evade the necessity of reforming their system and of changing their present mode
of life, they first complained of commutation, of the weight of
public taxes, of the insupportable debt of the Union, of the scarcity
of money, and of the cruelty of suffering the private creditors to call
for their just dues. This catalogue of complaints was listened to by
many. County conventions were formed, and the cry for the paper
money, subject to depreciation, as was declared by some of their
public resolves, was the clamor of the day. But notwithstanding
instructions to members of the General Court and petitions from
different quarters, the majority of that body were opposed to the
measure. Failing of their point, the disaffected in the first place
attempted, and in many instances succeeded, to stop the courts of
law, and to suspend the operations of government. . . .

It is impossible for me to determine "when and how they will
end;" as I see little probability that they will be brought to a period, and the dignity of government supported, without bloodshed.
When a single drop is drawn, the most prophetic spirit will not, in
my opinion, be able to determine when it will cease flowing. The
proportion of debtors run high in this State. Too many of them are
against the government. The men of property and the holders of the
public securities are generally supporters of our present constitution. Few of these have been in the field, and it remains quite
problematical whether they will in time so fully discover their own
interests as they shall be induced thereby to lend for a season part
of their property for the security of the remainder. If these classes of
men should not turn out on the broad scale with spirit, and the
insurgents should take the field and keep it, our constitution will be
overturned, and the federal government broken in upon by lopping
off one branch essential to the well being of the whole. This cannot
be submitted to by the United States with impunity. They must
send force to our aid; when this shall be collected, they will be equal
to *all* purposes . . .

☆   ☆   ☆

"ARE YOUR PEOPLE GETTING MAD?"   "Mad" here is not used
in the sense of "angry"; rather it refers to madness, or insanity.

GOODLY FABRIC   The goodly fabric is the government established under the Articles of Confederation. This question means,
"Are we to see our eight-year-old government destroyed?"

104

UNLESS THE TOTTERING SYSTEM . . . . HAVE SUPPORTED
"THE GOODLY FABRIC" Unless the government is supported
by a militia, it is in grave danger. But a government that must be
supported by arms is so far from the one that was established that
one can hardly say that one is supporting the original government.

BROUGHT TO A PERIOD Brought to an end.

FEDERAL GOVERNMENT . . . . OF THE WHOLE The "one
branch" refers to the state government. If the state constitution
is overthrown, the rebels will have broken in on the federal government as well, for the state government is an essential branch of
the federal government.

The Virginia Plan 1787

When the Constitutional Convention met in the spring of 1787 to
outline a new government, the delegates had only the ineffectual
Articles of Confederation to use as a guide. All the delegates knew
that the government could not follow this model. However, the
Virginia delegation, prior to their meeting in Philadelphia, had
adopted a plan of government which they presented to the Convention in late May.

This plan, called the Virginia Plan or Large-States Plan (*see
p. 3*) provided a framework that the delegates could build upon
and improve. It suggested a government composed of a two-house
legislature with representation based on population. The lower
house would be elected by the people, but the upper house would be
chosen by the lower house. The president would be chosen by the
legislature, too. This plan favored the large states since their representatives would outnumber those of smaller states.

While the details of this part of the plan were not accepted, one
device was to appear in the Constitution. A council of Revision
composed of the executive and part of the judiciary had a power of
veto over legislation. This balancing veto power among the legislature, executive, and judiciary was to play an important part in the
Constitution.

As you read, note the important provisions included in the plan
that were included in the Constitution.

DOCUMENT

(4) 1. *Resolved,* That the articles of the confederation ought to
be so corrected and enlarged, as to accomplish the objects
proposed by their institution, namely, common defence, security of
liberty, and general welfare.

2. *Resolved,* Therefore, That the right of suffrage, in the national legislature, ought to be proportioned to the quotas of contribution, or to the number of free inhabitants, as the one or the other may seem best, in different cases.

3. *Resolved,* That the national legislature ought to consist of two branches.

4. *Resolved,* That the members of the first branch of the national legislature ought to be elected by the people of the several States, every ——— for the term of ——— to be of the age of ——— years at least; to receive liberal stipends, by which they may be compensated for the devotion of their time to public service; to be ineligible to any office established by a particular State, or under the authority of the United States (except those peculiarly belonging to the functions of the first branch) during the term of service and for the space of ——— after its expiration; to be incapable of re-election for the space of ——— after the expiration of their term of service; and to be subject to recall.

5. *Resolved,* That the members of the second branch of the national legislature ought to be elected by those of the first, out of a proper number of persons nominated by the individual legislatures; to be of the age of ——— years, at least; to hold their offices for a term sufficient to ensure their independency; to receive liberal stipends, by which they may be compensated for the devotion of their time to the public service; and to be ineligible to any office established by a particular State, or under the authority of the United States, (except those peculiarly belonging to the functions of the second branch) during the term of service; and for the space of ——— after the expiration thereof.

6. *Resolved,* That each branch ought to possess the right of originating acts; that the national legislature ought to be empowered to enjoy the legislative right vested in Congress, by the confederation; and moreover to legislate in all cases to which the separate States are incompetent, or in which the harmony of the United States may be interrupted by the exercise of individual legislation; to negative all laws passed by the several States, contravening in the opinion of the national legislature, the articles of union, or any treaty subsisting under the authority of the union; and to call forth the force of the union against any member of the union failing to fulfil its duty under the articles thereof.

7. *Resolved,* That a national executive be instituted, to be chosen by the national legislature for the term of———years, to receive punctually, at stated times, a fixed compensation for the services rendered, in which no increase or diminution shall be made, so as to affect the magistracy existing at the time of the increase or diminution; to be ineligible a second time; and that,

besides a general authority to execute the national laws, it ought to enjoy the executive rights vested in congress by the confederation.

8. *Resolved,* That the executive, and a convenient number of the national judiciary, ought to compose a council of revision, with authority to examine every act of the national legislature, before it shall operate, and every act of a particular legislature before a negative thereon shall be final; and that the dissent of the said council shall amount to a rejection, unless the act of the national legislature be again passed, or that a particular legislature be again negatived by ———— of the members of each branch.

9. *Resolved,* That a national judiciary be established to hold their offices during good behavior, and to receive punctually, at stated times, fixed compensations for their services, in which no increase or diminution shall be made, so as to affect the person actually in office at the time of such increase or diminution—That the jurisdiction of the inferior tribunals shall be, to hear and determine . . . in the dernier resort, all piracies and felonies on the high seas; captures from an enemy; cases in which foreigners, or citizens of other States, applying to such jurisdictions, may be interested, or which respect the collection of the national revenue; impeachments of any national officer; and questions which involved the national peace or harmony.

10. *Resolved,* That provision ought to be made for the admission of States, lawfully arising within the limits of the United States, whether from a voluntary junction of government and territory, or otherwise, with the consent of a number of voices in the national legislature less than the whole.

11. *Resolved,* That a republican government, and the territory of each State (except in the instance of a voluntary junction of government and territory) ought to be guaranteed by the United States to each State.

12. *Resolved,* That provision ought to be made for the continuance of a congress, and their authorities and privileges, until a given day, after the reform of the articles of union shall be adopted, and for the completion of all their engagements.

13. That provision ought to be made for the amendment of the articles of union whensoever it shall seem necessary; and that the assent of the national legislature ought not to be required thereto.

14. *Resolved,* That the legislative, executive, and judiciary powers within the several States, ought to be bound by oath to support the articles of union.

15. *Resolved,* That the amendments, which shall be offered to the confederation by the convention, ought, at a proper time or times, after the approbation of congress, to be submitted to an assembly or assemblies of representatives, recommended by the

several legislatures, to be expressly chosen by the people to consider and decide thereon.

☆   ☆   ☆

PROPORTIONED TO THE QUOTAS OF CONTRIBUTION
The contributions referred to here would be taxes which in those days were often head taxes—each person had to pay the same amount of tax. The quota would be the total taxes in the state. Thus representation would be based on the total taxes each state paid and the states with larger populations would have larger representation.

IN THE DERNIER RESORT   In the last court of appeals.

The New Jersey Plan 1787

While the Virginia Plan *(see pp. 105–108)* was debated at the Philadelphia Convention, the delegates from some of the smaller states— such as New Jersey, Connecticut, Maryland, and Delaware—became increasingly concerned about certain features of that proposal; they feared control of a strong central government by the larger states. Consequently, a group of delegates drafted a counterplan designed to safeguard the rights of each individual, and more particularly the states with small populations. This new proposal, called the New Jersey Plan, furnished a rallying point for those opposed to the Virginia Plan.

The New Jersey Plan called for a revision of the Articles of Confederation with a Congress, like the Congress of the Confederation, in which each state would have equal representation. Yet the small state delegates, realizing the weaknesses of the Articles, proposed that Congress have the right to tax and to regulate commerce.

One of the most significant features of the New Jersey Plan was the statement that federal laws and treaties would be the "supreme law of the respective states." This concept, which was inserted into the completed Constitution in Article VI, Section 2, has created a more powerful federal government than any supporter of the New Jersey Plan visualized.

As the delegates continued to debate the essential features of these two plans, it became clear that the problem of representation was the major obstacle to the creation of a new government. The Convention solved the dilemma by a compromise; each state would have equal representation in the upper house and proportional representation in the lower house.

108

Which portions of this document were used in the Constitution? How many constitutional compromises can you trace to this document?

(5) 1. Resolved, That the Articles of Confeder^n ought to be so revised, corrected, and enlarged as to render the federal Constitution adequate to the exigencies of Government, and the preservation of the Union.

2. Resolved, That in addition to the Powers vested in the United States in Congress by the present existing Articles of Confederation, they be authorized to pass Acts for raising a Revenue by levying a Duty or Duties on all goods and Merchandise of foreign growth or manufacture imported into any part of the United States, — by Stamps on Paper Vellum or Parchment, — and by a Postage on all Letters and Packages passing through the general Post Office. To be applied to such federal purposes as they shall deem proper and expedient; to make rules and regulations for the collection thereof, and the same from time to time to alter and amend, in such manner as they shall think proper. To pass Acts for the regulation of Trade and Commerce, as well with foreign Nations, as with each other. Provided that all Punishments, Fines Forfeitures and Penalties to be incurred for contravening such Rules, and regulations shall be adjudged by the common Law Judiciary of the States in which any offence contrary to the true intent and meaning of such Rules and regulations shall be committed or perpetrated; with liberty of commencing in the first instance all suits or prosecutions for that purpose in the Superior Common Law Judiciary of such State; subject Nevertheless to an Appeal for the Correction of all errors, both in Law and Fact, in rendering Judgment, to the Judiciary of the United States.

3. Resolved, That whenever Requisitions shall be necessary, instead of the present Rule, the United States in Congress be authorized to make such Requisitions in proportion to the whole Number of white and other Free Citizens and Inhabitants of every age, sex and condition, including those bound to servitude for a Term of years, and three fifths of all other persons not comprehended in the foregoing description — (except Indians not paying Taxes): that if such Requisitions be not complied with, in the time to be specified therein, to direct the Collection thereof in the non complying States and for that purpose to devise and pass Acts directing and authorizing the same. Provided that none of the powers hereby vested in the United States in Congress shall be exercized without the Consent of at least —— States, and *in* that proportion,

109

if the number of confederated States should be hereafter encreased or diminished.

4. Resolved, That the U.S. in Congress be authorized to elect a fœderal Executive to consist of ———— Persons, to continue in office for the Term of ———— years; to receive punctually at Stated times a fixed compensation for the services by them rendered, in which no increase or diminution shall be made, so as to affect the persons composing the Executive at the time of such encrease or diminution; to be paid out of the Federal Treasury; to be incapable of holding any other Office or appointment during their time of service, and for ———— years thereafter; to be ineligible a second time, and removable on impeachment and conviction for Mal practice or neglect of duty—by Congress on application by a Majority of the Executives of the several States. That the Executive, besides a general authority to execute the federal Acts, ought to appoint all federal Officers not other wise provided for, and to direct all Military operations; provided that none of the persons composing the federal Executive shall on any occasion take command of any Troops so as personally to conduct any Military enterprise as general ["Officer" stricken out] or in any other capacity.

5. Resolved, That a federal Judiciary be established, to consist of a supreme Tribunal, the Judges of which to be appointed by the Executive, and to hold their Offices during good behavior; to receive punctually at stated times a fixed compensation for their services, in which no increase or diminution shall be made so as to effect the persons actually in Office at the time of such increase or diminution;—That the Judiciary so established shall have authority to hear and determine in the first instance on all impeachments of federal Officers, and by way of Appeal in the dernier resort in all cases touching the Rights and privileges of Embassadors; in all cases of captures from an Enemy; in all cases of Piricies and Felonies on the high Seas; in all cases in which Foreigners may be interested in the construction of any Treaty or Treaties, or which may arise on any Act or Ordinance of Congress for the Regulation of Trade, or the collection of the Federal Revenue: that none of the Judiciary Officers shall during the time they remain in Office be capable of receiving or holding any other Office or appointment during their time of service, or for ———— thereafter.

6. Resolved, That the Legislative, Executive, and Judiciary Powers within the several States ought to be bound by Oath to support the Articles of Union.

7. Resolved, That all Acts of the United States in Congress Assembled, made by virtue and pursuance of the Powers hereby vested in them, and by the Articles of Confederation, and all Treaties made and ratified under the authority of the United States, shall

be the supreme Law of the respective States, as far as those Acts or Treaties shall relate to the said States or their *citizens* ["subjects" stricken out]; and that the Judiciaries of the several States shall be bound thereby in their decisions, anything in the respective Laws of the Individual States to the Contrary notwithstanding.

And if any State, or any body of Men in any State, shall oppose or prevent the carrying into Execution such Acts or Treaties, the federal Executive shall be authorized to call forth the Powers of the confederated States, or so much thereof as may be necessary to enforce and compell an obedience to such Acts or an observance of such Treaties.

8. Resolved, That Provision ought to be made for the admission of New States into the Union.

9. Resolved, That Provision ought to be made for hearing and deciding upon all disputes arising between the United States and an Individual State respecting Territory.

10. Resolved, That the Rule for Naturalization ought to be the same in every State.

11. Resolved, That a Citizen of one State committing an Offence in an other State, shall be deemed guilty of the same offence, as if it had been committed by a Citizen of the State in which the offence was committed.

☆   ☆   ☆

Richard Henry Lee
on the Constitution 1787

Not all the patriots of 1776 were supporters of the Constitution when the ratification contest took place. In fact some of the Revolution's most militant leaders, such as Samuel Adams, were opposed to the document because they felt it took too many freedoms from the states.

The Virginia ratification controversy was no different. Patrick Henry and James Monroe, both noted Revolutionary War patriots, led the antifederalist opposition in Virginia. Richard Henry Lee, who in 1776 had declared in the Second Continental Congress that the colonies ought to be free and independent, wrote pamphlets to support the antifederalists.

Richard Henry Lee's statements, however, were not as bitterly opposed to the Constitution as were some of the documents that were written at this time. Lee's main objection to the new government was his fear that state governments would lose their power in being consolidated into one federal government. As you read, compare the

111

three possible forms of government Lee proposes with the government set up under the Constitution today. List the objections Lee had to the Constitution. Have Lee's objections to the Constitution proven to be valid?

(6) The present moment discovers a new face in our affairs.
Our object has been all along, to reform our federal system, and to strengthen our governments — to establish peace, order and justice in the community — but a new object now presents. The plan of government now proposed is evidently calculated totally to change, in time, our condition as a people. Instead of being thirteen republics, under a federal head, it is clearly designed to make us one consolidated government. Of this, I think, I shall fully convince you, in my following letters on the subject. This consolidation of the states has been the object of several men in this country for some time past. Whether such a change can ever be effected . . . without convulsions and civil wars; whether such a change will not totally destroy the liberties of this country — time only can determine. . . .

In the first place, I shall premise, that the plan proposed is a plan of accommodation — and that it is in this way only, and by giving up a part of our opinions, that we can ever expect to obtain a government founded in freedom and compact. This circumstance candid men will always keep in view, in the discussion of this subject.

The plan proposed appears to be partly federal, but principally however, calculated ultimately to make the states one consolidated government.

The first interesting question, therefore suggested, is, how far the states can be consolidated into one entire government on free principles. In considering this question extensive objects are to be taken into view, and important changes in the forms of government to be carefully attended to in all their consequences. The happiness of the people at large must be the great object with every honest statesman, and he will direct every movement to this point. If we are so situated as a people, as not to be able to enjoy equal happiness, and advantages under one government, the consolidation of the states cannot be admitted.

There are three different forms of free government under which the United States may exist as one nation; and now is, perhaps, the time to determine to which we will direct our views. 1. Distinct republics connected under a federal head. In this case the respective state governments must be the principal guardians of the peoples rights, and exclusively regulate their internal police; in them must rest the balance of government. The congress of the states, or federal head, must consist of delegates amenable to, and removable by the respective states: This congress must have general directing powers; powers to require men and monies of the states; to make treaties; peace and war; to direct the operations of armies, &c. Under this federal modification of government, the powers of congress would be rather advisory or recommendatory than coercive. 2. We may do away the federal state governments, and form or consolidate all the states into one entire government, with one executive, one judiciary, and one legislature, consisting of senators and representatives collected from all parts of the union: In this case there would be a compleat consolidation of the states. 3. We may consolidate the states as to certain national objects, and leave them severally distinct independent republics, as to internal police generally. Let the general government consist of an executive, a judiciary, and balanced legislature, and its powers extend exclusively to all foreign concerns, causes arising on the seas to commerce, imports, armies, navies, Indian affairs, peace and war, and to a few internal concerns of the community; to the coin, post offices, weights and measures, a general plan for the militia, to naturalization, *and, perhaps to bankruptcies,* leaving the internal police of the community, in other respects, exclusively to the state governments; as the administration of justice in all causes arising internally, the laying and collecting of internal taxes, and the forming of the militia according to the general plan prescribed. In this case there would be compleat consolidation, *quoad* certain objects only.

Touching the first, or federal plan, I do not think much can be said in its favor: The sovereignity of the nation, without coercive and efficient powers to collect the strength of it, cannot always be depended on to answer the purposes of government; and in a congress of representatives of foreign states, there must necessarily be an unreasonable mixture of powers in the same hands.

As to the second, or compleat consolidating plan, it deserves to be carefully considered at this time by every American: If it be impracticable, it is a fatal error to model our governments, directing our views ultimately to it.

The third plan, or partial consolidation, is, in my opinion, the only one that can secure the freedom and happiness of this people. I once had some general ideas that the second plan was practicable, but from long attention, and the proceedings of the convention, I am fully satisfied, that this third plan is the only one we can with safety and propriety proceed upon. Making this the standard to point out, with candor and fairness, the parts of the new constitution which appear to be improper, is my object. The convention appears to have proposed the partial consolidation evidently with a view to collect all powers ultimately, in the United States into one entire government; and from its views in this respect, and from the tenacity of the small states to have an equal vote in the senate, probably originated the greatest defects in the proposed plan.

Independent of the opinions of many great authors, that a free elective government cannot be extended over large territories, a few reflections must evince, that one government and general legislation alone never can extend equal benefits to all parts of the United States: Different laws, customs, and opinions exist in the different states, which by a uniform system of laws would be unreasonably invaded. The United States contain about a million of square miles, and in half a century will, probably contain ten millions of people; and from the center to the extremes is about 800 miles.

Before we do away the state governments or adopt measures that will tend to abolish them, and to consolidate the states into one entire government several principles should be considered and facts ascertained: — These, and my examination into the essential parts of the proposed plan, I shall pursue in my next.

☆   ☆   ☆

Federalist 10
1787

The debate over ratifying the Constitution in New York was fiercely fought. To convince the people of New York to ratify, Alexander Hamilton, John Jay, and James Madison wrote a series of articles for the newspapers. These articles, known as the Federalist papers, were a careful analysis of political theory.

This particular article was written by James Madison. It goes into great detail describing how factions, groups of people who have a special interest in common, operate in a government. For example, Madison had had great experience with seeing how men would try to support laws that would be to their state's interest at the Philadelphia Convention.

Although Madison sees the possibility of the factions' working against national interest, he predicts that the new government, which he calls the "republican government," will be so constructed that no faction can gain control. As you read these selections from *Federalist 10*, find out why Madison feels the republican government will keep the evil influences of factions to a minimum. Look for provisions that try to keep any group of men from gaining too much control. Madison helped frame the Constitution; can you see his influence?

(7) Among the numerous advantages promised by a well-constructed Union, none deserves to be more accurately developed than its tendency to break and control the violence of faction. . . . The valuable improvements made by the American constitutions on the popular models, both ancient and modern, cannot certainly be too much admired; but it would be an unwarrantable partiality to contend that they have as effectually obviated the danger on this side, as was wished and expected. . . .

By a faction, I understand a number of citizens, whether amounting to a majority or minority of the whole, who are united and actuated by some common impulse of passion, or of interest, adverse to the rights of other citizens, or to the permanent and aggregate interests of the community. . . .

As long as the reason of man continues fallible, and he is at liberty to exercise it, different opinions will be formed. As long as the connection subsists between his reason and his self-love, his opinions and his passions will have a reciprocal influence on each other; and the former will be objects to which the latter will attach themselves. The diversity in the faculties of men, from which the rights of property originate, is not less an insuperable obstacle to a uniformity of interests. The protection of these faculties is the first object of government. From the protection of different and unequal faculties of acquiring property, the possession of different degrees and kinds of property immediately results; and from the influence of these on the sentiments and views of the respective proprietors ensues a division of the society into different interests and parties. . . .

But the most common and durable source of factions has been the various and unequal distribution of property. Those who hold and those who are without property have ever formed distinct interests in society. Those who are creditors and those who are debtors fall under a like discrimination. A landed interest, a manufacturing interest, a mercantile interest, a moneyed interest with many lesser interests, grow up of necessity in civilized nations and divide them into different classes, actuated by different sentiments and views. The regulation of these various and interfering interests forms the principal task of modern legislation and involves the spirit of party and faction in the necessary and ordinary operations of the government. . . .

Shall domestic manufacturers be encouraged, and in what degree, by restrictions on foreign manufacturers? are questions which would be differently decided by the landed and the manufacturing classes, and probably by neither with a sole regard to justice and the public good. The apportionment of taxes on the various descriptions of property is an act which seems to require the most exact impartiality; yet there is, perhaps, no legislative act in which greater opportunity and temptation are given to a predominant party to trample on the rules of justice. Every shilling with which they overburden the inferior number is a shilling saved to their own pockets.

It is in vain to say that enlightened statesmen will be able to adjust these clashing interests and render them all subservient to the public good. Enlightened statesmen will not always be at the helm. Nor, in many cases, can such an adjustment be made at all without taking into view indirect and remote considerations, which will rarely prevail over the immediate interest which one party may find in disregarding the rights of another or the good of the whole. . . .

If a faction consists of less than a majority, relief is supplied by the republican principle, which enables the majority to defeat its sinister views by regular vote. It may clog the administration, it may convulse the society; but it will be unable to execute and mask its violence under the forms of the Constitution. When a majority is included in a faction, the form of popular government, on the other hand, enables it to sacrifice to its ruling passion or interest both the public good and the rights of other citizens. . . .

From this view of the subject it may be concluded that a pure democracy, by which I mean a society consisting of a small number of citizens who assemble and administer the government in person, can admit of no cure for the mischiefs of faction. A common passion or interest will, in almost every case, be felt by a majority of the whole; a communication and concert result from the form of government itself; and there is nothing to check the inducements to sacrifice the weaker party or an obnoxious individual. . . .

A republic, by which I mean a government in which the scheme of representation takes place, opens a different prospect and promises the cure for which we are seeking. . . .

The two great points of difference between a democracy and a republic are: first, the delegation of the government, in the latter, to a small number of citizens elected by the rest; secondly, the greater number of citizens, and greater sphere of country, over which the latter may be extended.

The effect of the first difference is, on the one hand, to refine and enlarge the public views, by passing them through the medium of a chosen body of citizens, whose wisdom may best discern the true interest of their country, and whose patriotism and love of justice will be least likely to sacrifice it to temporary or partial considerations. Under such a regulation, it may well happen that the public voice, pronounced by the representatives of the people, will be more consonant to the public good than if pronounced by the people themselves, convened for the purpose. On the other hand, the effect may be inverted. Men of factious tempers, of local prejudices, or of sinister designs may, by intrigue, by corruption, or by other means, first obtain the suffrages, and then betray the interests, of the people. . . .

The other point of difference is the greater number of citizens and extent of territory which may be brought within the compass of republican than of democratic government; and it is this circumstance principally which renders factious combinations less to be dreaded in the former than in the latter. . . . Extend the sphere and you take in a greater variety of parties and interests; you make it less probable that a majority of the whole will have a common motive to invade the rights of other citizens; or if such a common motive exists, it will be more difficult for all who feel it to discover their own strength and to act in unison with each other. . . .

Hence, it clearly appears that the same advantage which a republic has over a democracy, in controlling the effects of factions, is enjoyed by a large over a small republic — is enjoyed by the Union over the states composing it. Does the advantage consist in the substitution of representatives whose enlightened views and virtuous sentiments render them superior to local prejudices and to schemes of injustice? It will not be denied that the representation of the Union will be most likely to possess these requisite endowments. Does it consist in the greater security afforded by a greater variety of parties, against the event of any one party being able to outnumber and oppress the rest? In an equal degree does the increased variety of parties comprised within the Union, increase this security. Does it, in fine, consist in the greater obstacles opposed to the concert and accomplishment of the secret wishes of an unjust and interested majority? Here, again, the extent of the Union gives it the most palpable advantage. . . .

The influence of factious leaders may kindle a flame within their particular states but will be unable to spread a general conflagration through the other states. A religious sect may degenerate into a political faction in a part of the Confederacy; but the variety of sects dispersed over the entire face of it must secure the national councils against any danger from that source. A rage for paper money, for an abolition of debts, for an equal division of property, or for any other improper or wicked project will be less apt to pervade the whole body of the Union than a particular member of it; in the same proportion as such a malady is more likely to taint a particular county or district than an entire state.

In the extent and proper structure of the Union, therefore, we behold a republican remedy for the diseases most incident to republican government. And according to the degree of pleasure and pride we feel in being republicans, ought to be our zeal in cherishing the spirit and supporting the character of Federalists.

☆   ☆   ☆

Jefferson on
the Bill of Rights 1789

Many persons who opposed the ratification of the Constitution objected to it because a Bill of Rights was omitted. Those favoring ratification without a Bill of Rights contended that the restrictions in the Constitution against suspension of the writ of habeas corpus and provisions against bills of attainder and ex post facto laws were sufficient to curb any possible excesses by the federal government. They also argued that the states had bills of rights, making any federal statement unnecessary.

Thomas Jefferson believed that a Bill of Rights should be added to the Constitution. Although Jefferson did not attend the Philadelphia Convention, since he was in France representing the United States at the court of Louis XVI, he corresponded with many of his friends about domestic matters. In a letter written in Paris on March 15, 1789, to his close friend James Madison, Jefferson clearly revealed his reasons for hoping that a Bill of Rights would be adopted. As you read, summarize the reasons Jefferson wanted such a guarantee of individual rights.

(8) Your thoughts on the subject of the declaration of rights, in the letter of October the 17th, I have weighed with great satisfaction. Some of them had not occurred to me before, but were acknowledged just in the moment they were presented to my mind. In the arguments in favor of a declaration of rights, you omit one which has great weight with me; the legal check which it puts into the hands of the judiciary. This is a body, which, if rendered independent and kept strictly to their own department, merits great confidence for their learning and integrity. In fact, what degree of confidence would be too much, for a body composed of such men as Wythe, Blair and Pendleton? . . . The declaration of rights, is like all other human blessings, alloyed with some inconveniences, and not accomplishing fully its object. But the good in this instance, vastly overweighs the evil. I cannot refrain from making short answers to the objections which your letter states to have been raised. 1. That the rights in question are reserved, by the manner in which the federal powers are granted. Answer. A constitutive

act may, certainly, be so formed, as to need no declaration of rights. The act itself has the force of a declaration, as far as it goes; and if it goes to all material points, nothing more is wanting. In the draught of a constitution which I had once a thought of proposing in Virginia, and printed afterwards, I endeavored to reach all the great objects of public liberty, and did not mean to add a declaration of rights. Probably the object was imperfectly executed; but the deficiencies would have been supplied by others, in the course of discussion. But in a constitutive act which leaves some precious articles unnoticed, and raises implications against others, a declaration of rights becomes necessary, by way of supplement. This is the case of our new federal Constitution. This instrument forms us into one State, as to certain objects, and gives us a legislative and executive body for these objects. It should, therefore, guard us against their abuses of power, within the field submitted to them. 2. A positive declaration of some essential rights could not be obtained in the requisite latitude. Answer. Half a loaf is better than no bread. If we cannot secure all our rights, let us secure what we can. 3. The limited powers of the federal government, and jealousy of the subordinate governments, afford a security which exists in no other instance. Answer. The first member of this seems resolvable into the first objection before stated. The jealousy of the subordinate governments is a precious reliance. But observe that those governments are only agents. They must have principles furnished them, whereon to found their opposition. The declaration of rights will be the text, whereby they will try all the acts of the federal government. In this view, it is necessary to the federal government also; as by the same text, they may try the opposition of the subordinate governments. 4. Experience proves the inefficacy of a bill of rights. True. But though it is not absolutely efficacious under all circumstances, it is of great potency always, and rarely inefficacious. A brace the more will often keep up the building which would have fallen, with that brace the less. There is a remarkable difference between the characters of the inconveniences which attend a declaration of rights, and those which attend the want of it. The inconveniences of the declaration are, that it may cramp government in its useful exertions. But the evil of this is short-lived, moderate, and reparable. The inconveniences of the want of a declaration are permanent, afflicting and irreparable.

☆   ☆   ☆

THE RIGHTS . . . POWERS ARE GRANTED Jefferson here is referring to the understanding of the Constitution that all powers not specifically granted to Congress and the President are reserved to the people or the state governments. The "manner" was the limitations placed on the power of a government.

119

Jefferson and Hamilton on the Meaning of the Constitution 1791

The first serious disagreement over the interpretation of the Constitution came during the administration of George Washington in 1791. Alexander Hamilton, Secretary of the Treasury, had proposed the establishment of a Bank of the United States which would be owned partially by the government and partially by private individuals. Washington was uncertain about the bank's constitutionality and asked both Hamilton and his Secretary of State, Thomas Jefferson, to give him their opinions in the matter.

Jefferson argued against its constitutionality on the grounds that there were no specific provisions in the Constitution granting the government such powers.

Hamilton contended that the governments—both federal and state—could do virtually anything "not precluded by restrictions and exceptions specified in the constitution." Those disagreeing over the meaning of the Constitution have often used these different points of view as the basis of their arguments. Much of our political history has revolved around these two differing viewpoints of the real meaning of the Constitution. No one since 1791, however, has stated the case more clearly than these two great Americans. Washington took Hamilton's view and supported the creation of the bank.

DOCUMENT

(9) *Jefferson's letter to George Washington of February 15, 1791, giving his ideas on the constitutionality of the proposed Bank of the United States:*

I consider the foundation of the Constitution as laid on this ground: That "all powers not delegated to the United States, by the Constitution, nor prohibited by it to the States, are reserved to the States or to the people." [Tenth Amendment] To take a single step beyond the boundaries thus specially drawn around the powers of Congress, is to take possession of a boundless field of power, no longer susceptible of any definition.

The incorporation of a bank, and the powers assumed by this bill, have not, in my opinion, been delegated to the United States, by the Constitution.

1. They are not among the powers especially enumerated: for these are: 1st. A power to lay taxes for the purpose of paying the debts of the United States; but no debt is paid by this bill, nor any

tax laid. Were it a bill to raise money, its origination in the Senate would condemn it by the Constitution.

2. "To borrow money." But this bill neither borrows money nor ensures the borrowing it. The proprietors of the bank will be just as free as any other money holders, to lend or not to lend their money to the public. The operation proposed in the bill, first, to lend them two millions, and then to borrow them back again, cannot change the nature of the latter act, which will still be a payment, and not a loan, call it by what name you please.

3. To "regulate commerce with foreign nations, and among the States, and with the Indian tribes." To erect a bank, and to regulate commerce, are very different acts.

☆   ☆   ☆

(10) *Alexander Hamilton's opinion given to George Washington in which he takes a different view from that expressed by Jefferson in regard to the Bank of the United States: Dated: February 23, 1791.*

Now it appears to the Secretary of the Treasury, that this *general principle* is *inherent* in the very *definition* of *Government* and *essential* to every step of the progress to be made by that of the United States; namely—that every power vested in a Government is in its nature *sovereign*, and includes by *force* of the *term*, a right to employ all the *means* requisite, and fairly *applicable* to the attainment of the *ends* of such power; and which are not precluded by restrictions & exceptions specified in the constitution; or not immoral, or not contrary to the essential ends of political society.

This principle in its application to Government in general would be admitted as an axiom. And it will be incumbent upon those, who may incline to deny it, to *prove* a distinction; and to shew that a rule which in the general system of things is essential to the preservation of the social order is inapplicable to the United States.

The circumstances that the powers of sovereignty are in this country divided between the National and State Governments, does not afford the distinction required. It does not follow from this, that each of the *portions* of powers delegated to the one or to the other is not sovereign *with regard to its proper objects.* It will only *follow* from it, that each has sovereign power as to *certain things*, and not as to *other things.* To deny that the Government of the United States has sovereign power as to its declared purposes & trusts, because its power does not extend to all cases, would be equally to deny, that the State Governments have sovereign power in any case; because their power does not extend to every case. The tenth section of the first article of the constitution exhibits a long list of very important things which they may not do. And thus the United States would furnish the singular spectacle of a *political society* without *sovereignty*, or of a people *governed* without *government*.

☆   ☆   ☆

The Whiskey Rebellion 1794

One of the most difficult domestic problems facing George Washington as President was the open defiance of federal law by a large group of whiskey distillers and their friends living in western Pennsylvania. They bitterly resented an excise tax on whiskey and refused to pay it; in the summer of 1794 a group of about 2,000 armed men threatened to attack a small detachment of regular army troops stationed at Pittsburgh. Washington called up 15,000 militia from several states and ordered them to suppress the minor rebellion. In the face of such overwhelming force the Whiskey Rebellion collapsed.

Excerpts from a letter by George Washington to Major General Daniel Morgan, who had been ordered by the President to lead some of the troops, indicate his sentiments about those who would violate federal law.

Compare the outcome and effects of the Whiskey Rebellion with the outcome and effect of Shays' Rebellion (*see pp. 102–105*).

(11) . . . At that place, or at Bedford, my ulterior resolution must be taken, either to advance with the Troops into the Insurgent Counties of this State, or to return to Philadelphia for the purpose of meeting Congress the 3d. of next month.

Imperious circumstances alone can justify my absence from the Seat of Government whilst Congress are in Session; but if these, from the disposition of the People in the refractory Counties, and the state of the information I expect to receive at the advanced Posts, should appear to exist the lesser must yield to the greater duties of my office and I shall cross the mountains with the Troops; if not, I shall place the command of the combined force under the orders of Governor Lee of Virginia and repair to the Seat of Government.

I am perfectly in sentiment with you, that the business we are drawn out upon, should be effectually executed; and that the daring and factious spirit which has arisen (to overturn the laws, and to subvert the Constitution) ought to be subdued. If this is not done, there is, an end of and we may bid adieu to all government in this Country, except Mob and Club Govt. from whence nothing but anarchy and confusion can ensue; for if the minority, and a small one too, are suffered to dictate to the majority, after measures have undergone the most solemn discussions by the Representatives of the people, and their Will through this medium is enacted into a law; there can be no security for life, liberty or property; nor if the laws are not to govern, can any man know how to conduct himself with safety for there never was a law *yet made*, I conceive, that hit the taste *exactly* of every man, or every part of the community; of course, if this be a reason for opposition no law can be execd. at all witht. force and every man or set of men will in that case cut and carve for themselves; the consequences of which must be deprecated by all classes of men who are friends to order, and to the peace and happiness of the Country; but how can things be otherwise than they are when clubs and Societies have been instituted for the express purpose though clothed in another garb by their diabolical leader Gt [Genet] whose object was to sow sedition, to poison the minds of the people of this Country, and to make them discond. [discontented] with the Government of it, and who have labored indefatigably to effect these purposes.

☆   ☆   ☆

Marbury v. Madison 1803

Although the Constitution provided for a judicial branch of government, it did not specifically grant the court the right to interpret the Constitution. While some framers, such as Hamilton, felt the Supreme Court should have this right, it was not clear in the early years of the Republic who could decide whether an act of Congress was unconstitutional or what action might be taken about an unconstitutional law.

When the Sedition Act was passed in 1798, the question of unconstitutionality arose again. At that time Jefferson and Madison felt it was the responsibility of each state to decide on constitutionality (*see pp. 126–129*). This was an opinion that was to influence the attitudes and actions of many states, but particularly the Southern states, in the fifty years that were to follow. (*See Chapter 5 for details.*)

In 1803, however, the great Chief Justice John Marshall claimed the right of interpretation for the Supreme Court. In the historic *Marbury* v. *Madison* decision he stated that the Supreme Court has the duty to decide whether an act of Congress is unconstitutional, and that an act declared unconstitutional cannot be enforced. While the Supreme Court was deciding the case, however, it had to consider its own powers. Congress had passed a law in 1789 giving the Court certain powers that went beyond those granted by the Constitution; Marshall declared the 1789 act unconstitutional and said that it could not be enforced.

Marshall's statement of the Supreme Court's duty to interpret the constitutionality of laws, plus the future Court's exercising of this power of judicial review, has made the decision a landmark in constitutional history.

(12) The question, whether an act *repugnant* [*contrary*] to the constitution can become the law of the land, is a question deeply interesting to the United States; but, happily, not of an intricacy proportioned to its interest. It seems only necessary to recognize certain principles . . . to decide it. . . .

The constitution is either a superior *paramount* [*highest*] law, unchangeable by ordinary means, or it is on a level with ordinary legislative acts, and, like other acts, is alterable when the legislature shall please to alter it. . . .

If an act of the legislature, repugnant to the constitution, is void, does it, notwithstanding its invalidity, bind the courts, and oblige them to give it effect? Or, in other words, though it be not law, does it constitute a rule as operative as if it was a law? This would be to overthrow in fact what was established in theory; and would seem, at first view, an absurdity too gross to be insisted on. It shall, however, receive a more attentive consideration.

It is emphatically the province and duty of the judicial department to say what the law is. Those who apply the rule to particular cases, must of necessity expound and interpret that rule. If two laws conflict with each other, the courts must decide on the operation of each.

So if a law be in opposition to the constitution; if both the law and the constitution apply to a particular case, so that the court must either decide that case conformably to [in agreement with] the law, disregarding the constitution, or conforming to the constitution, disregarding the law, the court must determine which of these conflicting rules governs the case. This is the very essence of judicial duty. If, then, the courts are to regard the constitution, and the constitution is superior to any ordinary act of the legislature, the constitution, and not such ordinary act, must govern the case to which they both apply . . .

✯   ✯   ✯

OVERTHROW IN FACT . . . IN THEORY The question whether an unconstitutional act should be enforced is the one considered here. The "theory" is the statement that an unconstitutional act does not have the power of law and hence is unenforceable. Thus if the unconstitutional law were enforced ("in fact"), the fact of its enforcement would overthrow the theory.

IV. Footnotes

[1]Francis Newton Thorpe, ed., *The Federal and State Constitutions, Colonial Charters, and Other Organic Laws of the States, Territories, and Colonies Now or Heretofore Forming the United States of America* (Government Printing Office, Washington, D.C., 1909) I, 9–16.

[2]*Ibid.*, II, 957–962.

[3]*Papers of General Benjamin Lincoln*, Sparks Manuscripts (Harvard College Library, Cambridge, Mass.) LVII.

[4]Charles C. Tansill, ed., *Documents Illustrative of the Formation of the Union of the American States* (Government Printing Office, Washington, D.C., 1927) 957–959.

[5]*Ibid.*, 971–974.

[6]Paul Leicester Ford, ed., *Pamphlets on the Constitution of the United States* (Brooklyn, New York, 1888) 282–288.

[7]*The Federalist on the New Constitution, Written in the Year 1788 by Mr. Hamilton, Mr. Madison, and Mr. Jay* (Glazier, Masters and Smith, Hallowell, 1837) 43–49.

[8]Andrew A. Lipscomb, ed., *The Writings of Thomas Jefferson* (The Thomas Jefferson Memorial Association of the United States, Washington, D.C., 1904) VII, 309.

[9]Paul Leicester Ford, ed., *The Works of Thomas Jefferson* (G. P. Putnam's Sons, New York and London, 1904) VI, 198.

[10]Harold C. Surett, ed., *The Papers of Alexander Hamilton* (Columbia University Press, New York and London, 1965) VIII, 98, 103.

[11]John C. Fitzpatrick, ed., *The Writings of George Washington, July 1, 1793 — October 9, 1794* (Government Printing Office, Washington, D.C., 1940) XXXIII, 522–524.

[12]1 Cranch, 137 (1803).

V
States' and Federal Rights: What Is the Balance of Power?

The ratification of the Constitution did not automatically mean that the separate states would willingly grant powers to the federal government. In fact, much of the history of the seventy years after George Washington's presidency suggests that the national and state leaders could not decide just how the states were related to the federal government. In many different states people asked, "Does a state have the right to disobey a law it feels is unconstitutional?" "Do states have all powers not specifically given the federal government in the Constitution?" "Does a state have the right to leave the United States of America if it disagrees with the federal government's policies?"

These questions were asked and answered in many ways. Some historians feel that the questions were decisively answered by the Civil War. Since the states that tried to leave the Union did not succeed in their attempt, it became a fact of history that the federal government was the supreme power. Once a state joined the union, it had admitted that the union was more important than state interests. But from the nation's earliest years, we find disagreement about this question: How much authority does the Constitution give to the state and federal governments?

The Kentucky Resolution 1798

When Congress passed the Naturalization, Alien, and Sedition Act in 1798, the contest between the state and federal governments began. This law made naturalization difficult; it allowed the President to deport aliens and to punish those whose speeches or writings defamed the President and Congress. Not everyone agreed Congress had the power to pass these laws, and the Virginia and Kentucky legislatures sent protests to that effect.

Today the issues of the law have been decided; the federal government does have the right to regulate aliens and to fix the laws for naturalization. There is some question that the law abridged men's freedom of speech. However, the reasoning of the Kentucky Resolution forms the basis of the argument that dominated the North-South conflict that was to follow.

The Kentucky Resolution starts with a statement that all powers not specifically granted to the national government are powers granted to the state government. The Resolution accuses the government of having passed an act that it had no power to pass. And finally, the act is declared unconstitutional, hence null and void.

(1) Resolved, That the several States composing the United States of America, are not united on the principle of unlimited submission to their general government; but that by compact under the style and title of a Constitution for the United States and of amendments thereto, they constituted a general government for special purposes, delegated to that government certain definite powers, reserving each State to itself, the residuary mass of right to their own self-government; and that whensoever the general government assumes undelegated powers, its acts are unauthoritative, void, and of no force: That to this compact each State acceded as a State, and is an integral party, its co-States forming, as to itself, the other party: That the government created by this compact was not made the exclusive or final judge of the extent of the powers delegated to itself; since that would have made its discretion, and not the Constitution, the measure of its powers; but that as in all other cases of compact among parties having no common Judge, each party has an equal right to judge for itself, as well of infractions as of the mode and measure of redress. . . .

III. Resolved, That it is true as a general principle, and is also expressly declared by one of the amendments to the Constitution that: "the powers not delegated to the United States by the Constitution, nor prohibited by it to the States, are reserved to the States respectively, or to the people;" and that no power over the freedom of religion, freedom of speech, or freedom of the press being delegated to the United States by the Constitution, nor prohibited by it to the States, all lawful powers respecting the same did of right remain, and were reserved to the States, or to the people: That thus was manifested their determination to retain to themselves the right of judging how far the licentiousness of speech and of the press may be abridged without lessening their useful freedom, and how far those abuses which cannot be separated from their use should be tolerated rather than the use be destroyed; and thus also they guarded against all abridgment by the United States of the freedom of religious opinions and exercises, and retained to themselves the right of protecting the same, as this State, by a law passed on the general demand of its citizens, had already protected them from all human restraint or interference: And that in addition to this general principle and express declaration, another and more special provision has been made by one of the amendments to the Constitution which expressly declares, that "Congress shall make no law respecting an establishment of religion, or prohibiting the free exercise thereof, or abridging the freedom of speech, or of the press," thereby guarding in the same sentence, and under the same words, the freedom of religion, of speech, and of the press, insomuch, that whatever violates either, throws down the sanctuary which covers the others, and that libels, falsehoods, defamation equally with heresy and false religion, are withheld from the cognizance of Federal tribunals. That therefore the act of the Congress of the United States passed on the 14th day of July, 1798, entitled "An act in addition to the act for the punishment of certain crimes against the United States," which does abridge the freedom of the press, is not law, but is altogether void and of no effect.

IV. Resolved, That alien friends are under the jurisdiction and protection of the laws of the State wherein they are; that no power over them has been delegated to the United States, nor prohibited to the individual States distinct from their power over citizens; and it being true as a general principle, and one of the amendments to the Constitution having also declared that: the powers not delegated to the United States by the Constitution, nor prohibited by it to the States, are reserved to the States respectively, or to the people," the act of the Congress of the United States passed on the 22d day of June, 1798, entitled "An act concerning aliens," which assumes power over alien friends not delegated by the Constitution, is not law, but is altogether void and of no force. . . .

VI. Resolved, That the imprisonment of a person under the protection of the laws of this Commonwealth on his failure to obey the simple order of the President to depart out of the United States, as is undertaken by the said act entitled "An act concerning aliens," is contrary to the Constitution. . . .

This Commonwealth does therefore call on its co-States for an expression of their sentiments on the acts concerning aliens, and for the punishment of certain crimes herein before specified, plainly declaring whether these acts are or are not authorized by the Federal

Compact. And it doubts not that their sense will be so announced as to prove their attachment unaltered to limited government, whether general or particular, and that the rights and liberties of their co-States will be exposed to no dangers by remaining embarked on a common bottom [foundation] with their own: That they will concur with this Commonwealth in considering the said acts as so palpably against the Constitution as to amount to an undisguised declaration, that the compact is not meant to be the measure of the powers of the general government, but that it will proceed in the exercise over these States of all powers whatsoever: That they will view this as seizing the rights of the States and consolidating them in the hands of the general government with a power assumed to bind the States (not merely in cases made Federal) but in all cases whatsoever, by laws made, not with their consent, but by others against their consent: That this would be to surrender the form of government we have chosen, and to live under one deriving its powers from its own will, and not from our authority; and that the co-states, recurring to their natural right in cases not made Federal, will concur in declaring these acts void and of no force, and will each unite with this commonwealth in requesting their repeal at the next session of Congress.

☆ ☆ ☆

WHATEVER VIOLATES . . . . THE OTHERS When the right of free speech is abridged, the other rights of freedom of religion and freedom of the press are violated too because all three are guaranteed under the same amendment; violating one is violating them all.

AND IT DOUBTS . . . . LIMITED GOVERNMENT "It" refers to the state of Kentucky. Thus the state of Kentucky does not doubt that the other states will announce that they too still feel limited government is the best kind.

The Hartford Convention 1815

Many New Englanders opposed the War of 1812. They objected when the Secretary of War proposed incorporating state militias into the regular army. They claimed that the federal government had not adequately defended their coasts against British raiders; and they resented the trade restrictions imposed prior to the war. The war had cut off trade with Britain, and the merchants were angry about that, too. The Massachusetts legislature was angry enough to request other New England states to meet in convention to discuss grievances against the federal government. The proceedings of these meetings were secret, but the Convention issued a final report to the legislatures of the states.

The Hartford Convention report used language very similar to that of the Kentucky Resolution (*see pp. 126–129*), reaffirming the duty of each state to "interpose" if the national government acted in "deliberate, dangerous, and palpable infractions of the constitution."

While this document does not threaten the federal government with any specific action, it declares that a state can "interpose" itself between misuses of the federal government's power and the citizens of the state. Although the New England states do admit they have no right to openly rebel against the federal government (they later deplored the rebellion on the part of the Southern states), much of the reasoning contained in this protest was later used by the Southern states. As you read, compare the attitude of this Convention and that of the Kentucky legislature toward the federal government.

(2) The Convention is deeply impressed with a sense of the arduous nature of the commission which they were appointed to execute, of devising the means of defence against dangers, and of relief from oppressions proceeding from the acts of their own government, without violating constitutional principles, or disappointing the hopes of a suffering and injured people. To prescribe patience and firmness to those who are aleady exhausted by distress, is sometimes to drive them to despair, and the progress towards reform by the regular road, is irksome to those whose imaginations discern, and whose feelings prompt, to a shorter course. But when abuses, reduced to a system, and accumulated through a course of years, have pervaded every department of government, and spread corruption through every region of the state; when these are clothed with the forms of law, and enforced by an executive whose will is their source, no summary means of relief can be applied without recourse to direct and open resistance. This experiment, even when justifiable, cannot fail to be painful to the good citizen; and the success of the effort will be no security against the danger of the example. Precedents of resistance to the worst administration, are eagerly seized by those who are naturally hostile to the best. Necessity alone can sanction a resort to this measure; and it should never be extended in duration or degree beyond the exigency, until the people, not merely in the fervour of sudden excitement, but after full deliberation, are determined to change the constitution. . . .

The power of compelling the militia, and other citizens of the United States, by a forcible draft or conscription, to serve in the regular armies as proposed in a late official letter of the Secretary of War, is not delegated to Congress by the constitution, and the exercise of it would not be less dangerous to their liberties, than hostile to the sovereignty of the states. The effort to deduce this power from the right of raising armies, is a flagrant attempt to pervert the sense of the clause in the constitution which confers that right, and is incompatible with other provisions in that instrument. The armies of the United States have always been raised by contract, never by conscription, and nothing more can be wanting to a government possessing the power thus claimed to enable it to usurp the entire control of the militia, in derogation of the authority of the state, and to convert it by impressment into a standing army. . . .

That acts of Congress in violation of the constitution are absolutely void, is an undeniable position. It does not, however, consist with respect and forbearance due from a confederate state towards the general government, to fly to open resistance upon every infraction of the constitution. The mode and the energy of the opposition, should always conform to the nature of the violation, the intention of its authors, the extent of the injury inflicted, the determination manifested to persist in it, and the danger of delay. But in cases of deliberate, dangerous, and palpable infractions of the constitution, affecting the sovereignty of a state, and liberties of the people; it is not only the right but the duty of such a state to interpose its authority for their protection, in the manner best calculated to secure that end. When emergencies occur which are either beyond the reach of the judicial tribunals, or too pressing to admit of the delay incident to their forms, states which have no common umpire, must be their own judges, and execute their own decisions.

☆   ☆   ☆

South Carolina's Nullification Ordinance 1832

The ideas in the Kentucky Resolution and the Hartford Convention were again stated in the Ordinance of Nullification proclaimed by a South Carolina convention in November of 1832.

The South in general, and South Carolina in particular, were angered by the tariff laws that had been passed to protect New England's manufactured goods. Import duties were placed on foreign goods that would compete with New England's products. Manufacturers were helped by these tariffs because they could keep their prices high to make a profit; they would not have to set lower prices to compete with foreign goods. The South bought many of its manufactured goods from the North and had to pay what they thought were higher prices than necessary. Also, the South sent much of its cotton to England; and since England had manufactured goods to trade, England was not too happy about having to pay high tariffs in the United States.

In the fall of 1832 another protective tariff was passed, and the patience of the South was exhausted. While proclaiming their love for the Union and the Constitution, the South Carolina convention proclaimed that "Above all, she estimates as beyond all price, her LIBERTY." The convention declared that the tariff laws of the United States were "null, void, and no law, nor binding upon this state." The convention asserted its right to this declaration on the ground that the Congress had no constitutional power to pass the law in the first place.

The uniqueness of the Ordinance of Nullification is not in its stated belief that a state has a right to declare acts of Congress unconstitutional – that had already happened twice before – but that South Carolina made two threats that President Jackson found endangering to the Union. First, South Carolina declared that it would not obey the law – that the tariff was not to be collected in the state. Second, South Carolina declared its right to leave the Union if other states tried to blockade its ports or make the state obey the law in any other way.

Why would the President be more concerned when a state refuses to obey the law than when a state declares an act unconstitutional?

(3) *An Ordinance to Nullify certain acts of the Congress of the United States, purporting to be laws laying duties and imposts on the importation of foreign commodities.*

Whereas the Congress of the United States, by various acts, purporting to be acts laying duties and imposts on foreign imports, but in reality intended for the protection of domestic manufactures, and the giving of bounties to classes and individuals engaged in particular employments, at the expense and to the injury and oppression of other classes and individuals and by wholly exempting from taxation certain foreign commodities, such as are not produced or manufactured in the United States, to afford a pretext for imposing higher and excessive duties on articles similar to those intended to be protected, hath exceeded its just powers under the Constitution, which confers on it no authority to afford such protection, and hath violated the true meaning and intent of the Constitution, which provides for equality in imposing the burthens of taxation upon the several States and portions of the confederacy: And whereas the said Congress, exceeding its just power to impose taxes and collect revenue for the purpose of effecting and accomplishing the specific objects and purposes which the Constitution of the United States authorizes it to effect and accomplish, hath raised and collected unnecessary revenue for objects unauthorized by the Constitution:

We, therefore, the people of the State of South Carolina in Convention assembled, do declare and ordain, and it is hereby declared and ordained, that the several acts and parts of acts of the Congress of the United States, purporting to be laws for the imposing of duties and imposts on the importation of foreign commodities, and now having actual operation and effect within the United States, and, more especially, an act entitled "An act in alteration of the several acts imposing duties on imports," approved on the nineteenth day of May, one thousand eight hundred and twenty-eight, and also an act entitled "An act to alter and amend the several acts imposing duties on imports," approved on the fourteenth day of July, one thousand eight hundred and thirty-two, are unauthorized by the Constitution of the United States, and violate the true meaning and intent thereof, and are null, void, and no law, nor binding upon this State, its officers or citizens; and all promises, contracts, and obligations, made or entered into, or to be made or entered into, with purpose to secure the duties imposed by the said acts, and all judicial proceedings which shall be hereafter had in affirmance thereof, are and shall be held utterly null and void.

And it is further ordained, that it shall not be lawful for any of the constituted authorities, whether of this State or of the United States, to enforce the payment of duties imposed by the said acts within the limits of this State; but it shall be the duty of the Legislature to adopt such measures and pass such acts as may be necessary to give full effect to this ordinance, and to prevent the enforcement and arrest the operation of the said acts and parts of acts of the Congress of the United States within the limits of this State, from and after the 1st day of February next, and the duty of all other constituted authorities, and of all persons residing or being within the limits of this State, and they are hereby required and enjoined, to obey and give effect to this ordinance, and such acts and measures of the Legislature as may be passed or adopted in obedience thereto.

And we, the people of South Carolina, to the end that it may be fully understood by the Government of the United States, and the people of the co-States, that we are determined to maintain this, our ordinance and declaration, at every hazard, do further declare that we will not submit to the application of force, on the part of the Federal Government, to reduce this State to obedience; but that we will consider the passage, by Congress, of any act authorizing the employment of a military or naval force against the State of South Carolina, her constituted authorities or citizens; or any act abolishing or closing the ports of this State, or any of them, or otherwise obstructing the free ingress [entrance] and egress [exit] of vessels to and from the said ports, or any other act on the part of the Federal Government, to coerce the State, shut up her ports, destroy or harass her commerce, or to enforce the acts hereby declared to be null and void, otherwise than through the civil tribunals of the country, as inconsistent with the longer continuance of South Carolina in the Union; and that the people of this State will thenceforth hold themselves absolved from all further obligation to maintain or preserve their political connexion with the people of the other States, and will forthwith proceed to organize a separate Government, and do all other acts and things which sovereign and independent States may of right do.

Done in Convention at Columbia, the twenty-fourth day of November, in the year of our Lord one thousand eight hundred and thirty-two, and in the fifty-seventh year of the declaration of the independence of the United States of America.

☆　　☆　　☆

Jackson's Proclamation on Nullification 1833

President Andrew Jackson saw South Carolina's Nullification Ordinance as an extreme threat to the Union. He issued a proclamation in December of 1832 warning the South Carolinians of the dangers in attempting to nullify an act of Congress. He argued that it was the function of the courts, not the states, to declare an act unconstitutional. And he further stated that the Constitution is a compact, an agreement that is binding on the states.

Fortunately, South Carolina did not withdraw from the Union, because Congress was willing to compromise. Congress lowered the tariff that had caused South Carolina's actions, and in turn South Carolina repealed its Ordinance. But the compromise did not resolve the basic argument. Some states still did not agree with Jackson's view of the Union as an unbreakable compact; South Carolina was one of those states that did not agree.

(4) Whereas a convention assembled in the State of South Carolina have passed an ordinance by which they declare "that the several acts and parts of acts of the Congress of the United States purporting to be laws for the imposing of duties and imposts on the importation of foreign commodities . . . are unauthorized by the Constitution of the United States, and . . . are null and void and no law" . . . and . . .

Whereas the said ordinance prescribes to the people of South Carolina a course of conduct in direct violation of their duty as citizens of the United States . . . and having for its object the destruction of the Union. . . .

To preserve this bond of our political existence from destruction, . . . I, Andrew Jackson, President of the United States, have thought proper to issue this my proclamation, ... [and] warn them of the consequences that must inevitably result from an observance of the dictates of the convention. . . .

The ordinance is founded . . . on the strange position that any one state may not only declare an act of Congress void, but prohibit its execution: . . . . Our social compact, in express terms, declares that the laws of the United States, its Constitution, and treaties made under it are the supreme law of the land, and, for greater caution, adds "that the judges in every state shall be bound thereby, anything in the constitution or laws of any state to the contrary notwithstanding." . . .

I consider, then, the power to annul a law of the United States, assumed by one State, *incompatible with the existence of the Union, contradicted expressly by the letter of the Constitution, unauthorized by its spirit, inconsistent with every principle on which it was founded, and destructive of the great object for which it was formed.* . . .

Because the Union was formed by a compact, it is said the parties to that compact may, when they feel themselves aggrieved, depart from it; but it is precisely because it is a compact that they cannot. A compact is an agreement or binding obligation. It may by its terms have a sanction or penalty for its breach, or it may not. . . . An attempt, by force of arms, to destroy a government is an offense . . . and such government has the right by the law of self-defense to pass acts for punishing the offender. . . .

This, then, is the position in which we stand: A small majority of the citizens of one State in the Union have elected delegates to a State convention; that convention has ordained that all the revenue laws of the United States must be repealed, or that they are no longer a member of the Union. . . . And it is the intent of this instrument to *proclaim,* not only that the duty imposed on me by the Constitution "to take care that the laws be faithfully executed" shall be performed to the extent of the powers already vested in me by law, . . . but to warn the citizens of South Carolina . . . of the danger they will incur by obedience to the illegal and disorganizing ordinance of the convention. . . .

Fellow-citizens of my native State, let me not only admonish you, as the First Magistrate of our common country, not to incur the penalty of its laws, but use the influence that a father would over his children whom he saw rushing to certain ruin. . . .

The laws of the United States must be executed. I have no discretionary power on the subject; my duty is emphatically pronounced in the Constitution. Those who told you that you might peaceably prevent their execution deceived you; they could not have been deceived themselves. They know that a forcible opposition could alone prevent the execution of the laws, and they know that such an opposition must be repelled. . . .

Fellow citizens, the momentous case is before you. On your undivided support of your Government depends the decision of the great question it involves — whether your sacred Union will be preserved and the blessing it secures to us as one people shall be perpetuated. . . .

☆   ☆   ☆

The Compromise of 1850

The annexation of Texas in 1845 and the addition to the United States in 1848 of vast new territories as a result of the Mexican War brought the slavery issue to the point of explosion. The gold rush of 1849 had given California a population large enough for admission to the Union as a free state. Slavery existed in Texas, and there were bitter quarrels over the fate of the extensive territory between Texas and California. Would these territories be organized with or without slavery?

The intensity of feeling between the North and the South was so strong that many believed secession or civil war was imminent. To avoid the break South Carolina had threatened twenty years before, the problem was solved temporarily by the Great Compromise of 1850. The Compromise permitted new territories to decide the slavery issue for themselves.

Excerpts from Henry Clay's speech to the Senate in January of 1850, the speech that was the basis of the compromise, are quoted below.

(5) It being desirable, for the peace, concord, and harmony of the Union of these States, to settle and adjust amicably all existing questions of controversy between them arising out of the institution of slavery upon a fair, equitable, and just basis: therefore,

1. *Resolved,* That California, with suitable boundaries, ought, upon her application to be admitted as one of the States of this Union without the imposition by Congress of any restriction in respect to the exclusion or introduction of slavery within these boundaries.

2. *Resolved,* That as slavery does not exist by law, and is not likely to be introduced into any of the territory acquired by the United States from the republic of Mexico, it is inexpedient for Congress to provide by law either for its introduction into, or exclusion from, any part of the said territory; and that appropriate territorial governments ought to be established by Congress in all of the said territory, not assigned as the boundaries of the proposed State of California, without the adoption of any restriction or condition on the subject of slavery.

3. *Resolved,* That the western boundary of the State of Texas ought to be fixed on the Rio del Norte [Rio Grande], commencing one marine league from its mouth, and running up that river to the southern line of New Mexico; thence with that line eastwardly, and so continuing in the same direction to the line as established between the United States and Spain, excluding any portion of New Mexico, whether lying on the east or west of that river.

4. *Resolved,* That it be proposed to the State of Texas, that the United States will provide for the payment of all that portion of the legitimate and bona fide public debt of that State contracted prior to its annexation to the United States, and for which the duties on foreign imports were pledged by the said State to its creditors, not exceeding the sum of ——— dollars, in consideration of the said duties so pledged having been no longer applicable to that object after the said annexation, but having thenceforward become payable to the United States; and upon the condition, also, that the said State of Texas shall, by some solemn and authentic act of her legislature or of a convention, relinquish to the United States any claim which it has to any part of New Mexico.

5. *Resolved,* That it is inexpedient to abolish slavery in the District of Columbia whilst that institution continues to exist in the State of Maryland, without the consent of that State, without the consent of the people of the District, and without just compensation to the owners of slaves within the District.

6. *But, resolved,* That it is expedient to prohibit, within the

District, the slave trade in slaves brought into it from States or places beyond the limits of the District. . . .

7. *Resolved,* That more effectual provision ought to be made by law, according to the requirement of the constitution, for the restitution and delivery of persons bound to service or labor in any State, who may escape into any other State or Territory in the Union. And,

8. *Resolved,* That Congress has no power to promote or obstruct the trade in slaves between the slaveholding States; but that the admission or exclusion of slaves brought from one into another of them, depends exclusively upon their own particular laws.

☆ ☆ ☆

Southern Support of the Compromise of 1850

After the Compromise of 1850 was enacted, a convention of those Southern states that approved the measure was held in Milledgeville, Georgia. The issue of the right of a state to leave the Union came up again in another form. This time the convention asserted that a state is bound to the nation as long as the nation upholds the "rights and principles it was designed to perpetuate." And while the wording was not harsh, the Southern states clearly showed they intended to leave the Union if any of the provisions of the Compromise were broken.

As you read, compare the Southern states' attitude toward the compact that holds the Union together with Andrew Jackson's understanding of the compact.

DOCUMENT

(6) To the end that the position of this State may be clearly apprehended by her Confederates of the South and of the North, and that she may be blameless of all future consequences —

Be it resolved by the people of Georgia in Convention assembled,

First. That we hold the American Union secondary in importance only to the rights and principles it was designed to perpetuate. That past associations, present fruition, and future prospects, will bind us to it so long as it continues to be the safe-guard of those rights and principles.

Second. That if the thirteen original Parties to the Compact, bordering the Atlantic in a narrow belt, while their separate interests were in embryo, their peculiar tendencies scarcely developed, their revolutionary trials and triumphs still green in memory, found

Union impossible without compromise, the thirty-one of this day may well yield somewhat in the conflict of opinion and policy, to preserve that Union which has extended the sway of Republican Government over a vast wilderness to another ocean, and proportionately advanced their civilization and national greatness.

Third. That in this spirit the State of Georgia has maturely considered the action of Congress, embracing a series of measures for the admission of California into the Union, the organization of Territorial Governments for Utah and New Mexico, the establishment of a boundary between the latter and the State of Texas, the suppression of the slave-trade in the District of Columbia, and the extradition of fugitive slaves, and (connected with them) the rejection of propositions to exclude slavery from the Mexican Territories, and to abolish it in the District of Columbia; and, whilst she does not wholly approve, will abide by it as a permanent adjustment of this sectional controversy.

Fourth. That the State of Georgia, in the judgment of this Convention, will and ought to resist, even (as a last resort) to a disruption of every tie which binds her to the Union, any future Act of Congress abolishing Slavery in the District of Columbia, without the consent and petition of the slave-holders thereof, or any Act abolishing Slavery in places within the slave-holding States, purchased by the United States for the erection of forts, magazines, arsenals, dock-yards, navy-yards, and other like purposes; or in any Act suppressing the slave-trade between slave-holding States; or in any refusal to admit as a State any Territory applying, because of the existence of Slavery therein; or in any Act prohibiting the introduction of slaves into the Territories of Utah and New Mexico; or in any Act repealing or materially modifying the laws now in force for the recovery of fugitive slaves.

Fifth. That it is the deliberate opinion of this Convention, that upon the faithful execution of the Fugitive Slave Bill by the proper authorities, depends the preservation of our much loved Union.

☆   ☆   ☆

The Impending Crisis of the South 1858

Most Southerners felt that a prosperous future for the South meant retaining slavery, and they agreed that a threat to slavery would justify the Southern states' leaving the Union. But probably the most devastating attack on the economic disadvantages of slavery came from a non-slave-owning North Carolinian named Hinton Helper. In 1858 he published *The Impending Crisis of the South,* in which he demonstrated why the South had failed to develop economically and intellectually. The language of the book was so strong that the volume was banned in many parts of the South.

As you read, list the reasons Hinton Helper thought the North had developed economically. How do these reasons suggest that the South would be at an economic disadvantage if it were to leave the Union?

DOCUMENT

(7) It is a fact well known to every intelligent Southerner that we are compelled to go to the North for almost every article of utility and adornment, from matches, shoepegs and paintings up to cotton mills, steamships and statuary; that we have no foreign trade, no princely merchants, nor respectable artists; that in comparison with the free states, we contribute nothing to the literature, polite arts and inventions of the age; that, for want of profitable employment at home, large numbers of our native population find themselves necessitated to emigrate to the West, whilst the free states retain not only the larger proportion of those born within their own limits, but induce, annually, hundreds of thousands of foreigners to settle and remain amongst them; that almost everything produced at the North meets with ready sale, while, at the same time, there is no demand, even among our own citizens for the productions of Southern industry; that owing to the absence of a proper system of business amongst us, the North becomes, in one way or another, the proprietor and dispenser of all our floating wealth, and that we are dependent on Northern capitalists for the means necessary to build our railroads, canals, and other public improvements; that if we want to visit a foreign country, even though it may lie directly South of us, we find no convenient way of getting there except by taking passage through a Northern port; and that nearly all the profits arising from the exchange of commodities, from insurance and shipping offices, and from the thousand and one industrial pursuits of the country, accrue to the North, and are there invested in the erection of those magnificent cities and stupendous works of art which dazzle the eyes of the South, and attest the superiority of free institutions!

The North is the Mecca of our merchants, and to it they must and do make two pilgrimages per annum—one in the spring and one in the fall. All our commercial, mechanical, manufactural, and literary supplies come from there. We want Bibles, brooms, buckets

and books, and we go to the North; . . . we want furniture, crock-
ery, glassware and pianos, and we go to the North; we want toys,
primers, school books, fashionable apparel, machinery, medicines,
tombstones, and a thousand other things, and we go to the North
for them all. Instead of keeping our money in circulation at home,
by patronizing our own mechanics, manufacturers, and laborers, we
send it all away to the North, and there it remains; it never falls into
our hands again.

☆   ☆   ☆

Alabama Ordinance of Secession 1861

In 1860 Abraham Lincoln, the head of the then new Republican
party, was elected to the presidency. This new party had been associated with the resistance to the spread of slavery to new territories.
When the election results were finally in, in late December of 1860,
South Carolina seceded. The causes that led up to this move were
many, but the threat of a President who was not sympathetic to
slavery was a blow the South was unwilling to take. The Ordinance
of Secession printed below was Alabama's statement of agreement
with South Carolina's action, and is also the culminating document
on the question of whether or not a state has a right to leave the
Union. The South had done what it said it had a right to do.

DOCUMENT

(8) Whereas, the election of Abraham Lincoln and Hannibal
Hamlin to the offices of President and Vice-President of
the United States of America by a sectional party avowedly hostile
to the domestic institutions and to the peace and security of the
people of the State of Alabama, preceded by many and dangerous
infractions of the Constitution of the United States by many of the
States and people of the Northern section, is a political wrong of so
insulting and menacing a character as to justify the people of the
State of Alabama in the adoption of prompt and decided measures
for their future peace and security; Therefore,

Be it declared and ordained by the people of the State of Alabama
in Convention assembled, That the State of Alabama now withdraws,
and is hereby withdrawn, from the Union known as "the United
States of America," and henceforth ceases to be one of said
United States, and is, and of right ought to be, a sovereign and
independent State.

Section 2. *Be it further declared and ordained by the People of the State of Alabama in convention assembled,* That all the powers over the territory of said State and over the people thereof heretofore delegated to the Government of the United States of America be, and they are hereby, withdrawn from said Government, and are hereby resumed and vested in the people of the State of Alabama.

Be it resolved by the people of Alabama in convention assembled, That the people of the States of Delaware, Maryland, Virginia, North Carolina, South Carolina, Florida, Georgia, Mississippi, Louisiana, Texas, Arkansas, Tennessee, Kentucky, and Missouri be, and are hereby, invited to meet the people of the State of Alabama, by their delegates in convention, on the 4th day of February, A.D. 1861, at the city of Montgomery, in the State of Alabama, for the purpose of consulting with each other as to the most effectual mode of securing concerted and harmonious action in whatever measures may be deemed most desirable for our common peace and security.

And be it further resolved, That the president of this convention be, and is hereby, instructed to transmit forthwith a copy of the foregoing preamble, ordinance, and resolutions to the Governors of the several States named in said resolutions.

☆ ☆ ☆

Jefferson Davis's Farewell Address to the Senate 1861

Secession by the Southern states on the eve of the Civil War was not an easy or a happy decision for those Southerners with any insight into the consequences of their actions. Jefferson Davis, who in 1861 was elected to the Presidency of the Confederate States of America, had long served his state and the United States government. A Mississippi planter, Davis had been a member of the House of Representatives, an officer in the Mexican War, and Secretary of War in the cabinet of President Franklin Pierce; at the time Mississippi seceded from the Union he represented his state in the Senate of the United States. Like many of his colleagues who later served the Confederacy, Davis looked upon secession as the last resort, the final remedy to protect what he considered to be the just interests of the South.

Possibly one of the most emotionally charged addresses ever made in the United States Senate was delivered by Senator Jefferson Davis on January 21, 1861. He made the formal announcement that Mississippi had seceded from the Union and also delivered his farewell address to that august body, which was filled with many of his personal friends who would shortly be on opposite sides of the battle lines.

Davis's speech contains little that is new in the argument over secession; his statements rely on the seventy years of proclamations, resolves, and ordinances that have stated this position. But perhaps his speech, more than any other, shows the difficult decision Southerners faced when they were asked to choose between loyalty to their states and loyalty to the Union.

(9) I rise, Mr. President, for the purpose of announcing . . . that the State of Mississippi . . . has declared her separation from the United States. Under these circumstances, of course, my functions are terminated here. . . .

[Senators know] . . . that I have for many years advocated, as an essential attribute of State sovereignty, the right of a State to secede from the Union. Therefore, if I had not believed there was justifiable cause; if I had thought that Mississippi was acting without sufficient provocation, or without an existing necessity, I should still under my theory of Government, because of my allegiance to the State of which I am a citizen, have been bound by her action. I however, may be permitted to say that I do think she has justifiable cause, and I approve her act. I conferred with her people before that act was taken, counseled them then that if the state of things which they apprehended should exist when the convention met, they should take the action which they have now adopted. . . .

When you deny to us the right to withdraw from a Government which thus perverted threatens to be destructive of our rights, we but tread in the path of our fathers when we proclaim our independence, and take the hazard. This is done not in hostility to each other, not to injure any section of the country, not even for our pecuniary benefit; but from the high and solemn motive of defending and protecting the rights we inherited, and which it is our sacred duty to transmit unshorn to our children. . . . I am sure I feel no hostility to you, Senators from the North. I am sure there is not one of you, whatever sharp discussion there may have been between us, to whom I cannot now say, in the presence of my God, I wish you well; and such, I am sure, is the feeling of the people whom I represent towards those whom you represent. I therefore feel that I but express their desire when I say I hope, and they hope, for peaceful relations with you, though we must part. They may be mutually beneficial to us in the future, as they have been in the past, if you so will it. . . .

Whatever offense I have given which has not been redressed, or for which satisfaction has not been demanded, I have, Senators, in this hour of our parting, to offer you my apology for any pain which, in heat of discussion, I have inflicted. I go hence unencumbered of the remembrance of any injury received, and having discharged the duty of making the only reparation in my power for any injury offered.

Mr. President, and Senators, . . . it only remains for me to bid you a final adieu.

☆   ☆   ☆

Economic Effects of Secession 1861

The secession of the Southern states brought a mixed reaction in the North. Many abolitionists, who opposed slavery on moral grounds, thought if the Southerners would not free their slaves it was better that they were out of the Union. Undoubtedly a much larger group in the North, headed by President-elect Abraham Lincoln, believed that the union of all the states must be preserved. Some felt the loss of the South would have no economic effect on the North, but others thought the South absolutely indispensable to Northern prosperity.

As you read this editorial from the Manchester, New Hampshire, *Union Democrat* titled "Let Them Go," list the reasons the editor feels that the economic well-being of the North is linked to the South. Compare this point of view with Helper's statement about the economic advantages in the North *(see pp. 139–141)*. Which man's opinion proved correct in light of the outcome of the Civil War?

DOCUMENT

(10) Some of our Republican friends affect to be very indifferent to the secession of the Southern states. "Let them go — we can get along very well without them."

No you can't. Consider a moment. The line of separation will be the line of the free and the slave states. We shall divide in anger. The Southern Confederacy will not employ our ships or buy our goods. What is our shipping without it? Literally nothing. The transportation of cotton and its fabrics employs more ships than all other trades. The first result will be, that Northern ships and ship owners will go to the South. They are doing it even now. It is very clear that the South gains by this process, and we lose.

In the manufacturing department, we now have the almost exclusive supply of 10,000,000 of people. Can this market be cut off, and we not feel it? Our mills run now—why? Because they have the cotton, and may nearly as well have the manufactured goods as the stock, on hand. But they will not run long. We hear from good authority that some of them will stop in sixty days. We don't need any authority—everyone knows they must stop if our national troubles are not adjusted. An inflexible law cannot be violated. The shoe business is completely prostrate. Why? Because, while we have sent $10,000,000 worth of shoes to the South per year, we now send greatly less, and very soon we shall send less still. One branch of business suffers with another—one man suffers with another.

Our city owes its origin and growth to the Southern trade—to the Union. We cannot afford to "let the South go," if she may be retained by any fair compromise, as we believe she may be. If the time shall come when the people *realize* the fact that the Union is permanently dissolved, real estate will depreciate one half in a single year. —Our population will decrease with the decline of business, and matters will go on in geometrical progression from bad to worse—until all of us will be swamped in utter ruin. Let men consider—apply the laws of business, and see if they can reach any different conclusion.

No—we *must not* "let the South go." It is easy and honorable to keep her. Simply recognize in the neighborhood of states those principles of equity and courtesy which we would scorn to violate in our social relations at home—that is all. Let New Hampshire treat Virginia as we should treat our neighbors. Do we vilify them, watch for chances to annoy them, clear up to the line of the law, and sometimes beyond it, and encourage hostile raids against them? Is that good neighborhood? Then, let not one state practice it against another.

☆   ☆   ☆

Reconstruction Follows War 1867

Some historians might even go so far as to say that the Civil War was fought over this issue of a state's right to leave the Union. But history is not so simple that only one factor can explain a war. The Civil War was fought between two sections of the country that had widely different interests to protect. The South had developed its agricultural life to a high degree. The invention of the cotton gin made cotton growing profitable for Southern planters. And cotton growing was even more profitable when slaves were used. The South had little industry, since Southerners could make a living selling cotton. The North had no need for slaves, and slaves had all but vanished there because the North made its money through manufacturing. New England was most famous for its textile industry, but Northern factories made many other products as well.

Neither section wanted to risk seeing its way of life threatened. Northerners did not want slavery to spread because other slave states would be sympathetic with the South. These sympathetic states would vote with the Southern states in Congress. Southern states did not want many new states to enter the Union without slavery because these states would side with the North. Soon there might be enough states to end slavery over the protests of the South. Southerners felt that an end to slavery would mean the end of their profitable cotton growing. The South tried to resolve these fears by leaving the Union, but the Northern states, led by President Lincoln, were willing to fight the South to bring the Union back together.

After the North won, the nation was plunged into Reconstruction. Long before the end of the Civil War, Abraham Lincoln maintained that the Southern states should be treated like prodigal sons: they had temporarily left their home, but they were still part of the family. It was in this spirit that Lincoln used the immortal words "with malice toward none; with charity for all" in his second inaugural address in 1865, shortly before the end of the great conflict.

There were others, however, who believed that the defeated Confederate States should be treated like conquered enemies. The death of Lincoln removed the major support for the idea that reconstruction of the South should be carried on in a moderate manner. By 1867 Congress adopted a stern, harsh Reconstruction Act which delighted those who felt that the South should be punished for its sins. One of the supporters of this attitude was Thaddeus Stevens, a member of the House of Representatives. Excerpts from one of his speeches in the House are quoted below.

DOCUMENT

(11) . . . Mr. Stevens, in his speech upon introducing the bill, did not attempt to conceal its positive and peremptory character. "It provides," said he, "that the ten disorganized States shall be divided into five military districts; that the Commander of the Army shall take charge of them, through his officers not below the rank of Brigadier-General, who shall have the general supervision of the peace, quiet and protection of the people, loyal and disloyal, who reside within those precincts; and that to do so, he may use, as the law of nations would authorize him to do, the legal tribunals whenever he may deem them competent; but these tribunals are to be considered of no validity *per se*, of no intrinsic force, of no force in consequence of their origin; the question being

wholly within the power of the conqueror, and to remain until that conqueror shall permanently supply their place with something else. This is the whole bill. It does not need much examination. One night's rest after its reading is enough to digest it."

☆   ☆   ☆

Amnesty for the South 1871

The bitterness that marked Thaddeus Stevens' speech supporting the Reconstruction Act crept into the Fourteenth Amendment, which was designed to punish those who had been the public officials of the Confederacy. This amendment required that officials who had sworn to uphold the Constitution and later upheld the Confederacy were disbarred from a number of offices; only a two-thirds vote of Congress could change this ruling.

In his 1871 annual Message to Congress, President Ulysses S. Grant said that enough time had passed since the end of the war for Congress to grant amnesty to this particular group. It was most fitting that this suggestion should come from the President who, as a general, had led the Union armies to victory on the field of battle. After heated debate Congress passed the Amnesty Act in May, 1872; the act applied to all but about five hundred of the highest ranking Confederate officials. Although Reconstruction did not end until 1877, when the last federal troops were removed from South Carolina and Louisiana, the Amnesty Act was an important step in healing wartime wounds.

DOCUMENT

(12) More than six years having elapsed since the last hostile gun was fired between the armies then arrayed against each other—one for the perpetuation, the other for the destruction, of the Union—it may well be considered whether it is not now time that the disabilities imposed by the fourteenth amendment should be removed. That amendment does not exclude the ballot, but only imposes the disability to hold offices upon certain classes. When the purity of the ballot is secure, majorities are sure to elect officers reflecting the views of the majority. I do not see the advantage or propriety of excluding men from office merely because they were before the rebellion of standing and character sufficient to be elected to positions requiring them to take oaths to support the Constitution, and admitting to eligibility those entertaining precisely the same views, but of less standing in their communities. It may be

said that the former violated an oath, while the latter did not; the latter did not have it in their power to do so. If they had taken this oath, it can not be doubted they would have broken it as did the former class. If there are any great criminals, distinguished above all others for the part they took in opposition to the Government, they might, in the judgment of Congress, be excluded from such an amnesty.

This subject is submitted for your careful consideration.

☆　　☆　　☆

An Attitude Toward Governmental Power Today 1965

Since the Civil War the right of a state to leave the Union has not been seriously questioned—no state has tried. And the early conflicts over a state's right to declare an act of Congress unconstitutional has been resolved by the Supreme Court's clear assumption of that right. The United States today has a much stronger federal government than it had one hundred years ago, but this strength has not gone unquestioned, particularly when the government exercises power in areas where states feel it has no right to do so.

In the past ten years the issue over the power of the federal government has centered on recent civil rights legislation. *(See Chapter 9.)* Some states have felt the civil rights laws were unconstitutional because they violated, for example, the state's right to determine voting practices. The Supreme Court has generally upheld civil rights legislation. Therefore, those in opposition to the legislation have felt the Supreme Court has gone beyond its power to interpret the Constitution.

This speech titled "The Role of the Supreme Court as the Interpreter of the Constitution" by Senator Sam J. Ervin, Jr., of North Carolina, reflects the view of those who oppose both a powerful central government and the recent Supreme Court decisions that favored the government's activities. Although his attack is directed mostly against the Supreme Court, find those places where the senator asserts the rights of states to direct their affairs.

DOCUMENT

(13) The men who composed the Constitutional Convention of 1787 were wise men. They had read the history of the long and bitter struggle of man for freedom, and had found this shocking but everlasting truth inscribed upon each page of that

history: No man or set of men can be safely trusted with governmental power of an unlimited nature. As a consequence, they were determined, above all things, to establish a government of laws and not of men.

To prevent the exercise of arbitrary power by the Federal Government, they embodied in the Constitution the doctrine of the separation of governmental powers. In so doing, they utilized this doctrine in a twofold way. They delegated to the Federal Government the powers necessary to enable it to discharge its functions as a central government, and they left to each State the power to regulate its own internal affairs. It was this use of the doctrine of the separation of powers which prompted Chief Justice Salmon P. Chase to make this trenchant observation in *Texas* v. *White* (7 Wall. (U. S.) 700): "The Constitution, in all its provisions, looks to an indestructible Union, composed of indestructible States."

In their other utilization of the doctrine of the separation of governmental powers, the members of the Convention 1787 vested the power to make laws in the Congress, the power to execute laws in the President, and the power to interpret laws in the Supreme Court and such inferior courts as the Congress might establish. Moreover, they declared, in essence, that the legislative, the executive, and the judicial powers of the Federal Government should forever remain separate and distinct from each other.

This brings me to my subject: The role of the Supreme Court as the interpreter of the Constitution. . . .

Since the meaning of a written constitution is fixed when it is adopted and is not different at any subsequent time when a court has occasion to pass upon it, Judge Cooley was justified in declaring in his "Constitutional Limitations" that "a court * * * which should allow a change in public sentiment to influence it in giving to a written constitution a constitution not warranted by the intention of its founders would be justly chargeable with reckless disregard of official oath and public duty.". . .

If the thesis that a majority of the members of the Supreme Court have the rightful power to change the meaning of the Constitution under the guise of interpreting it every time a sitting Justice wavers in mind or a newly appointed Justice ascends the bench should find permanent acceptance, the Constitution would become to all practical intents and purposes an uncertain and unstable document of no beneficial value to the country. Yea, more than this, it would become a constant menace to sound government at all levels, and to the freedom of the millions of Americans who are not at liberty to join Supreme Court Justices in saying that Supreme Court decisions on constitutional questions are not binding on them. . . .

If the America which George Washington and the other Founding Fathers created is to endure, Supreme Court Justices as well as Presidents and Congresses must heed what he said in his Farewell Address to the American people. I quote his words:

"It is important likewise, that the habits of thinking in a free country should inspire caution in those intrusted with its administration, to confine themselves within their respective constitutional spheres, avoiding in the exercise of the powers of one department, to encroach upon another. The spirit of encroachment tends to consolidate the powers of all the departments in one, and thus to create, whatever the form of government, a real despotism. A just estimate of that love of power and proneness to abuse it which predominate in the human heart is sufficient to satisfy us of the truth of this position."

☆　　☆　　☆

V. Footnotes

[1]N. S. Shaler, *Kentucky* (New York, 1893) 409–416.

[2]Theodore Dwight, *History of the Hartford Convention* (N. and J. White, New York, 1833) 352–361.

[3]*Public Documents: The Senate of the United States*, Twenty-Second Congress, 2nd session (Duff Green, Washington, D.C., 1832) I, 36–39.

[4]James D. Richardson, comp., *A Compilation of the Messages and Papers of the Presidents, 1789–1897* (Government Printing Office, Washington, D.C., 1898) II, 640–656.

[5]*U.S. Senate Journal*, 31st Congress, 1st session, 118 ff.

[6]Alexander H. Stephens, *A Constitutional View of the Late War Between the States, etc.* (National Publishing Co., Philadelphia, 1870) II, 676–677.

[7]Hinton Rowan Helper, *The Impending Crisis of the South: How to Meet It* (A. B. Burdick, New York, 1860) 21–23.

[8]*A Compilation of the War of the Rebellion: Official Records of the Union and Confederate Armies*, series 4, 1 (Government Printing Office, Washington, D.C., 1900) 43–44.

[9]*Congressional Globe*, 36th Congress, 2nd Session, January 21, 1861, 487.

[10]Howard Cecil Perkins, ed., *Northern Editorials on Secession* (D. Appleton-Century, New York, 1942) 591–592.

[11]James B. Blaine, *Twenty Years of Congress: from Lincoln to Garfield* (The Henry Bill Publishing Co., Norwich, Conn., 1886) II, 251.

[12]James D. Richardson, comp., *A Compilation of the Messages and Papers of the Presidents, 1789–1897* (Government Printing Office, Washington, D.C., 1898) VII, 153.

[13]*Congressional Record*, 89th Congress, 1st Session, July 16, 1965, 16493–16495.

VI
Should Suffrage
Be Limited?

Many of the amendments of the Constitution deal with the liberalization of voting laws. The Fifteenth Amendment extended the right to vote to all men regardless of race; direct voting for senators was granted by the Seventeenth Amendment; and women gained the right to vote with the Nineteenth Amendment. This extension of suffrage (which means the right to vote) was necessary because at the beginning of our nation's history voting laws were very restrictive.

When the colonists began to have a voice in their governments, women and slaves were automatically excluded from voting. There was no precedent for woman suffrage, since women in England had not voted. Slaves did not have the right to vote because they were considered to be property. Also, the colonies that did allow suffrage had differing restrictions. For example, in Virginia property owners had the right to vote, but in the Massachusetts Bay Colony voters also had to be church members.

When the colonies became a union under the Constitution, many of the states kept their voting laws intact. In that era few people were educated, and those that were, were for the most part the wealthy property owners. In one sense some people felt that the laws had been made with the best interests of the country in mind; these laws gave those best able to govern—the educated—the right to govern. But American society changed; people had more time to think about their government, and more schools were opened to educate more people. Forty years after the founding of the country, men were beginning to question the idea that property ownership was a qualification upon which the right to vote should be based.

Since that time, although the history of suffrage has been one of continually extending the right to vote to more and more people, there have been areas of disagreement. The suffrage movement has not stopped; it is still continuing today.

An Argument against Universal Suffrage 1821

In 1821 New York State was considering a new state constitution. One of the proposals of the constitution was that the state should permit universal male suffrage. At this time many other states were gradually abolishing property qualifications. At the Convention, James Kent, a prominent New Yorker, delivered the following speech, which reflected the alarm many people felt at the idea of universal suffrage.

As you read, find what the original constitution required for suffrage. For what two reasons did Kent fear universal suffrage? Have these reasons proved to be sound?

DOCUMENT

(1) I hope that what I may have to say will be kindly received, for it will be well intended. But, if I thought otherwise, I should still prefer to hazard the loss of the little popularity which I might have in this house. . . .

The Senate has hitherto been elected by the farmers of the state—by the free and independent lords of the soil, worth at least $250 in freehold state, over and above all debts charged thereon. The governor has been chosen by the same electors, and we have hitherto elected citizens of elevated rank and character. Our assembly has been chosen by freeholders possessing a freehold of the value of $50, or by persons renting a tenement of the yearly value of $5, and who have been rated and actually paid taxes to the state. By the report before us, we propose to annihilate, at one stroke, all those property distinctions and to bow before the idol of universal suffrage. That extreme democratic principle, when applied to the legislative and executive departments of the government, has been regarded with terror, by the wise men of every age, because in every European republic, ancient and modern, in which it has been tried, it has terminated disastrously, and been productive of corruption, injustice, violence, and tyranny. And dare we flatter ourselves that we are a peculiar people, who can run the career of history, exempted from the passions which have disrupted and corrupted the rest of mankind? If we are like other races of men, with similar follies and vices, then I greatly fear that our posterity will have reason to deplore in sackcloth and ashes, the delusion of the day. . . . .

Now, sir, I wish to preserve our senate as the representative of the landed interest. I wish those who have an interest in the soil, to retain this exclusive possession of a branch in the legislature, as a stronghold in which they may find safety through all the vicissitudes which the state may be destined, in the course of Providence, to experience. I wish them to be always enabled to say that their freeholds cannot be taxed without their consent. The men of no property, together with the crowds of dependents, connected with great manufacturing and commercial establishments, and the motley and undefinable population of crowded ports, may, perhaps, at some future day, under skillful management, predominate in the assembly, and yet we should be perfectly safe if no laws could pass without the free consent of the owners of the soil. That security we at present enjoy; and it is that security which I wish to retain.

The apprehended danger from the experiment of universal suffrage applied to the whole legislative department, is no dream of the imagination. It is too mighty an excitement for the mortal constitution of man to endure. The tendency of universal suffrage, is to jeopardize the rights of property, and the principles of liberty. . . . There is a tendency in the poor to covet and to share the plunder of the rich; in the debtor to relax or avoid the obligation of contracts; in the majority to tyrannize over the minority, and trample down their rights; in the indolent and the profligate, to cast the whole burthens [burdens] of society upon the industrious and the virtuous; and *there is a tendency in ambitious and wicked men to inflame these combustible materials.* It requires a vigilant government, and a firm administration of justice, to counteract that tendency. . . .

☆ ☆ ☆

An Argument for Universal Suffrage 1828

Although James Kent and many others deplored the idea of universal suffrage, during the 1820's and 1830's state after state continued to abandon property qualifications for voting. America was becoming more democratic in its political institutions, and those who applauded the trend soon outnumbered those who feared it.

James Fenimore Cooper, who is better known today for his novels than for his political writings, favored this extension of democracy. The selection below is taken from *Notions of the Americans: Picked Up by a Travelling Bachelor*, a book he wrote while living in Europe. Written as a series of letters sent home to Europe by a traveler in the United States, the book was an attempt to explain American democracy to Europeans. In this selection his fictional traveler is telling about an American election.

(2) After quitting the poll, we familiarly discussed the merits and demerits of this system of popular elections. In order to extract the opinions of my friend, several of the more obvious and ordinary objections were stated with a freedom that induced him to speak with some seriousness.

"You see a thousand dangers in universal suffrage," he said, "merely because you have been taught to think so, without even having seen the experiment tried. The Austrian would be very apt to say, under the influence of mere speculation too, that it would be fatal to government to have any representation at all; and a vizier of the Grand Turk might find the mild exercise of the laws, which is certainly practiced in Austria proper, altogether fatal to good order. . . .

"There can be no doubt that, under a bald theory, a representation would be all the better if the most ignorant, profligate, and vagabond part of the community were excluded from the right of voting. It is just as true that if all the rogues and corrupt politicians, even including those who read Latin and have well-lined pocket-books, could be refused the right of voting, honest men would fare all the better. But as it is very well known that the latter are not, nor cannot well be excluded from the right of suffrage anywhere except in despotism, we have come to the conclusion that it is scarcely worth while to do so much violence to natural justice, without sufficient reason, as to disenfranchise a man merely because he is poor. Though a trifling *qualification* of property may sometimes be useful in particular conditions of society, there can be no greater fallacy than its *representation*. The most vehement declaimers in favor of the justice of the representation of property overlook two or three very important points of the argument. A man may be a voluntary associate in a joint-stock company and justly have a right to a participation in its management in proportion to his pecuniary interest, but life is not a chartered institution. . . . If men, when a little better than common, were anything like perfect,

154

we might hope to see power lodged with safety in the hands of a reasonable portion of the enlightened without any danger of its abuse. But the experience of the world goes to prove that there is a tendency to monopoly wherever power is reposed in the hands of the minority. Nothing is more likely to be true than that twenty wise men will unite in opinions in opposition to a hundred fools; but nothing is more certain than that, if placed in situations to control all the interests of their less gifted neighbors, the chance is that fifteen or sixteen of them would pervert their philosophy to selfishness . . . . Since the hour of the Revolution, the habits, opinions, laws, and I may say principles of the Americans are getting daily to be more democratic. We are perfectly aware that, while the votes of a few thousand scattered individuals can make no great or lasting impression on the prosperity or policy of the country, their dissatisfaction at being excluded might give a great deal of trouble. I do not mean to say that the suffrage may not, in most countries, be extended too far. I only wish to show you that it is not here. . . ."

☆   ☆   ☆

Democracy in America 1835

The election of Andrew Jackson to the presidency in 1828 is frequently referred to as the "beginning of democracy" in America. Jackson was of humble background and was the first occupant of the White House who was considered a "man of the people." During the Jacksonian period manhood suffrage became almost universal. The average man had, for the first time, come into his own in the United States. This feeling of the equality of mankind (slaves were the exception) has been effectively described in Alexis de Tocqueville's *Democracy in America*, published in France in 1835. De Tocqueville came to the United States in 1831 to study prison reform, but during his visit he observed virtually every aspect of life and brilliantly portrayed in his writings the spirit of the vigorous new nation. As you read, compare De Tocqueville's attitude toward government with John Locke's (see pp. 64–66) and Jefferson's (see pp. 91–95).

DOCUMENT

(3) In America the aristocratic element has always been feeble from its birth; and if at the present day it is not actually destroyed, it is at any rate so completely disabled that we can scarcely assign to it any degree of influence on the course of affairs.

The democratic principle, on the contrary, has gained so much strength, by time, by events, and by legislation, as to have become not only predominant, but all-powerful. No family or corporate authority can be perceived; very often one cannot even discover it in any very lasting individual influence.

America, then, exhibits in her social state an extraordinary phenomenon. Men are there seen on a greater equality in point of fortune and intellect, or, in other words, more equal in their strength, than in any other country of the world, or in any age of which history has preserved the remembrance.

The political consequences of such a social condition as this are easily deducible.

It is impossible to believe that equality will not eventually find its way into the political world, as it does everywhere else. To conceive of men remaining forever unequal upon a single point, yet equal on all others, is impossible; they must come in the end to be equal upon all.

Now, I know of only two methods of establishing equality in the political world; rights must be given to every citizen, or none at all to anyone. For nations which are arrived at the same stage of social existence as the Anglo-Americans, it is, therefore, very difficult to discover a medium between the sovereignty of all and the absolute power of one man: and it would be vain to deny that the social condition which I have been describing is just as liable to each of these consequences.

There is, in fact, a manly and lawful passion for equality that excites men to wish all to be powerful and honored. This passion tends to elevate the humble to the rank of the great; but there exists also in the human heart a depraved taste for equality, which impels the weak to attempt to lower the powerful to their own level and reduces men to prefer equality in slavery to inequality with freedom. Not that those nations whose social condition is democratic naturally despise liberty; on the contrary, they have an instinctive love of it. But liberty is not the chief and constant object of their desires; equality is their idol: they make rapid and sudden efforts to obtain liberty and, if they miss their aim, resign themselves to their disappointment; but nothing can satisfy them without equality, and they would rather perish than lose it.

On the other hand, in a state where the citizens are all practically equal, it becomes difficult for them to preserve their independence against the aggressions of power. No one among them being strong enough to engage in the struggle alone with advantage, nothing but a general combination can protect their liberty. Now, such a union is not always possible.

From the same social position, then, nations may derive one

or the other of two great political results; these results are extremely different from each other, but they both proceed from the same cause.

The Anglo-Americans are the first nation who, having been exposed to this formidable alternative, have been happy enough to escape the dominion of absolute power. They have been allowed by their circumstances, their origin, their intelligence, and especially by their morals to establish and maintain the sovereignty of the people.

Whenever the political laws of the United States are to be discussed, it is with the doctrine of the sovereignty of the people that we must begin.

The principle of the sovereignty of the people, which is always to be found, more or less, at the bottom of almost all human institutions, generally remains there concealed from view. It is obeyed without being recognized, or if for a moment it be brought to light, it is hastily cast back into the gloom of the sanctuary.

"The will of the nation" is one of those expressions that have been most largely abused by the wily and the despotic of every age. Some have seen the expression of it in the purchased suffrages of a few of the satellites of power; others, in the votes of a timid or an interested minority; and some have even discovered it in the silence of a people, on the supposition that the fact of submission established the right to command.

In America the principle of the sovereignty of the people is neither barren or concealed, as it is with some other nations; it is recognized by the customs and proclaimed by the laws. . . .

When a nation begins to modify the elective qualifications, it may easily be foreseen that, sooner or later, that qualification will be entirely abolished. There is no more invariable rule in the history of society: the further electoral rights are extended, the greater is the need of extending them; for after each concession the strength of the democracy increases, and its demands increase with its strength. The ambition of those who are below the appointed rate is irritated in exact proportion to the great number of those who are above it. The exception at last becomes the rule, concession follows concession, and no stop can be made short of universal suffrage.

At the present day the principle of the sovereignty of the people has acquired in the United States, all the practical development that the imagination can conceive. It is unencumbered by those fictions that are thrown over it in other countries, and it appears in every possible form, according to the exigency of the occasion. Sometimes the laws are made by the people in a body, as at Athens; and sometimes its representatives, chosen by universal suffrage, transact business in its name and under its immediate supervision.

In some countries a power exists which, though it is in a degree foreign to the social body, directs it, and forces it to pursue a certain track. In others the ruling force is divided, being partly within and partly without the ranks of the people. But nothing of this kind is to be seen in the United States; there society governs itself for itself. All power centers in its bosom, and scarcely an individual is to be met with who would venture to conceive or, still less, to express the idea of seeking it elsewhere. The nation participates in the making of its laws by the choice of its legislators, and in the execution of them by the choice of the agents of the executive government; it may almost be said to govern itself, so feeble and so restricted is the share left to the administration, so little do the authorities forget their popular origin and the power from which they emanate. . . .

☆   ☆   ☆

Declaration of Women's Rights 1848

Although the country had established universal manhood suffrage by 1848, the position of women and slaves had not progressed since colonial days. Laws concerning property, divorce, and the rights of husbands were made by men. A few women vigorously resented their legal and economic subservience to men. Some of these women met in the first Women's Rights Convention in Seneca Falls, New York, in 1848 and adopted a Declaration of Rights and Sentiments. Although these women were filled with angry frustration at the position they felt they were forced to occupy, they realized even at that early day that they must acquire the right to vote; for if women had the right to vote for their lawmakers, they would have some voice in the laws they lived under.

DOCUMENT

(4) When, in the course of human events, it becomes necessary for one portion of the family of man to assume among the people of the earth a position different from that which they have hitherto occupied, but one to which the laws of nature and of nature's God entitle them, a decent respect to the opinions of mankind requires that they should declare the causes that impel them to such a course.

We hold these truths to be self-evident: that all men and women are created equal; that they are endowed by their Creator with certain inalienable rights; that among these are life, liberty, and the pursuit of happiness. . . .

The history of mankind is a history of repeated injuries and usurpations on the part of man toward woman, having in direct object the establishment of an absolute tyranny over her. To prove this, let facts be submitted to a candid world.

He has never permitted her to exercise her inalienable right to the elective franchise.

He has compelled her to submit to laws, in the formation of which she had no voice.

He has withheld from her rights which are given to the most ignorant and degraded men—both natives and foreigners.

Having deprived her of this first right of a citizen, the elective franchise, thereby leaving her without representation in the halls of legislation, he has oppressed her on all sides.

He has made her, if married, in the eye of the law, civilly dead.

He has taken from her all right in property, even to the wages she earns.

He has made her, morally, an irresponsible being, as she can commit many crimes with impunity, provided they be done in the presence of her husband. In the covenant of marriage, she is compelled to promise obedience to her husband, he becoming, to all intents and purposes, her master—the law giving him power to deprive her of her liberty, and to administer chastisement.

He has so framed the laws of divorce, as to what shall be the proper causes, and in cases of separation, to whom the guardianship of the children shall be given, as to be wholly regardless of the happiness of women—the law, in all cases, going upon a false supposition of the supremacy of man, and giving all power into his hands.

After depriving her of all rights as a married woman, if single, and the owner of property, he has taxed her to support a government which recognizes her only when her property can be made profitable to it. . . .

He has monopolized nearly all the profitable employments, and from those she is permitted to follow, she receives but a scanty remuneration. He closes against her all the avenues to wealth and distinction which he considers most honorable to himself. As a teacher of theology, medicine, or law, she is not known.

He has denied her the facilities for obtaining a thorough education, all colleges being closed against her.

He allows her in Church, as well as State, but a subordinate position, claiming Apostolic authority for her exclusion from the ministry, and, with some exceptions, from any public participation in the affairs of the Church.

He has created a false public sentiment by giving to the world a different code of morals for men and women, by which moral delinquencies which exclude women from society, are not only tolerated, but deemed of little account in man. . . .

Now, in view of this entire disfranchisement of one-half the people of this country, their social and religious degradation — in view of the unjust laws above mentioned, and because women do feel themselves aggrieved, oppressed, and fraudulently deprived of their most sacred rights, we insist that they have immediate admission to all the rights and privileges which belong to them as citizens of the United States. . . .

Resolved, That all laws which prevent woman from occupying such a station in society as her conscience shall dictate, or which place her in a position inferior to that of man, are contrary to the great precept of nature, and therefore of no force or authority. . . .

Resolved, That it is the duty of the women of this country to secure to themselves their sacred right to the elective franchise.

☆　　☆　　☆

For the Right to Vote 1908

A small group of energetic women kept alive the spirit of the Seneca Falls conference and continued to press for woman suffrage. These women had to answer all types of arguments against their demands; they were warned they would lose their femininity, they were told they did not have the minds to understand complex political issues, and they were told that most women didn't want to vote. The fire and determination of this group is reflected in the following speeches delivered by Mrs. Judith H. Douglas and Mrs. Frances S. Potter in addresses to the Annual National Suffrage Convention held in 1908.

DOCUMENT

(5) Only one thing can make me see the justness of woman being classed with the idiot, the insane and the criminal and that is, if she is willing, if she is satisfied to be so classed, if she is contented to remain in the circumscribed limits which corrupt customs and perverted application of the Scriptures have marked out for her. It is idiotic not to want one's liberty; it is insane not to value one's inalienable rights and it is criminal to neglect one's God-given responsibilities. God placed woman originally in the same sphere with man, with the same inspirations and aspirations, the same emotions and intellect and accountability. . . . The Chinamen for centuries have taken peculiar means for restricting women's activities by binding the feet of girl babies and yet there remains the significant fact that, after centuries of constraint, God continues to send the female child into the world with feet well

formed, with a foundation as substantial to stand upon as that of the male child. As in this instance, so in all cases of restriction put upon women, they do not come from God but from man, beginning at birth. . . . For thousands of centuries woman has heard what sphere God wanted her to move in from men, God's self-ordained proxies. The thing for woman to do is to blaze the way of her sex so thoroughly that sixteen-year-old boys in the next generation will not dare ask a scholarly woman incredulously if she really thinks women have sense enough to vote. Woman can enter into the larger sphere her great Creator has assigned her only when she has an equal voice with man in forming public opinion, which crystalizes customs; only when her voice is heard in the pulpit, applying Scripture to man and woman equally, and when it is heard in the Legislature. Only then can be realized the full import of God's words when He said, "It is not well for man to be alone."

☆ ☆ ☆

Then, Mrs. Potter addressed the convention:

DOCUMENT

(6) Louis XIV said an infamous thing when he declared: "I am the State," but he announced his position frankly. He was an autocrat and he said so. It was a more honest and therefore less harmful position than that of a majority of voters in our country today. Can it help but confuse and deteriorate one sex, trained to believe and call itself living in a democracy, to say silently year by year at the polls, "I am the State"? Can it help but confuse and deteriorate the other sex, similarly trained to acquiescence year after year in a national misrepresentation and a personal no-representation? This fundamental insincerity of our so-called democracy is as insidious an influence upon the minds and morals of our franchised men, our unfranchised women and our young Americans of both sexes, as hypocrisy is to a church member or spurious currency to a bank. It is to be remembered that the evils which are pointed out in our commonwealth today are not the evils of a democracy but of an amorphous something which is afraid to be a democracy. Whether the opposition to women's voting be honestly professed, or whether it is concealed under chivalrous idolatry, distrust and skepticism are behind it. . . . When pushed to the wall, objectors to woman suffrage now-a-days take refuge behind one of two platitudes: The first is used too often by women whose public activities ought logically to make them suffragists — the assertion that equal suffrage is bound to come in time, but that at present there are more pressing needs. "Let us get the poor better housed and fed," these women say. "Let us get our schools improved and our cities cleaned up and then we shall have time to take up the cause of equal suffrage." Is not this a

161

survival of that old vice of womankind, indirection? . . . The suffrage issue should not be put off but should be placed first, as making the other issues easier and more permanent. . . .

This brings me to the other platitude. How often we are told, "Women themselves do not want it; when they do it will be given to them." That is to say, when an overwhelming majority of women want what they ought to have, then they can have it. Extension of suffrage never has been granted on these terms. No great reform has gone through on these terms. In an enlightened State wanting is not considered a necessary condition to the granting of education or the extension of any privilege. . . .

☆   ☆   ☆

Against Woman Suffrage 1918

The woman suffrage movement finally succeeded when the Nineteenth Amendment was added to the Constitution in 1920. The spirit of the women who fought for the cause, the patriotic contributions of women during the First World War (1914–1918), and the changing times helped convince the country that it was time women should vote.

But the amendment had to pass through the House of Representatives for debate before it ever got to the people. And the House was far from being in total agreement as to the wisdom of the bill. Frank Clark of Florida made a speech that was somewhat typical of the arguments of those who were opposed to the proposed amendment. While Representative Clark's statements may have been a bit extreme in predicting the destruction of the American home if woman suffrage took effect, the vehemence of his argument suggests why women had to wait so long for the passage of the Nineteenth Amendment.

DOCUMENT

(7) I want to say, in conclusion, that if I had no other objection to woman suffrage, I should oppose it because, in my humble judgment, the conferring of the franchise on woman will tend to disrupt the family, which is the unit of society, and when you disrupt the family you destroy the home, which in America is the foundation stone of the Republic. Nothing can convince me that a thing which is not only liable, but almost certain, to create discord in the families of men can ever prove beneficial to this country. If this resolution should pass and the proposed

amendment should be ratified by three-fourths of the States of the Union, then we would find a condition where the wife would either blindly follow the husband in the casting of her vote or she would disagree with his views and have her vote counted in opposition to his. If the former is to be the case, then it occurs to me that all will agree that this would be an entirely superfluous and useless piece of legislation, as the only result would be to practically double the number of votes cast without changing in the slightest the political complexion of the State or the Nation, but adding largely to the expense of holding our elections. If the latter should be the case, then we would find the husband and wife constantly engaged in political disputation, which would grow warmer, more heated, and more acrimonious as the campaign advanced, until finally a veritable conflagration of domestic infelicity would be kindled, consuming the marital tie, destroying the home, and sending the children, to all intents and purposes, orphans out on the cold charity of the world to become charges on the State. It may be said that this picture is overdrawn, but, sir, it is not. Man and wife to live happily together must be in harmony. They must think alike, act alike, have the same ideals of life, and look forward with like vision to the happy consummation "beyond the vale." . . .

. . . These four—home, mother, wife, and heaven—are the corner stones of our governmental structure, and if either be destroyed, the Republic will crumble to decay and self-government among men will pass from the earth. Ridicule it, if you please; sneer at it, if you will; but I shall never cease to reverence and love the sweet, womanly wife and mother who, in the fear of God and with queenly dignity presides over an American home. Hers is the proudest place in the economy of the universe. Talk about rights, about influence, about power—all mankind is at her feet, and she wields a scepter more powerful than that of any king or potentate, the scepter of wifely fidelity and motherly love. (*Applause.*)

☆ ☆ ☆

John Austin Moon on Woman Suffrage 1918

John Austin Moon of Tennessee also delivered a speech in the House of Representatives in opposition to the Nineteenth Amendment. Moon argued against the amendment on grounds other than that woman suffrage would break up home and family; rather, he felt, the law would tend to undermine the Constitution. While few people would today agree with the logical structure of his argument, many of his points are echoed today when Congress debates laws that are designed to secure the right to vote for minority groups.

As you read, find Moon's main objection to the amendment. How valid is the objection in light of Article V of the Constitution, which provides for the amending process?

DOCUMENT

(8) For the gratification of those most excellent women and men who desire the passage of the pending woman's suffrage amendment to the United States Constitution I would be much pleased to vote to submit it for ratification to the States, but my sense of duty and my loyalty to the platform of the national Democracy and to the principles of my party and obedience to the will of an overwhelming majority of the people I represent forbids that I do so. It is not because I have any opposition to women exercising the right of franchise that I cast a negative vote on this amendment, but because of the manner in which it is sought to be obtained. A restrictive amendment upon the rights and liberties of the people of a State attached to the Federal Constitution can not be desired by any person who has given careful thought to our system of government and the basis upon which local rights and liberty rests. . . .

Logically, no man can deny that a woman is entitled to all the rights and privileges, including the right of suffrage, that men enjoy; nor has man the moral right to determine whether it is best for women to exercise the right to vote or not. Women should be permitted to determine for themselves that which they think is best for them. For men to determine that women ought not to vote is to destroy the equal justice to which the sexes are entitled. The power, aside from the moral right, however, to make men and women equal at the ballot box under existing law rests with the qualified voters. The qualified voters are men, and women therefore have no voice under the Constitution and law as it exists in securing their own enfranchisement. It therefore becomes the duty of men under our dual system of government to determine the manner in which it shall be done, if they conclude it shall be done at all. There are two methods by which women may be entitled to equal political rights with men. One is by amendment to the Federal Constitution, the other is by amendment by each State to its constitution or by its law if permitted under the State constitution to grant suffrage to women. A large number of the States have already granted suffrage to women. They have exercised their political power and sovereignty in the matter and determined in the interest of the rights of women. Other States might be of the opinion that it is not proper to grant this power to women. The proposed Federal amendment, if passed, would deprive the State of its legal right to determine its electorate. It may be said that the amendments that have already been passed to the Federal Constitution that are restrictive of the rights of States do also pro tanto deprive the State of sovereign power. That, so far as it goes, is true, but it affords no reason why the State should be further deprived of sovereignty, nor are the powers of which the States are deprived under the Federal Constitution essential to the maintenance of local self-government. The enumerated powers of the Federal Government under the Constitution are those powers which are essential to the transaction of the greater functions of government that are national in their nature. They do not restrict the States in the most vital function that enables them to maintain local self-government. When you deprive a State of the right to say who its electors are or place restrictions upon the State in determining the qualifications of its electors, you strike down absolutely and unconditionally the life of its sovereignty.

☆   ☆   ☆

The Voting Rights Act of 1965

The fight to secure the right to vote for all adult citizens of the United States did not end with the Nineteenth Amendment. Although the Fifteenth Amendment gave all adult male citizens the right to vote regardless of race or creed, the amendment was not fully in effect in some parts of the country. In some states minority groups were kept from voting by restrictive registration laws.

In 1965 Congress passed the Voting Rights Act for the purpose of enforcing the "Fifteenth Amendment to the Constitution and for other purposes." While it was designed to secure the right to vote for all minority groups, it was passed in response to the Negro minority's objections that they did not have the right to vote in some Southern states. The law outlawed the poll tax and literacy test as methods of determining who should vote; both of these devices had been used by some states to keep Negroes from voting.

To assure the enforcement of the law, Congress provided that federal examiners could make lists of eligible voters. These would then be sent to local election officials and to state and national attorneys general.

There has been bitter disagreement about the constitutionality of this bill, particularly in states that have had federal examiners

165

come to compile voting lists. Some people have argued that each state has the right to make its own voting laws according to Article I, section 4, clause 1 of the Constitution (*see pp. 15–16*).

DOCUMENT

(9) To enforce the fifteenth amendment of the Constitution of the United States, and for other purposes.

Be it enacted by the Senate and House of Representatives of the United States of America in Congress assembled, That this Act shall be known as the "Voting Rights Act of 1965."

SEC. 2. No voting qualification or prerequisite to voting, or standard, practice, or procedure shall be imposed or applied by any State or political subdivision to deny or abridge the right of any citizen of the United States to vote on account of race or color.

SEC. 3. (a) Whenever the Attorney General institutes a proceeding under any statute to enforce the guarantees of the fifteenth amendment in any State or political subdivision the court shall authorize the appointment of Federal examiners by the United States Civil Service Commission in accordance with section 6 to serve for such period of time and for such political subdivision as the court shall determine is appropriate to enforce the guarantees of the fifteenth amendment. . . .

SEC. 4. (a) To assure that the right of citizens of the United States to vote is not denied or abridged on account of race or color, no citizen shall be denied the right to vote in any Federal, State, or local election because of his failure to comply with any test or device in any State with respect to which the determinations have been made under subsection (b). . . .

(c) The phrase "test or device" shall mean any requirement that a person as a prerequisite for voting or registration for voting (1) demonstrate the ability to read, write, understand, or interpret any matter, (2) demonstrate any educational achievement or his knowledge of any particular subject, (3) possess good moral character, or (4) prove his qualifications by the voucher of registered voters or members of any other class.

(d) For purposes of this section no State or political subdivision shall be determined to have engaged in the use of tests or devices for the purpose or with the effect of denying or abridging the right to vote on account of race or color if (1) incidents of such use have been few in number and have been promptly and effectively corrected by State or local action, (2) the continuing effect of such incidents has been eliminated, and (3) there is no reasonable probability of their recurrence in the future.

(e) (1) Congress hereby declares that to secure the rights under the fourteenth amendment of persons educated in American-flag schools in which the predominant classroom language was other than English, it is necessary to prohibit the States from conditioning the right to vote of such persons on ability to read, write, understand, or interpret any matter in the English language.

(2) No person who demonstrates that he has successfully completed the sixth primary grade in a public school in, or a private school accredited by, any State or territory, the District of Columbia, or the Commonwealth of Puerto Rico in which the predominant classroom language was other than English, shall be denied the right to vote in any Federal, State, or local election because of his inability to read, write, understand, or interpret any matter in the English language, except that in States in which State law provides that a different level of education is presumptive of literacy, he shall demonstrate that he has successfully completed an equivalent level of education in a public school in, or a private school accredited by, any State or territory, the District of Columbia, or the Commonwealth of Puerto Rico in which the predominant classroom language was other than English.

SEC. 7. . . . (b) Any person whom the examiner finds, in accordance with instructions received under section 9 (b), to have the qualifications prescribed by State law not inconsistent with the Constitution and laws of the United States shall promptly be placed on a list of eligible voters. . . . The examiner shall certify and transmit such list, and any supplements as appropriate, at least once a month, to the offices of the appropriate election officials, with copies to the Attorney General and the attorney general of the State, and any such lists and supplements thereto transmitted during the month shall be available for public inspection on the last business day of the month and in any event not later than the forty-fifth day prior to any election. The appropriate State or local election official shall place such names on the official voting list. Any person whose name appears on the examiner's list shall be entitled and allowed to vote in the election district of his residence unless and until the appropriate election officials shall have been notified that such person has been removed from such list in accordance with subsection (d). . . .

SEC. 10. (a) The Congress finds that the requirement of the payment of a poll tax as a precondition to voting (i) precludes persons of limited means from voting or imposes unreasonable financial hardship on such persons as a precondition to their exercise of the franchise, (ii) does not bear a reasonable relationship to any legitimate State interest in the conduct of elections, and (iii) in some areas has the purpose or effect of denying persons the right to vote because of race or color. Upon the basis of these findings, Congress declares that the constitutional right of citizens to vote is denied or abridged in some areas by the requirement of the payment of a poll tax as a precondition to voting.

☆   ☆   ☆

The Supreme Court Decision on the Voting Rights Act 1966

The Voting Rights Act of 1965 was criticized in many Southern states and by citizens across the country because some people felt the federal government was overstepping its rights. In 1966 the Supreme Court ruled that the key provisions of the law were constitutional because the law was a valid means of implementing the Fifteenth Amendment. In the decision in the case of *South Carolina* v. *Katzenbach* the Supreme Court showed that it had little sympathy with the laws that had denied Negroes the right to vote.

DOCUMENT

(10) These provisions of the Voting Rights Act of 1965 are challenged on the fundamental ground that they exceed the powers of Congress and encroach on an area reserved to the States by the Constitution. South Carolina and certain of the *amici curiae* also attack specific sections of the Act for more particular reasons. They argue that the coverage formula prescribed in §4 (a)–(d) violates the principle of the equality of States, denies due process by employing an invalid presumption and by barring judicial review of administrative findings, constitutes a forbidden bill of attainder, and impairs the separation of powers by adjudicating guilt through legislation. They claim that the review of new voting rules required in §5 infringes Article III by directing the District Court to issue advisory opinions. They contend that the assignment of federal examiners authorized in §6(b) abridges due process by precluding judicial review of administrative findings and impairs the separation of powers by giving the Attorney General judicial functions; also that the challenge procedure prescribed in §9 denies due process on account of its speed. Finally, South Carolina and certain of the *amici curiae* maintain that §§4(a) and 5, buttressed by §14(b) of the Act, abridge due process by limiting litigation to a distant forum. . . .

After enduring nearly a century of widespread resistance to the Fifteenth Amendment, Congress has marshalled an array of potent weapons against the evil, with authority in the Attorney General to employ them effectively. Many of the areas directly affected by this development have indicated their willingness to abide by any restraints legitimately imposed upon them. We here hold that the portions of the Voting Rights Act properly before us are a valid means for carrying out the commands of the Fifteenth Amendment. Hopefully, millions of non-white Americans will now be able to participate for the first time on an equal basis in the government under which they live. We may finally look forward to the day when truly "the right of citizens of the United States to vote shall not be denied or abridged by the United States or by any State on account of race, color, or previous condition of servitude."

The bill of complaint is

Dismissed.

☆　　☆　　☆

VI. *Footnotes*

[1]*Reports of the Proceedings and Debates of the Convention of 1821 Assembled for the Purpose of Amending the Constitution of the State of New York* (E. and E. Hosford, Albany, N. Y., 1821) 219–221.

[2]James Fenimore Cooper, *Notions of the Americans: Picked Up by a Travelling Bachelor* (Henry Colburn, London, 1828) I, 352–356.

[3]Alexis de Tocqueville, *Democracy in America,* Henry Reeve, trans., second American edition (George Adlard, New York, 1838) 35–39.

[4]Elizabeth Cady Stanton, Susan B. Anthony, and Ida Husted Harper, eds., *The History of Woman Suffrage* (The Hollenbeck Press, Indianapolis, 1902) I, 70.

[5]Ida Husted Harper, ed., *The History of Woman Suffrage* (National American Woman Suffrage Association, New York, 1922) V, 222.

[6]*Ibid.,* 228.

[7]*Congressional Record,* 65th Congress, 2nd Session, January 10, 1918, LVI, 785–786.

[8]*Ibid.,* 765.

[9]*Public Law 89–110,* 89th Congress, S. 1564, August 6, 1965.

[10]*Supreme Court of the United States* (March 7, 1966) no. 22, pp. 17, 31.

VII

Should Government
Protect the Individual
by Regulating Business?

After the Civil War there was little question that Northern industry would soon outstrip Southern cotton growing in economic importance. The small textile mills that had formed the base of the North's industry grew. When steam engines replaced waterfalls as the main source of power, mills could be built close to the source of raw materials. The new mills and factories needed people to work in them. Since most families lived on farms and the men were needed at home, the earliest factory workers were women and children. Another source of manpower for these factories was the immigrants who poured into New York and made their way to Eastern and Northern factory towns.

The immigrants, women, and children who worked in these factories lived close to their work in overcrowded, unsafe, and unhealthful housing. Besides working long hours under poor conditions in the factories, the workers had to face equally bad conditions at home. And these conditions multiplied and worsened as the mill towns grew. The larger cities, which became the main trading centers for these manufactured goods, bulged with an additional population, too. By the turn of the century, living conditions had become so bad that thoughtful people felt they must find a way to help these workers.

The President, Congress, many governors, and the mayors of large cities were concerned about the poverty of the factory workers. Often these people would place the blame for the problems on the rich factory owners and other leaders of industry. But few reformers agreed on the solution to this problem, and others actually felt that these problems were just a result of human nature, not to be worried about at all. Just as the strongest animal would survive in the jungle, so would the strongest man be most successful in life. Such an idea was encouraged by an important economic and political philosophy that was influential during the nineteenth century. This philosophy, called *laissez-faire*, derived its name from the French phrase that means "let people do what they choose." *Laissez-faire* encouraged a government that did as little as possible to regulate the lives and activities of the people. In fact, the theory held that the greatest good would come to the greatest number of people if each person looked out for his own interest.

The *laissez-faire* philosophy was further strengthened by the writings of Herbert Spencer, the English philosopher, who developed a theory that became known as social Darwinism. Spencer saw a parallel between the social order and the biological world. Just as Darwin saw an evolution in the world of plants and animals, Spencer saw an evolution in political, social, and economic institutions. Spencer concluded that it was either useless or harmful to try to influence the outcome of the economic and social order. Passing a law to regulate the economy would be like passing a law to make water run uphill.

The economic successes of a few people under a *laissez-faire* system convinced many people that the social order in the United States was quite acceptable. Social Darwinism led some to rationalize that the poor were poor because they were the least strong in the evolution of the social order. And the system worked; the United States was becoming a wealthy manufacturing nation with a rising middle-class society that could overlook the poor working conditions and the poverty brought about by the factory system.

Of course, not everyone believed in social Darwinism and *laissez-faire*. Many government officials, private citizens, and journalists were concerned with the economic and social evils that were shaping each individual's life. They were dedicated to freeing the immigrants, the poor, and the displaced farmers from the narrow circle of poverty. To these reformers, *laissez-faire* and social Darwinism were just excuses to ignore poverty. So, with differing degrees of success, they worked to develop laws to change the economic, political, and social order. The contest between those who wanted to change the system and those who said, "It works, let's not tamper with it," was a long one. (Many people still argue about it today.)

One of the important institutions in the decisions for and against social change was the Supreme Court. When Congress passed social legislation, the new laws were usually contested by some citizens. The Supreme Court then had to decide on the constitutionality of each piece of social legislation.

This chapter and the next one both demonstrate the changing role of government in protecting people who need help. The following chapter deals with the role of government in individual welfare after 1929. The documents in this chapter fall into an earlier period when there was a growing consciousness of the necessity for protecting citizens' welfare by outlining the rights of corporations and the rights of their employees. As you read, notice whether each selection supports or wants to reform big business, whether the Supreme Court supports or discourages the reform, and what role the government plays in the dispute.

William Graham Sumner on Wealth and Individualism 1902

One of the chief spokesmen for a *laissez-faire* system was not a businessman but a college professor, William Graham Sumner. Sumner was an Episcopal minister who became a professor of political and social science at Yale in 1872. For over thirty years, until his death in 1910, he wrote numerous books and articles that were to influence many during this period.

Sumner was a social Darwinist. He defended the workings of the economic system and praised the men who had used it to gain wealth. As you read selections from his essay "Concentration of Wealth," see if you can discover why Sumner placed such a high value on being wealthy and why he had little or no desire to reform the situation of the poor.

(1) I have tried to set forth the economic necessity for the concentration of wealth; and I maintain that this is the controlling consideration. Those who care most about the concentration of wealth are indifferent to this consideration; what strikes them most is the fact that there are some rich men. I will, therefore, try to show that this fact also is only another economic justification of the concentration of wealth. . . .

What matters it then that some millionaires are idle, or silly, or vulgar; that their ideas are sometimes futile and their plans grotesque, when they turn aside from money-making? How do they differ in this from any other class? The millionaires are a product of natural selection, acting on the whole body of men to pick out those who can meet the requirement of certain work to be done. In this respect they are just like the great statesmen, or scientific men, or military men. It is because they are thus selected that wealth — both their own and that intrusted to them — aggregates under their hands. Let one of them make a mistake and see how quickly the concentration gives way to dispersion. They may fairly be regarded as the naturally selected agents of society for certain work. They get high wages and live in luxury, but the bargain is a good one for society. There is the intensest competition for their place and occupation. This assures us that all who are competent for this function will be employed in it, so that the cost of it will be reduced to the lowest terms; and furthermore that the competitors will study the proper conduct to be observed in their occupation. This will bring discipline and the correction of arrogance and masterfulness.

☆   ☆   ☆

Munn v. *Illinois* 1877

Early in the history of the country's industrial growth, railroads became big business. The development of railroads posed serious problems for individuals, communities, states, and the nation at large. Railroad companies had a great deal of power, for they determined the routes new rail lines were to take. This power was especially important west of the Mississippi River, where companies could create towns where none had existed or could bypass existing towns and thus rob them of prosperity.

Once the tracks were laid, the communities along the route were economically dependent upon the railroads, since the companies were free to fix the rates charged for hauling freight. The railroad could paralyze a community by charging excessive rates. Likewise, the railroads could influence the general business community by charging high rates to one firm and allowing another business to ship its freight at lower rates.

By 1870 a number of states had begun to pass laws to regulate railroad rates. The railroad companies protested and took the laws to court, claiming the states had no legal right to fix the charges of privately owned corporations such as theirs. The states felt that they did have a right to fix the rates, since the privately owned companies were affecting the welfare of the community.

In the decision *Munn* v. *Illinois* the Supreme Court permitted state regulation on the grounds that a state has a right to restrain an individual from injuring another; and a law regulating rates was a kind of "police power" instead of an infringement of private property. Why was this a very important decision? Do you think it was a wise one?

(2) When one becomes a member of society, he necessarily parts with some rights or privileges which, as an individual not affected by his relations to others, he might retain. "A body politic," as aptly defined in the preamble of the Constitution of Massachusetts, "is a social compact by which the whole people covenants with each citizen, and each citizen with the whole people, that all shall be governed by certain laws for the common good." This does not confer power upon the whole people to control rights which are purely and exclusively private . . . but it does authorize the establishment of laws requiring each citizen to so conduct himself, and so use his own property, as not unnecessarily to injure another. . . . From this source come the police powers, which, as was said by Mr. Chief Justice Taney in the *License Cases* . . . "are nothing more or less than the powers of government inherent in every sovereignty . . . that is to say . . . the power to govern men and things." Under these powers the government regulates the conduct of its citizens one towards another, and the manner in which each shall use his own property, when such regulation becomes necessary for the public good. In their exercise it has been customary in England from time immemorial, and in this country from its first colonization, to regulate ferries, common carriers, hackmen, bakers, millers, wharfingers, innkeepers, & c., and in so doing to fix a maximum of charge to be made for services rendered, accommodations furnished, and articles sold. To this day, statutes are to be found in many of the States upon some or all these subjects; and we think it has never yet been successfully contended that such legislation came within any of the constitutional prohibitions against interference with private property. . . .

☆   ☆   ☆

The Growth of the Standard Oil Company 1883

Of all the success stories concerning the business tycoons who emerged after the Civil War, none surpasses that of John D. Rockefeller. At sixteen, Rockefeller earned fifty cents a day as an assistant bookkeeper; at forty-one, he controlled ninety percent of all petroleum refined in the United States and was worth millions of dollars.

Perhaps it was the way in which he controlled the petroleum industry that made his success so unusual, for he was one of the first to see the benefits of controlling an entire industry from raw material to finished product. Thus he gained control of oil fields, refineries, transportation, pipelines, and petroleum distribution centers; the growth of Rockefeller's Standard Oil was spectacular.

For some people the success of Standard Oil in developing an efficient business was cause enough to let the business go its own course. One of these people was Senator J. N. Camden of West Virginia, who had been associated with Rockefeller. In 1883 Camden wrote an article explaining and justifying the growth of the Standard Oil Company. As you read his article, try to summarize why Camden thinks Rockefeller did the oil industry a great service. In light of the Supreme Court's decision in *Munn* v. *Illinois* (*see pp. 173–174*), did the Standard Oil Company do a great service to the nation as a whole? What are the disadvantages to the community of a business that is so big?

DOCUMENT

(3) In order to appreciate what the Standard Oil Company has achieved, it is first necessary to glance at the condition of the oil industry at the time when this company entered it. . . .

. . . The universality of speculation; the utter disregard of the laws of supply and demand, aggravated by the haste of each land-owner to multiply his wells and get as large a share as possible of the underlying oil pool which his neighbors were sucking up; the lack of handling facilities, resulting in prodigal waste; the apparent instability of the whole business, which was hourly expected to vanish, and in many instances did vanish as suddenly as it had appeared—all this conspired to make the oil regions a pandemonium of excitement and confusion, and the simple statement of a man's connection with oil was a severe blow to his credit. The refining of oil at this early period was on a basis but little better than that of its production. Processes were extremely crude, and their product would to-day be unmerchantable for illuminating purposes. Still the demand for it was great and growing, and refineries multiplied. The competent and the incompetent rushed into the business in shoals, until the refining capacity of the country was more than three times the demand for consumption. Reaction, failures, and demoralization were the inevitable consequences.

The refiners recognized the dangerous and demoralized condition into which the excessive capacity of the refineries had brought them. . . . Various efforts were made to correct this evil of overproduction, through pools and running arrangements restricting capacity; but pools were broken, and agreements were ineffectual, until the lowest ebb in the oil business was reached. By this time bankruptcy had overtaken a large portion of the refining interest, and was threatening all. Such in general was the situation out of which was developed the Standard Oil Company, as a necessity, to arrest the conditions which were driving all connected with the business to bankruptcy and ruin. . . . Without entering into the details of their progress,—how the principal refining interests were first united under the management of the Standard Company, and how others gradually came into coöperation, whilst those less hopeful of the future of the business were bought out for money; how ineligibly located or poorly equipped refineries were dismantled and others better adapted to their purposes were improved,—it is only necessary to state that their success was such as to vindicate the wisdom of their broad plans and to establish the superiority of their business methods. It did more than this. It demonstrated that, under such firm and intelligent control, the oil business had possibilities which the doubting ones and the public generally had not seen, and this demonstration was followed by an antagonism to the company such as all great and successful organizations have to meet. . . .

☆   ☆   ☆

Andrew Carnegie Defends Trusts 1889 – 1900

Andrew Carnegie's life was a success story. In 1848 he worked in a cotton mill in Pittsburgh as a poor immigrant bobbin boy, but by 1859, when he was only twenty-four years old, he had become a superintendent of the Pennsylvania Railroad. He then turned to steel manufacturing and developed a great industrial giant, the Carnegie Steel Company. In 1901 he sold the company for $250,000,000 and it became part of the newly created United States Steel Corporation.

Carnegie wrote books and articles about the America of his day. He was greatly influenced by the writings of Herbert Spencer and defended big businesses and trusts like his own as the inevitable growth of industry and finance. Selections from two of his articles are quoted below. The first article, entitled "The Bugaboo of Trusts," was written in 1889. In this article Carnegie uses the Standard Oil Company (see pp. 174–176) and the sugar industry as examples of trusts (huge businesses that control most of an industry).

The second article, "Popular Illusions About Trusts," published in 1900, is an even stronger defense of the methods of business in a *laissez-faire* system. As you read both of these articles, list the reasons why Carnegie believes trusts were good for all people. Can you find a reason why Carnegie might have defended trusts on grounds other than social Darwinism? How similar are Sumner's, Camden's, and Carnegie's defenses of big business? Against whom do you think these men defended the workings of big business?

(4) We have given the genesis of trusts and combinations in their several forms. The question is, Do they menace the permanent interest of the nation? Are they a source of serious danger? Or are they to prove, as many other similar forms have proved, mere passing phases of unrest and transition? To answer this question let us follow the operation of the manufacturing trust which we have in imagination created, salt or sugar, nails, beams, or lead or copper; it is all the same. The sugar refiners, let us say, have formed a Trust after competing one with another through years of disastrous business, and all the sugar manufactured in the country in existing factories is sold through one channel at advanced prices. Profits begin to grow. Dividends are paid, and those who before saw their property vanishing before their eyes are now made happy. The dividends from that part of a man's capital invested in the sugar business yield him profit far above the capital he has invested in various other affairs. The prices of sugar are such that the capital invested in a new factory would yield enormously. He is perhaps bound not to enlarge his factory or to enter into a new factory, but his relatives and acquaintances soon discover the fresh opportunity for gain. He can advise them to push the completion of a small factory, which, of course, must be taken into the Trust. Or, even if he does not give his friends this intimation, capital is always upon the alert, especially when it is bruited about that a Trust has been formed, as in the case of sugar, and immediately new sugar manufactories spring up, as if by magic. The more successful the Trust, the surer these off-shoots are to sprout. Every victory is a defeat. Every factory that the Trust buys is the sure creator of another, and so on, *ad infinitum,* until the bubble bursts. The sugar refiners have tried to get more from capital in a special case than capital yields in general. They have endeavored to raise a part of the ocean of capital above the level of the surrounding waters, and over their bulwarks the floods have burst, and capital, like water, has again found its level. It is true that to regain this level a longer or a shorter period may be required, during which the article affected may be sold to the consumer in limited quantities at a higher rate than before existed. But for this the consumer is amply recompensed in the years that follow, during which the struggle between the discordant and competitive factories becomes severer than it ever was before, and lasts till the great

law of the survival of the fittest vindicates itself. Those factories and managers that can produce to the best advantage eventually close the less competent. Capital wisely managed yields its legitimate profit. After a time, the growth of demand enables capital to receive an unusual profit. This in turn attracts fresh capital to the manufacture, and we have a renewal of the old struggle, the consumer reaping the benefit.

Such is the law, such has been the law, and such promises to be the law for the future; for, so far, no device has yet been devised that has permanently thwarted its operation. Given freedom of competition, and all combinations or trusts that attempt to exact from the consumer more than a legitimate return upon capital and services, write the charter of their own defeat. We have many proofs that this great law does not sleep and that it will not be suppressed.

☆   ☆   ☆

(5) If there be in human history one truth clearer and more indisputable than another, it is that the cheapening of articles, whether of luxury or of necessity or of those classed as artistic, insures their more general distribution and is one of the most potent factors in refining and lifting a people, and in adding to its happiness. In no period of human activity has this great agency been so potent or so wide-spread as in our own. Now, the cheapening of all these good things, whether it be in the metals, in textiles, or in food, or especially in books and prints, is rendered possible only through the operation of the law which may be stated thus: cheapness is in proportion to the scale of production. To make ten tons of steel a day would cost many times as much per ton as to make one hundred tons; to make one hundred tons would cost double as much per ton as a thousand; and to make one thousand tons per day would cost greatly more than to make ten thousand tons. Thus, the larger the scale of operation the cheaper the product. The huge steamship of twenty thousand tons burden carries its ton of freight at less cost, it is stated, than the first steamships carried a pound. It is, fortunately, impossible for man to impede, much less to change, this great and beneficent law, from which flow most of his comforts and luxuries, and also most of the best and most improving forces in his life.

In an age noted for inventions, we see the same law running through these. Inventions facilitate big operations, and in most instances require to be worked upon a great scale. Indeed, as a rule, the great invention which is beneficent in its operation would be useless unless operated to supply a thousand people where ten were supplied before. Every agency in our day labors to scatter the good

178

things of life, both for mind and body, among the toiling millions. Everywhere we look we see the inexorable law ever producing bigger and bigger things. One of the most notable illustrations of this is seen in the railway freight-car. When the writer entered the service of the Pennsylvania Railroad seven to eight tons were carried upon eight wheels; to-day they carry fifty tons. The locomotive has quadrupled in power. The steamship to-day is ten times bigger, the blast-furnace has seven times more capacity, and the tendency everywhere is still to increase. The contrast between the hand printing-press of old and the elaborate newspaper printing-machine of to-day is even more marked.

We conclude that this overpowering, irresistible tendency toward aggregation of capital and increase of size in every branch of product cannot be arrested or even greatly impeded, and that, instead of attempting to restrict either, we should hail every increase as something gained, not for the few rich, but for the millions of poor, seeing that the law is salutary, working for good and not for evil. Every enlargement is an improvement, step by step, upon what has preceded. It makes for higher civilization, for the enrichment of human life, not for one, but for all classes of men. It tends to bring to the laborer's cottage the luxuries hitherto enjoyed only by the rich, to remove from the most squalid homes much of their squalor, and to foster the growth of human happiness relatively more in the workman's home than in the millionaire's palace. It does not tend to make the rich poorer, but it does tend to make the poor richer in the possession of better things, and greatly lessens the wide and deplorable gulf between the rich and the poor. Superficial politicians may, for a time, deceive the uninformed, but more and more will all this be clearly seen by those who are now led to regard aggregations as injurious.

☆   ☆   ☆

Ida Tarbell on Standard Oil 1904

Many people did not feel that trusts were good for all people. These reformers said a great deal about the immorality of big business. For instance, some felt that Rockefeller had used unscrupulous practices in building his business and that his success was not an adequate excuse for being unethical. These reformers were not willing to accept the argument that big businesses were good merely because they were efficient.

Ida Tarbell, a militant reformer, wrote articles and books to expose unethical business practices and to arouse public support for legislation to curb such businesses. Selections from her book *The*

History of Standard Oil are quoted below. As you read, note the ways in which she thinks Standard Oil has used unethical practices or harmed the lives of people. How can you tell Ida Tarbell is not in sympathy with big business?

(6) While there can be no doubt that the determining factor in the success of the Standard Oil Company in securing a practical monopoly of the oil industry has been the special privileges it has enjoyed since the beginning of its career, it is equally true that those privileges alone will not account for its success. Something besides illegal advantages has gone into the making of the Standard Oil Trust. Had it possessed only the qualities which the general public has always attributed to it, its overthrow would have come before this. But this huge bulk, blackened by commercial sin, has always been strong in all great business qualities — in energy, in intelligence, in dauntlessness. It has always been rich in youth as well as greed, in brains as well as unscrupulousness. If it has played its great game with contemptuous indifference to fair play, and to nice legal points of view, it has played it with consummate ability, daring and address. The silent, patient, all-seeing man who has led it in its transportation raids has led it no less successfully in what may be called its legitimate work. Nobody has appreciated more fully than he those qualities which alone make for permanent stability and growth in commercial ventures. He has insisted on these qualities, and it is because of this insistence that the Standard Oil Trust has always been something besides a fine piece of brigandage, with the fate of brigandage before it, that it has been a thing with life and future. . . .

Very often people who admit the facts, who are willing to see that Mr. Rockefeller has employed force and fraud to secure his ends, justify him by declaring, "It's business." That is, "It's business" has come to be a legitimate excuse for hard dealing, sly tricks, special privileges. It is a common enough thing to hear men arguing that the ordinary laws of morality do not apply in business. Now, if the Standard Oil Company were the only concern in the country guilty of the practices which have given it monopolistic power, this story never would have been written. Were it alone in these methods, public scorn would long ago have made short work of the Standard Oil Company. But it is simply the most conspicuous type of what can be done by these practices. The methods it employs with such acumen, persistency, and secrecy are employed by all sorts of business men, from corner grocers up to bankers. If exposed, they are excused on the ground that this is business. If the point is pushed, frequently the defender of the practice falls back on the Christian doctrine of charity, and points that we are erring mortals and must allow for each other's weaknesses!—an excuse which, if carried to its legitimate conclusion, would leave our business men weeping on one another's shoulders over human frailty, while they picked one another's pockets.

One of the most depressing features of the ethical side of the matter is that instead of such methods arousing contempt they are more or less openly admired. And this is logical. Canonize "business success," and men who make a success like that of the Standard Oil Trust become national heroes! The history of its organization is studied as a practical lesson in money-making. It is the most startling feature of the case to one who would like to feel that it is possible to be a commercial people and yet a race of gentlemen. Of course such practices exclude men by all the codes from the rank of gentlemen, just as such practices would exclude men from the sporting world or athletic field. There is no gaming table in the world where loaded dice are tolerated, no athletic field where men must not start fair. Yet Mr. Rockefeller has systematically played with loaded dice, and it is doubtful if there has ever been a time since 1872 when he has run a race with a competitor and started fair. Business played in this way loses all its sportsmanlike qualities. It is fit only for tricksters. . . .

And what are we going to do about it? For it is *our* business. We, the people of the United States, and nobody else, must cure whatever is wrong in the industrial situation, typified by this narrative of the growth of the Standard Oil Company. That our first task is to secure free and equal transportation privileges by rail, pipe and waterway is evident. It is not an easy matter. It is one which may require operations which will seem severe; but the whole system of discrimination has been nothing but violence, and those who have profited by it cannot complain if the curing of the evils they have wrought bring hardship in turn on them. At all events, until the transportation matter is settled, and settled right, the monopolistic trust will be with us, a leech on our pockets, a barrier to our free efforts.

As for the ethical side, there is no cure but in an increasing scorn of unfair play—an increasing sense that a thing won by breaking the rules of the game is not worth the winning. When the business man who fights to secure special privileges, to crowd his competitor off the track by other than fair competitive methods, receives the same summary disdainful ostracism by his fellows that the doctor or lawyer who is "unprofessional," the athlete who abuses the rules, receives, we shall have gone a long way toward making commerce a fit pursuit for our young men. ☆ ☆ ☆

The New York Tenements in the 1890's

Although trusts and monopolies were certainly not completely responsible for the social conditions of the poor in the 1890's, slums spread as workers for factories flocked to our large cities. Many slum dwellers were very poor, sick, starving, or unemployed. The slums came from unplanned and uncontrolled industrialization; the solution to their evils would take a great deal of thought and hard work and remains a problem today.

Before anything could be done to ease the slum conditions, the public had to be made aware of the desperate condition of the people who lived in tenements. Jacob Riis was a journalist who was very much concerned about these people. Trying to stir the public conscience, he wrote a book called *How the Other Half Lives*. Parts of his description of slum life follow.

(7) Suppose we look into . . . No.—Cherry Street. Be a little careful, please! The hall is dark and you might stumble over the children pitching pennies back there. Not that it would hurt them; kicks and cuffs are their daily diet. They have little else. Here where the hall turns and dives into utter darkness is a step, and another, and another. A flight of stairs. You can feel your way, if you cannot see it. Close? Yes! What would you have? All the fresh air that ever enters these stairs comes from the hall-door that is forever slamming, and from the windows of dark bedrooms that in turn receive from the stairs their sole supply of the elements God meant to be free, but man deals out with such niggardly hand. That was a woman filling her pail by the hydrant you just bumped against. The sinks are in the hallway, that all the tenants may have access—and all be poisoned alike by their summer stenches. Hear that pump squeak! It is the lullaby of tenement-house babes. In summer, when a thousand thirsty throats pant for a cooling drink in this block, it is worked in vain. But the saloon, whose open door you passed in the hall, is always there. The smell of it has followed you up. Here is a door. Listen! That short hacking cough, that tiny, helpless wail—what do they mean? They mean that the soiled bow of white you saw on the door downstairs will have another story to tell—Oh! a sadly familiar story—before the day is at an end. The child is dying of measles. With half a chance it might have lived; but it had none. That dark bedroom killed it. . . .

This gap between dingy brick-walls is the yard. That strip of smoke-colored sky up there is the heaven of these people. Do you wonder the name does not attract them to the churches? That baby's parents live in the rear tenement here. She is at least as clean as the steps we are now climbing. There are plenty of houses with half a hundred such in them. The tenement is much like the one in front we just left, only fouler, closer, darker. . . . A hundred thousand people lived in rear tenements in New York last year. . . .

☆   ☆   ☆

The Sherman Anti-Trust Act 1890

John D. Rockefeller built the Standard Oil Company as a trust company. A trust company issues certificates to people who own stock in another company; these people in turn give the control of their company to the new trust company. The trust certificates pay profits to all those who own them, but the certificates do not give their owners a say in managing the new trust company.

The trust—or monopoly, as it was sometimes called—was so successful that other industries began to use this device, too: the "beef trust," the "tobacco trust," the "whiskey trust," the "money trust," and the "sugar trust" soon followed. While such men as William Graham Sumner and Andrew Carnegie vehemently defended this kind of big business, others began to criticize trusts for not functioning for the welfare of the entire nation. Many people saw that large companies, in growing into large trusts, used unscrupulous practices to force competitors to give up the management of their companies. And these people felt that when one large trust controlled an industry, it kept any other business from competing, it could set unfair prices, and it would work against the welfare of the individuals who bought the products of the industry. Congress responded to the public's discontent and passed the Sherman Anti-Trust Act in 1890. Excerpts from the law follow.

DOCUMENT

(8) SEC. 1. Every contract, combination in the form of trust or otherwise, or conspiracy, in restraint of trade or commerce among the several States, or with foreign nations, is hereby declared to be illegal. Every person who shall make any such contract or engage in any such combination or conspiracy, shall be deemed guilty of a misdemeanor, and, on conviction thereof, shall be punished by fine not exceeding five thousand dollars, or by

imprisonment not exceeding one year, or by both said punishments, in the discretion of the court.

Sec. 2. Every person who shall monopolize, or attempt to monopolize, or combine or conspire with any other person or persons, to monopolize any part of the trade or commerce among the several States, or with foreign nations, shall be deemed guilty of a misdemeanor, and, on conviction thereof, shall be punished by fine not exceeding five thousand dollars, or by imprisonment not exceeding one year, or by both said punishments. . . .

SEC. 3. Every contract, combination in form of trust or otherwise, or conspiracy, in restraint of trade or commerce in any Territory of the United States . . . is hereby declared illegal. Every person who shall make any such contract or engage in any such combination or conspiracy, shall be deemed guilty of a misdemeanor, and, on conviction thereof, shall be punished by fine not exceeding five thousand dollars, or by imprisonment not exceeding one year, or by both said punishments. . . .

SEC. 4. The several circuit courts of the United States are hereby invested with jurisdiction to prevent and restrain violations of this act; and it shall be the duty of the several district attorneys . . . , under the direction of the Attorney-General, to institute proceedings in equity to prevent and restrain such violations. . . .

SEC. 7. Any person who shall be injured in his business or property by any other person or corporation by reason of anything forbidden or declared to be unlawful by this act, may sue therefor in any circuit court of the United States in the district in which the defendant resides or is found, without respect to the amount in controversy, and shall recover threefold the damages by him sustained, and the costs of suit, including a reasonable attorney's fee.

SEC. 8. That the word "person," or "persons," wherever used in this act shall be deemed to include corporations and associations existing under or authorized by the laws of either the United States, the laws of any of the Territories, the laws of any State, or the laws of any foreign country.

☆　　☆　　☆

Theodore Roosevelt's New Nationalism 1910

Before and during the time William McKinley was President (1897–1901), government had difficulty passing laws to regulate big business effectively. State and federal governments felt a great deal of pressure from business; when the state legislature would press for laws that would help labor unions, businessmen could threaten to cut off funds to their political party. In fact, some people went so far as to say that state legislatures (and the United States Senate, which was elected by these legislatures) were controlled or had been bought by big business.

McKinley was assassinated in 1901, and Theodore Roosevelt became President. Roosevelt was far from a timid President. Although he did not set out purposely to persuade Congress to legislate against big business, many of the laws passed during his administration were unpopular with business. It soon became clear that Roosevelt would not be controlled by business interests. He effectively enforced the Sherman Anti-Trust Act *(see pp. 183–184)*, favored legislation which secured for the Interstate Commerce Commission the power to regulate the rates of railroads, saw the Pure Food and Drug Act passed to control unsanitary conditions in the meat-packing and other industries, suggested legislation to secure workmen's compensation for transportation employees injured due to negligence on the part of employers, and encouraged conservation programs that helped the government regulate business's use of natural resources. Business resented these controls, but times were changing and business wasn't quite as powerful as it had once been.

After he left the presidency, Roosevelt was still active in politics. During one of his speaking tours he gave the following speech, in which he called for a "New Nationalism" that would, in effect, continue many of the programs he had started. As you read parts of his speech, note how Roosevelt thinks government and business should operate in the future.

DOCUMENT

(9) We come here to-day to commemorate one of the epoch-making events of the long struggle for the rights of man — the long struggle for the uplift of humanity. Our country — this great republic — means nothing unless it means the triumph of a real democracy, the triumph of popular government, and, in the long run, of an economic system under which each man shall be guaranteed the opportunity to show the best that there is in him. That is why the history of America is now the central feature of the history of the world; for the world has set its face hopefully toward our democracy; and, O my fellow citizens, each one of you carries on your shoulders not only the burden of doing well for the sake of your own country, but the burden of doing well and of seeing that this nation does well for the sake of mankind. . . .

Now, this means that our government, national and state, must be freed from the sinister influence or control of special interests. Exactly as the special interests of cotton and slavery threatened our political integrity before the Civil War, so now the great special business interests too often control and corrupt the men and methods of government for their own profit. We must drive the special interests out of politics. . . . The Constitution guarantees protection to property, and we must make that promise good. But it does not give the right of suffrage to any corporation.

The true friend of property, the true conservative, is he who insists that property shall be the servant and not the master of the commonwealth; . . .

Combinations in industry are the result of an imperative economic law which cannot be repealed by political legislation. The effort at prohibiting all combination has substantially failed. The way out lies, not in attempting to prevent such combinations, but in completely controlling them in the interest of the public welfare. . . .

No man should receive a dollar unless that dollar has been fairly earned. Every dollar received should represent a dollar's worth of service rendered—not gambling in stocks, but service rendered. The really big fortune, the swollen fortune, by the mere fact of its size acquires qualities which differentiate it in kind as well as in degree from what is possessed by men of relatively small means. Therefore, I believe in a graduated income tax on big fortunes, and in another tax which is far more easily collected and far more effective—a graduated inheritance tax on big fortunes, properly safeguarded against evasion and increasing rapidly in amount with the size of the estate. . . .

No man can be a good citizen unless he has a wage more than sufficient to cover the bare cost of living, and hours of labor short enough so that after his day's work is done he will have time and energy to bear his share in the management of the community, to help in carrying the general load. We keep countless men from being good citizens by the conditions of life with which we surround them. We need comprehensive workmen's compensation acts, both state and national laws to regulate child labor and work for women, and especially, we need in our common schools not merely education in book learning, but also practical training for daily life and work.

The object of government is the welfare of the people. The material progress and prosperity of a nation are desirable chiefly so far as they lead to the moral and material welfare of all good citizens.

☆   ☆   ☆

Child Labor in 1918

In the early, small textile mills many factory owners felt a responsibility for the health and welfare of the children in their employ. As the factory system developed, control of industry passed from the small family operator to giant companies. Many Americans bitterly opposed the continued use of child labor because large companies often showed no concern for the children's health and welfare. Still, many Americans believed that the responsibility for the child's welfare rested with his parents and not with the government or the factory owners. Because of this belief, few reforms were attempted.

However, after the reform movement had received encouragement from Theodore Roosevelt, people began to think that the state and federal governments had a responsibility to prevent abuses of children. Therefore, Congress passed a law to prevent children from working in factories engaged in interstate commerce. Using its constitutional power to regulate interstate commerce, Congress could regulate the methods by which the goods were manufactured.

Reuben Dagenhart was one of the children who had been working in a North Carolina factory twelve hours a day. His case was brought before the Supreme Court to test whether Congress had the right to ban child labor. The Supreme Court decision *Hammer* v. *Dagenhart* declared that the law was not constitutional. As you read selections from this decision, find the two reasons the Court ruled against Congress in this law.

(10) DOCUMENT The controlling question for decision is: Is it within the authority of Congress in regulating commerce among the states to prohibit the transportation in interstate commerce of manufactured goods, the product of a factory in which, within thirty days prior to their removal therefrom, children under the age of fourteen have been employed or permitted to work, or children between the ages of fourteen and sixteen years have been employed or permitted to work more than eight hours in any day, or more than six days in any week, or after the hour of seven o'clock P.M. or before the hour of six o'clock A.M.?

The power essential to the passage of this act, the Government contends, is found in the commerce clause of the Constitution which authorizes Congress to regulate commerce with foreign nations and among the States. . . .

. . . it is insisted that adjudged cases in this court establish the doctrine that the power to regulate given to Congress includes the authority to prohibit the movement of ordinary commodities and therefore that the subject is not open for discussion. The cases demonstrate the contrary. . . .

In each of these instances the use of interstate transportation was necessary to the accomplishment of harmful results. In other words, although the power over interstate transportation was to regulate, that could only be accomplished by prohibiting the use of the facilities of interstate commerce to the effect the evil intended.

This element is wanting in the present case. The thing intended to be accomplished by this statute is the denial of the facilities of interstate commerce to those manufacturers in the states who employ children within the prohibited ages. The act in its effect does not regulate transportation among the states, but aims to standardize the ages at which children may be employed in mining and manufacturing within the states. The goods shipped are of themselves harmless. The act permits them to be freely shipped after thirty days from the time of their removal from the factory. When offered for shipment, and before transportation begins, the labor of their production is over, and the mere fact that they were intended for interstate commerce transportation does not make their production subject to federal control under the commerce power. . . .

The power of the states to regulate their purely internal affairs by such laws as seem wise to the local authority is inherent and has never been surrendered to the general government. . . . To sustain this statute would not be in our judgment a recognition of the lawful exertion of congressional authority over interstate commerce, but would sanction an invasion by the federal power of the control of a matter purely local in its character, and over which no authority has been delegated to Congress in conferring the power to regulate commerce among the states. . . .

Thus the act in a twofold sense is repugnant to the Constitution. It not only transcends the authority delegated to Congress over commerce but also exerts a power as to a purely local matter to which the federal authority does not extend. The far reaching result of upholding this act cannot be more plainly indicated than by pointing out that if Congress can thus regulate matters entrusted to local authority by prohibition of the movement of commodities in interstate commerce, all freedom of commerce will be at an end, and the power of the states over local matters may be eliminated, and thus our system of government be practically destroyed.

For these reasons we hold that this law exceeds the constitutional authority of Congress. . . .

☆   ☆   ☆

Reuben Dagenhart's Opinion of
Hammer *v.* Dagenhart 1924

The Supreme Court held that the child labor law had exceeded the authority of Congress *(see pp. 187–188).* But the question came up again and again: Could the government constitutionally act to protect individual citizens? In 1941 the Court reversed its 1918 decision and declared, "The conclusion is inescapable that *Hammer* v. *Dagenhart* was a departure from the principles which have prevailed in the interpretation of the Commerce Clause both before and since the decision and that such vitality, as a precedent, as it then had has long since been exhausted. It should be and now is overruled."

Many years passed before the 1918 decision was reversed. In the meantime, several years after the first ruling, a reporter asked Reuben Dagenhart his opinion of the decision that bore his name. As you read selections from his answer, pay careful attention to the attitudes of the reporter and Reuben Dagenhart. In how many places do you find one of these men saying one thing but meaning another? Do you think Reuben Dagenhart may feel that his individual welfare was sacrificed to a constitutional principle? Why do you think so?

DOCUMENT

(11) This is the story of an ungrateful child. The story of a lad for whom all the machinery of the American judiciary was turned to preserve his constitutional rights and who, after six years, has not yet brought himself to give thanks.

The boy is Reuben Dagenhart, of Charlotte, North Carolina.

Six years ago, Federal Judge James E. Boyd, of the western North Carolina district, interposed the majesty of law in Reuben's behalf. Some months later Chief Justice White and Justices Day, Van Devanter, McReynolds, and Pitney did the same. They declared . . . that the Congress of the United States could not take away from young Reuben Dagenhart his "constitutional" right to work more hours every day than a boy of fourteen ought to work. . . .

And should not the Dagenhart boys be grateful for that?

Well, Reuben isn't.

I found him at his home in Charlotte. He is about the size of the office boy—weighs one hundred five pounds, he told me. But he is a married man with a child. He is twenty years old.

"What benefit," I asked him, "did you get out of the suit which you won in the United States Supreme Court?" . . .

"I don't see that I got any benefit. I guess I'd been a lot better off if they hadn't won it.

"Look at me! A hundred and five pounds, a grown man and no education. I may be mistaken, but I think the years I've put in the cotton mills have stunted my growth. They kept me from getting any schooling. I had to stop school after the third grade and now I need the education I didn't get. . . . From twelve years old on, I was working twelve hours a day—from six in the morning till seven at night, with time out for meals. And sometimes I worked nights besides. Lifting a hundred pounds and I only weighed sixty-five pounds myself." . . .

"Just what did you and John get out of that suit, then?" was asked.

"Why, we got some automobile rides when them big lawyers from the North was down here. Oh, yes, and they bought both of us a coca-cola! That's all we got out of it."

"What did you tell the judge when you were in court?"

"Oh, John and me never was in court! Just Paw was there. John and me was just little kids in short pants. I guess we wouldn't have looked like much in court. We were working in the mill while the case was going on. But Paw went up to Washington." . . .

"It would have been a good thing for all the kids in this state if that law they passed had been kept. Of course, they do better now than they used to. You don't see so many babies working in the factories, but you see a lot of them that ought to be going to school."

☆   ☆   ☆

Woodrow Wilson's New Freedom 1912

Theodore Roosevelt's years in the White House suggested that the years of politically influential big business were numbered. By 1912 there was little question that the country had moved into a new era of reform. Reform was to take place in many areas with differing degrees of success—in city slums, in working conditions, in wage reforms, and in promoting labor unions. One of the early signs that reform was here to stay was the issue of big business that was raised in the presidential campaign of 1912.

Although there were three major candidates for the presidency in 1912—President Taft (the incumbent), Roosevelt, and Woodrow Wilson—the most important candidates were Roosevelt and Wilson. The campaign took a new turn because Roosevelt and Wilson disagreed on how far the government should go in regulating business.

Roosevelt (*see pp. 184–186*) saw government as overseeing and regulating business, but Wilson wanted to go further and destroy the trusts, which he felt were harming competition in business. When the votes were in, the American public had decided that it wanted the further reforms that Wilson promised.

As you read parts of Wilson's campaign speech, compare the positions of big business and government with Roosevelt's New Nationalism speech. Then compare this speech with William Graham Sumner's article (*see pp. 172–173*). Decide why Roosevelt says, "I am for big business, and I am against the trusts." How had attitudes changed during the forty years since 1872?

DOCUMENT

(12) Gentlemen say, they have been saying for a long time, and, therefore, I assume that they believe, that trusts are inevitable. . . .

I admit the popularity of the theory that the trusts have come about through the natural development of business conditions in the United States, and that it is a mistake to try to oppose the processes by which they have been built up, because those processes belong to the very nature of business in our time, and that therefore the only thing we can do, and the only thing we ought to attempt to do, is to accept them as inevitable arrangements and to make the best out of it that we can by regulation.

I answer, nevertheless, that this attitude rests upon a confusion of thought. . . .

A trust is formed in this way: a few gentlemen "promote" it—that is to say, they get it up, being given enormous fees for their kindness. . . . The argument of the promoters is, not that every one who comes into the combination can carry on his business more efficiently than he did before; the argument is: we will assign to you as your share . . . five times what you could have sold your business for to an individual competitor who would have to run it on an economic and competitive basis. We can afford to buy it at such a figure because we are shutting out competition. We can afford to make the stock of the combination half a dozen times what it naturally would be and pay dividends on it, because there will be nobody to dispute the prices we shall fix.

Talk of that as sound business? Talk of that as inevitable? It is based upon nothing except power. It is not based upon efficiency. It is no wonder that the big trusts are not prospering in proportion to such competitors as they still have . . . ; they are prospering freely only in those fields to which competition has no access. Read the statistics of the Steel Trust, if you don't believe it. Read the statistics of any trust. They are constantly nervous about competition, and they are constantly buying up new competitors in order to narrow the field. The United States Steel Corporation is gaining in its supremacy in the American market only with regard to the cruder manufactures of iron and steel, but wherever, as in the field of more advanced manufactures of iron and steel, it has important competitors, its portion of the product is not increasing, but is decreasing, and its competitors, where they have a foothold, are often more efficient than it is.

Why? Why, with the unlimited capital and innumerable mines and plants everywhere in the United States, can't they beat the other fellows in the market? Partly because they are carrying too much. Partly because they are unwieldy. Their organization is imperfect. They bought up inefficient plants along with efficient, and they have got to carry what they have paid for, even if they have to shut some of the plants up in order to make any interest on their investments; or, rather, . . . on their alleged capitalization. Here we have a lot of giants staggering along under an almost intolerable weight of artificial burdens, which they have put on their own backs, and constantly looking about lest some little pigmy with a round stone in a sling may come out and slay them. . . . I'll undertake to put a water-logged giant out of business any time, if you will give me a fair field and as much credit as I am entitled to, and let the law do what from time immemorial law has been expected to do,—see fair play—.

. . . the big trusts, the big combinations, are the most wasteful, the most uneconomical, and, after they pass a certain size, the most inefficient, way of conducting the industries of this country.

A notable example is the way in which Mr. Carnegie was bought out of the steel business. Mr. Carnegie could build better mills and make better steel rails and make them cheaper than anybody else connected with what afterward became the United States Steel Corporation. They didn't dare leave him outside. He had so much more brains in finding out the best processes; he had so much more shrewdness in surrounding himself with the most successful assistants; he knew so well when a young man who came into his employ was fit for promotion and was ripe to put at the head of some branch of his business and was sure to make good, that he could undersell every mother's son of them in the market for steel rails. And they bought him out at a price that amounted to three or four times,—I believe actually five times,—the estimated value of his properties and of his business, because they couldn't beat him in competition. And then in what they charged afterward for their product,—the product of his mills included,—they made us pay the interest on the four or five times the difference.

192

That is the difference between a big business and a trust. A trust is an arrangement to get rid of competition, and a big business is a business that has survived competition by conquering in the field of intelligence and economy. A trust does not bring efficiency to the aid of business; it *buys efficiency out of business*. I am for big business, and I am against the trusts. Any man who can survive by his brains, any man who can put the others out of the business by making the thing cheaper to the consumer at the same time that he is increasing its intrinsic value and quality I take off my hat to, and I say: "You are the men who build up the United States, and I wish there were more of you."

☆   ☆   ☆

VII. Footnotes

[1]William Graham Sumner, *The Challenge of Facts and Other Essays*, Albert Galloway Keller, ed. (Yale University Press, New Haven, 1914) III, 88–90.

[2]94 U.S. 124–126.

[3]J. N. Camden, "The Standard Oil Company," *North American Review* (1883) CXXXVI, 183–185.

[4]Andrew Carnegie, "The Bugaboo of Trusts," *North American Review* (February, 1889) CXLIX, 144–146.

[5]Andrew Carnegie, "Popular Illusions About Trusts," *The Century Magazine* (May, 1900) XXXVIII, 145.

[6]Ida M. Tarbell, *The History of the Standard Oil Company* (McClure, Phillips and Co., New York, 1904) II, 231–291.

[7]Jacob Riis, *How the Other Half Lives* (Charles Scribner's Sons, New York, 1904) 43 ff.

[8]*The Statutes at Large of the United States of America, 1889–1891*, XXVI, 209–10.

[9]William E. Leuchtenburg, ed., *The New Nationalism, Theodore Roosevelt* (Prentice-Hall, Englewood Cliffs, N.J., 1961) 21–38.

[10]247 U.S. 251.

[11]Grace Abbott, *The Child and the State* (University of Chicago Press, Chicago, Ill., 1938) I, 515–516.

[12]Woodrow Wilson, *The New Freedom* (Doubleday, Page and Co., New York, 1913) 163–181.

VIII

What Role Should Government Play in Individual Welfare?

In the years between 1920 and 1930 there was a pause in the reform movement. The nation became wealthy and forgot about the slums the reformers had so vividly pictured. In the early twenties United States manufacturers had just finished producing large numbers of weapons for the First World War. After manufacturing had adjusted to peacetime, these factories produced many other kinds of goods for people to buy. A feeling of prosperity and well-being spread over the country. Banks lent money to small businessmen. These small businesses in turn expanded shops and factories and made more money on the additional goods they could manufacture and sell. Prices of stocks began to rise, and people who had never before bought stocks saw in the stock market a quick way to make money. Securities could be bought for a small down payment and, when the price rose, they could be sold at a profit.

While so many people had so much – good wages and stock market profits – few people were willing to complain about the social problems that were being ignored. In effect, the years of the twenties were a time when the nation stepped back from the reforming zeal of Roosevelt and Wilson. Big business was in favor, since most people felt such businesses were responsible for the country's prosperity. While the trusts of the 1880's no longer flourished, business enjoyed the patronage of a government that set high tariffs to protect their products and did not worry too much about the Sherman Anti-Trust Act.

During this time of prosperity, most people forgot the issues of the great trusts and the slum dwellers. But when the Great Depression began, people faced many of the same problems themselves and could not solve them. Then our country had to answer some important questions: What should government do to help? Does the Constitution allow a man the right to starve? Should each man work to solve his own problems or should someone help him? As you read, notice how these questions are handled in this period. Then compare the attitudes of this period with the attitudes after 1872 (*see Chapter* 7). Remember that some people did not agree with all these programs. Why did they criticize them?

The Stock Market Crash 1929

Between the years 1920 and 1930 there seemed to be no visible end to prosperity. Why worry about the poor? Most people's wages were very good and they lived comfortably. Life seemed to improve every day!

However, in October 1929 the nation discovered that dizzying profits and swollen prosperity could be wiped away by one severe ten-day plunge of the stock market. When the stock market fell, optimism about the health of the economy evaporated. Banks were faced with frightened people wanting to withdraw their money to keep it safely at home. The banks in turn had to stop lending money and called in loans to meet their demands. Businesses reduced the number of their employees and cut their output of products because people could not afford to buy any longer. Since this hardship lasted for almost ten years, poverty became chronic. People who until the time of the depression had made a good living could not even get a job. More people than ever before were out of work.

The stock market crash described in the following selection was the beginning of a new era of social problems. The author was hopeful that it was just temporary, but it was the beginning of a long period when the nation had to think about the government's responsibility for the welfare of the economy and for the welfare of individuals affected by such erratic changes as this depression caused.

DOCUMENT

(1) **Worst Stock Crash Stemmed By Banks; 12,894,650-Share Day Swamps Market; Leaders Confer, Find Conditions Sound**

The most disastrous decline in the biggest and broadest stock market of history rocked the financial district yesterday. In the very midst of the collapse five of the country's most influential bankers hurried to the office of J. P. Morgan & Co., and after a brief conference gave out word that they believe the foundations of the market to be sound, that the market smash has been caused by technical rather than fundamental considerations, and that many sound stocks are selling too low.

Suddenly, the market turned about on buying orders thrown into the pivotal issues, and before the final quotations were tapped out, four hours and eight minutes after the 3 o'clock bell, most stocks had regained a measurable part of their losses.

The break was one of the widest in the market's history, although the losses at the close were not particularly large, many having been recouped by the afternoon rally.

It carried down with it speculators, big and little, in every part of the country, wiping out thousands of accounts. It is probable that if the stockholders of the country's foremost corporations had not been calmed by the attitude of leading bankers and the subsequent rally, the business of the country would have been seriously affected. Doubtless business will feel the effects of the drastic stock shake-out, and this is expected to hit the luxuries most severely. . . .

The total losses cannot be accurately calculated, because of the large number of markets and the thousands of securities not listed on any exchange. However, they were staggering, running into billions of dollars. Fear struck the big speculators and little ones, big investors and little ones. Thousands of them threw their holdings into the whirling Stock Exchange pit for what they would bring. Losses were tremendous and thousands of prosperous brokerage and bank accounts, sound and healthy a week ago, were completely wrecked in the strange debacle, due to a combination of circumstances, but accelerated into a crash by fear. . . .

Under these circumstances of late tickers and spreads of 10, 20, and at times 30 points between the tape prices and those on the floor of the Exchange, the entire financial district was thrown into hopeless confusion and excitement. Wild-eyed speculators crowded the brokerage offices, awed by the disaster which had overtaken many of them. They followed the market literally "in the dark," getting but meager reports via the financial news tickers which printed the Exchange floor prices at ten-minute intervals.

Rumors, most of them wild and false, spread throughout the Wall Street district and thence throughout the country. One of the reports was that eleven speculators had committed suicide. A peaceful workman atop a Wall Street building looked down and saw a big crowd watching him, for the rumor had spread that he was going to jump off. Reports that the Chicago and Buffalo Exchanges had closed spread throughout the district, as did rumors that the New York Stock Exchange and the New York Curb Exchange were going to suspend trading. These rumors and reports were all found, on investigation, to be untrue. . . .

☆   ☆   ☆

Unemployment During the Great Depression 1932

In 1932 the number of persons unemployed was estimated at one-fourth of the labor force of the United States! Some of the unemployed moved in with relatives who had jobs. Others were fortunate enough to get an occasional job now and then. But millions were dependent on charity for the necessities of food and shelter.

The following selection is part of testimony before a Congressional committee concerning the fate of the unemployed in the city of Philadelphia in 1932. Notice in what ways the families managed to stretch their money in order to eat at all. What do you believe should be done at times like this?

(2) MR. DE SCHWEINITZ. When I appeared before the Subcommittee of the Committee on Manufacturers last December, I stated that there were 238,000 persons out of work in Philadelphia and that we estimated unemployment in the city in ordinary times to be between 40,000 and 50,000. There are now 298,000 persons out of work. In other words, whereas in December our unemployment was a little less than five times what one might call normal unemployment, to-day it is six times normal unemployment.

In December I told you that 43,000 families were receiving relief. Today 55,000 families are receiving relief.

In December our per family grant was $4.39 per week per family. It is now $4.23 per family. Of this $4.23 per family, about $3.93 is an allowance for food. This is about two-thirds of the amount needed to provide a health-maintaining diet. . . . I want to tell you about an experience we had in Philadelphia when our private funds were exhausted and before public funds became available.

On April 11 we mailed to families the last food orders which they received from private funds. It was not until April 22 that the giving of aid to families from public funds began, so that there was a period of about 11 days when many families received nothing. We have received reports from workers as to how these families managed. The material I am about to give you is typical, although it is based on a small sample. We made an intensive study of 91 families to find out what happened when the food orders stopped.

In a little less than 9 percent of these families there were pregnant mothers and in a little more than one third of the families children of nursing age.

This is how one of these families managed.

One woman said she borrowed 50 cents from a friend and bought stale bread for $3\frac{1}{2}$ cents per loaf, and that is all they had for eleven days except for one or two meals.

With the last food order another woman received she bought dried vegetables and canned goods. With this she made a soup and whenever the members of the family felt hungry they just ate some of the soup.

Here is a family of a pregnant mother and three children. They had only two meals a day and managed by having breakfast about 11 o'clock in the morning and then advancing the time of their evening meal. Breakfast consisted of cocoa, and bread and butter: the evening meal of canned soup.

One woman went along the docks and picked up vegetables that fell from the wagons. Sometimes the fish vendors gave her fish at the end of the day. On two different occasions this family was without food for a day and a half.

One family had nothing the day the food order stopped until 9 o'clock at night. Then the mother went to a friend's house and begged for a loaf of bread. This woman finally got two days' work at 75 cents a day. She bought a little meat and made a stew from vegetables picked up which they cooked over again every day to prevent its spoiling.

Another family's food consisted of potatoes, rice, bread, and coffee, and for a period of a day and a half they had no food at all.

SENATOR COSTIGAN. Are the cases you are citing typical or extreme?

MR. DE SCHWEINITZ. They are typical. I could tell you about many others, but while tragic it would become monotonous, and a few will illustrate the situation as well as many.

Here is another family which for two days had nothing to eat but bread, and during most of the rest of the time they had only two meals a day. Their meals consisted of bread and coffee for breakfast, and bread and raw or cooked carrots for dinner.

The gas company was careful not to turn off gas in a great many of these families, so in some instances food could be cooked.

Another family did not have food for two days. Then the husband went out and gathered dandelions and the family lived on them.

Here is another family which for two and half days went without food.

Still another family thinking to get as much as possible with their last food order bought potatoes and for 11 days lived only on them.

I should also like to say that when we talk to people who ask about unemployment they say, ' Well, people manage to get along somehow or other, don't they? You do not have very many people who really drop dead of starvation." That is perfectly true. Actually, death from starvation is not a frequent occurrence. You do not often hear about casualties of that sort. This is because people live in just the way that I have described. They live on inadequacies, and because they live on inadequacies the thing does not become dramatic and we do not hear about it. Yet the cost in human suffering is just as great as if they starved to death overnight.

SENATOR COSTIGAN. What you say is not only shockingly true but Senator Copeland, of New York, has recently reported cases of known starvation this past winter.

MR. DE SCHWEINITZ. The hospitals have had definite cases of starvation. . . .

A great many people raise the question as to whether the unemployed are a good-for-nothing lot and are out of work because of their own fault. They are not. We have definite studies to show that they had had long and good work records and that they are active, earnest human beings. All they want is a job.

SENATOR WAGNER. No really intelligent person asserts that to-day.

MR. DE SCHWEINITZ. No intelligent person, no; but lots of persons raise that question.

SENATOR WAGNER. I said intelligent persons.

MR. DE SCHWEINITZ. Yes; we are agreed on that.

I want to repeat that to-day the unemployed are upstanding, intelligent, earnest, capable people, but if we put the children in these families under a period of malnutrition such as they are going through to-day, what sort of people are we going to have 20 years from now, and what will we say at that time about them? What kind of working people will they be if we continue treating them as we are treating them now? . . .

SENATOR COSTIGAN. . . . One other question, Mr. de Schweinitz. Are World War veterans among the recipients of your relief?

MR. DE SCHWEINITZ. Oh, yes; a great many.

SENATOR COSTIGAN. They are suffering with the rest?

MR. DE SCHWEINITZ. There is no distinction. We have all creeds, all groups, all races; everyone is suffering together.

In Philadelphia, in large areas, no rent is being paid at all, and the landlords, the small landlords, are suffering terribly in a great many instances and sometimes by reason of their own losses they have been obliged to come to us for help. ☆ ☆ ☆

The American Farmer and the Great Depression 1932

During the 1920's, while their fellow Americans were enjoying a prosperity which some believed would never end, farmers were in financial trouble. They were not prospering the way the industrial sector of the nation was.

While agriculture still produced food for the cities and raw materials for the factories, farming had undergone dramatic changes after the Civil War. Farm machines and better farming techniques made it possible for a farmer to raise a great deal more food than the country needed. Since most farmers benefited from these agricultural improvements, more food was raised per acre than ever before. Who would buy the extra food? The surpluses remained unsold, and because so much food was available, low prices were paid for the rest.

Farmers complained of financial trouble in the 1920's. But the Great Depression, which lasted almost ten years after 1929, plunged them into deeper economic chaos. The following account is part of a statement made to a congressional committee in 1932; it describes the plight of the farmers and the agricultural regions during this period. The statement points out that it is possible to have overproduction of food and underconsumption (in other words, starvation) at the same time. Why does the author feel this is so?

DOCUMENT

(3) During the last three months I have visited, as I said, some 20 States of this wonderfully rich and beautiful country. Here are some of the things I heard and saw: In the State of Washington I was told that the forest fires raging in that region all summer and fall were caused by unemployed timber workers and bankrupt farmers in an endeavor to earn a few honest dollars as fire fighters. The last thing I saw on the night I left Seattle was a number of women searching for scraps of food in the refuse piles of the principal market of that city. A number of Montana citizens told me of thousands of bushels of wheat left in the fields uncut on account of its low price that hardly paid for harvesting. In Oregon I saw thousands of bushels of apples rotting in the orchards. Only absolutely flawless apples were still salable, at from 40 to 50 cents a box containing 200 apples. At the same time, there are millions of children who, on account of the poverty of their parents, will not eat one apple this winter.

While I was in Oregon the Portland *Oregonian* bemoaned the fact that thousands of ewes were killed by the sheep raisers because they did not bring enough in the market to pay the freight on them. And while Oregon sheep raisers fed mutton to the buzzards, I saw men picking for meat scraps in the garbage cans in the cities of New York and Chicago. I talked to one man in a restaurant in Chicago. He told me of his experience in raising sheep. He said that he had killed 3,000 sheep this fall and thrown them down the canyon, because it cost $1.10 to ship a sheep, and then he would get less than a dollar for it. He said he could not afford to feed the sheep, and he would not let them starve, so he just cut their throats and threw them down the canyon.

The roads of the West and Southwest teem with hungry hitch-hikers. The camp fires of the homeless are seen along every railroad track. I saw men, women, and children walking over hard roads. Most of them were tenant farmers who had lost their all in the late slump in wheat and cotton. Between Clarksville and Russellville, Ark., I picked up a family. The woman was hugging a dead chicken under a ragged coat. When I asked her where she had procured the fowl, first she told me she had found it dead in the road, and then added in grim humor, "They promised me a chicken in the pot, and now I got mine."

In Oklahoma, Texas, Arkansas, and Louisiana I saw untold bales of cotton rotting in the fields because the cotton pickers could not keep body and soul together on 35 cents paid for picking 100 pounds. The farmers' cooperatives who loaned the money to the planters to make the crops allowed the planters $5 a bale. That means 1,500 pounds of seed cotton for the picking of it, which was in the neighborhood of 35 cents a pound. A good picker can pick about 200 pounds of cotton a day, so that the 70 cents would not provide enough pork and beans to keep the picker in the field, so that there is fine staple cotton rotting down there by the hundreds and thousands of tons.

As a result of this appalling overproduction on the one side and the staggering underconsumption on the other side, 70 percent of the farmers of Oklahoma were unable to pay the interest on their mortgages. Last week one of the largest and oldest mortgage companies in that State went into the hands of the receiver. In that and other States we have now the interesting spectacle of farmers losing their farms by foreclosure and mortgage companies losing their recouped holdings by tax sales.

The farmers are being pauperized by the poverty of industrial populations and the industrial populations are being pauperized by the poverty of the farmers. Neither has the money to buy the product of the other, hence we have overproduction and underconsumption at the same time and in the same country.

☆　　☆　　☆

Roosevelt's Idea of Government 1932

When the stock market crash occurred, Herbert Hoover was President. As the nation's leader he was deeply concerned about the suffering of the people and tried to alleviate it by encouraging states to start public projects, by trying to influence bankers to lend money to businessmen, and by encouraging businessmen to cut hours of work rather than firing employees. Hoover felt the depression was caused by international economic difficulties over which he had little control. The depth of the depression, coupled with Hoover's belief that the government did not have the power to relieve individual suffering (that was a state and local responsibility), meant that by 1932 there was still little relief for the vast number of unemployed and the destitute farmers.

In 1932 there was an important presidential election in which the American people were given a choice of governments. Franklin D. Roosevelt had a theory quite different from Hoover's about the nature of the depression and the way to relieve it. Roosevelt thought the depression was a domestic problem and that the American people, with the strong support of their government, could restore the country to prosperity. As you read Roosevelt's speech, answer these questions about Roosevelt's philosophy: Which historical events preceded the growth of giant corporations? What rights does Roosevelt feel belong to every man? How is this philosophy different from the individualism of one hundred years before? Under what circumstances should the government act as an economic regulator?

DOCUMENT

(4) The issue of Government has always been whether individual men and women will have to serve some system of Government or economics, or whether a system of Government and economics exists to serve individual men and women. This question has persistently dominated the discussion of Government for many generations. . . .

Hamilton, and his friends, building toward a dominant centralized power were . . . defeated in the great election of 1800, by Mr. Jefferson's party. Out of that duel came the two parties, Republican and Democratic, as we know them today.

So began, in American political life, the new day, the day of the individual against the system, the day in which individualism was made the great watchword of American life. The happiest of economic conditions made that day long and splendid. On the Western frontier, land was substantially free. No one, who did not shirk the task of earning a living, was entirely without opportunity to do so. Depressions could, and did, come and go; but they could not alter the fundamental fact that most of the people lived partly by selling their labor and partly by extracting their livelihood from the soil, so that starvation and dislocation were practically impossible. At the worst there was always the possibility of climbing into a covered wagon and moving west where the untilled prairies afforded a haven for men to whom the East did not provide a place. So great were our natural resources that we could offer this relief not only to our own people, but to the distressed of all the world; we could invite immigration from Europe, and welcome it with open arms. . . .

It was in the middle of the nineteenth century that a new force was released and a new dream created. The force was what is called the industrial revolution, the advance of steam and machinery and the rise of the forerunners of the modern industrial plant. The dream was the dream of an economic machine, able to raise the standard of living for everyone; to bring luxury within the reach of the humblest; to annihilate distance by steam power and later by electricity, and to release everyone from the drudgery of the heaviest manual toil. . . .

In retrospect we can now see that the turn of the tide came with the turn of the century. We were reaching our last frontier; there was no more free land and our industrial combinations had become great uncontrolled and irresponsible units of power within the State. Clear-sighted men saw with fear the danger that opportunity would no longer be equal; that the growing corporation, like the feudal baron of old, might threaten the economic freedom of individuals to earn a living. In that hour, our anti-trust laws were born. . . .

A glance at the situation today only too clearly indicates that equality of opportunity as we have known it no longer exists. Our industrial plant is built; the problem just now is whether under existing conditions it is not overbuilt. Our last frontier has long since been reached, and there is practically no more free land. More than half of our people do not live on the farms or on lands and cannot derive a living by cultivating their own property. There is no safety valve in the form of a Western prairie to which those thrown out of work by Eastern economic machines can go for a new start. We are not able to invite the immigration from Europe to share our endless plenty. We are now providing a drab living for our own people. . . .

Just as freedom to farm has ceased, so also the opportunity in business has narrowed. It still is true that men can start small enterprises, trusting to native shrewdness and ability to keep abreast of competitors; but area after area has been preempted altogether by the great corporations, and even in the fields which still have no great concerns, the small man starts under a handicap. The unfeeling statistics of the past three decades show that the independent business man is running a losing race. . . . Recently a careful study was made of the concentration of business in the United States. It showed that our economic life was dominated by some six hundred odd corporations who controlled two-thirds of American industry. Ten million small business men divided the other third. More striking still, it appeared that if the process of concentration goes on at the same rate, at the end of another century we shall have all American industry controlled by a dozen corporations, and run by perhaps a hundred men. Put plainly, we are steering a steady course toward economic oligarchy, if we are not there already. . . .

Just as in older times the central Government was first a haven of refuge, and then a threat, so now in a closer economic system the central and ambitious financial unit is no longer a servant of the national desire, but a danger. I would draw the parallel one step farther. We did not think because national government had become a threat in the 18th century that therefore we should abandon the principle of national Government. Nor today should we abandon the principle of strong economic units called corporations, merely because their power is susceptible of easy abuse. In other times we dealt with the problem of an unduly ambitious central Government by modifying it gradually into a constitutional democratic Government. So today we are modifying and controlling our economic units.

As I see it, the task of Government in its relation to business is to assist the development of an economic declaration of rights, an economic constitutional order. This is the common task of statesman and business man. It is the minimum requirement of a more permanently safe order of things. . . .

Every man has a right to life; and this means that he has also a right to make a comfortable living. He may by sloth or crime decline to exercise that right; but it may not be denied him. We have no actual famine or dearth; our industrial and agricultural mechanism can produce enough and to spare. Our Government formal and informal, political and economic, owes to everyone an avenue to possess himself of a portion of that plenty sufficient for his needs, through his own work.

Every man has a right to his own property; which means a right to be assured, to the fullest extent attainable, in the safety of his savings. By no other means can men carry the burdens of those parts of life which, in the nature of things, afford no chance of labor: childhood, sickness, old age. In all thought of property, this right is paramount; all other property rights must yield to it. If, in accord with this principle, we must restrict the operations of the speculator, the manipulator, even the financier, I believe we must accept the restriction as needful, not to hamper individualism but to protect it. . . .

The Government should assume the function of economic regulation only as a last resort, to be tried only when private initiative inspired by high responsibility, with such assistance and balance as Government can give, has finally failed. As yet there has been no final failure, because there has been no attempt; and I decline to assume that this Nation is unable to meet the situation.

☆   ☆   ☆

Hoover's Commentary on the New Deal 1934

In his acceptance speech to the Democratic convention in the summer of 1932, Roosevelt promised the nation a "New Deal." The term "New Deal" stuck to Roosevelt's later economic programs that were designed to bring the country out of the depression. Roosevelt's "New Deal" began with a special session of Congress during his first hundred days in office. Roosevelt soon secured legislation to relieve the banking crisis, organized relief agencies, organized a Civilian Conservation Corps to provide jobs for unemployed young men, secured power to start agencies to help the nation recover from the depression, and tried to establish relief for the overproduction of farmers that had kept prices of farm products down.

Although all this activity was encouraging to those people who felt that the solution to the economic crisis was government intervention, to men with views like Hoover's, Roosevelt's activities were a frightening abuse of governmental power. Never before had a president used the federal government in so many areas or in such an extensive program of reform, control, and relief. In 1934 Hoover published a volume, *The Challenge to Liberty,* which outlined his own philosophy of government and criticized Roosevelt's administration. As you read selections from Hoover's writings, notice what he feels is the greatest danger Americans face in maintaining their liberty. Have his predictions about the evil effects of additional government power proved wholly correct? Compare Hoover's views and *laissez-faire.* How are they alike? How are they different?

DOCUMENT

(5) One may disagree and keep silent as to the justification of some of these measures if they are to be limited to "emergency," for in the march of a great people that is relatively unimportant if that is all of it. Then these dangers and stresses will disappear

as an eddy in the stream of national life. The important thing is whether this drift from essential liberties is to be permanent. If not permanent, these emergency measures will have served the purpose of having exhausted the pent-up panaceas of à generation and broken them on the wheel of resistant human behaviour and the spirit of a people with a heritage of liberty.

The threat of the continuance of these "emergency" acts is a threat to join the Continental retreat of human progress backward through the long corridor of time. In the demands for continuance there lies a mixture of desperate seeking for justification of their adoption and subtle ambitions of those advocating other philosophies. Whatever the motive, the promise of permanence now stares the American people starkly in the face. It is not the mere evolution of an economic procedure that this Regimentation implies — it steps off the solid highways of true American Liberty into the dangerous quicksands of governmental dictation. . . .

Our American System and its great purpose are builded upon the positive conception that "men are endowed by their Creator with certain unalienable Rights, that among these are Life, Liberty, and the pursuit of Happiness"; that the purpose and structure of government is to protect these rights; that upon them the government itself shall not encroach. From these liberties has come that unloosing of creative instincts and aspirations which have builded this, the greatest nation of all time. . . .

Yet today forces have come into action from ignorance, panic, or design which, either by subtle encroachment or by the breaking down of their safeguards, do endanger their primary purpose. These liberties are of urgent practical importance. The very employment upon which millions depend for their bread is today delayed because of the disturbance of confidence in their security. . . .

Even partial regimentation cannot be made to work and still maintain live democratic institutions. Representative government will sooner or later be at conflict with it along the whole front, both in the incidentals of daily working and in the whole field of free choice by the people. If it be continued the Congress must further surrender its checks and balances on administration and its free criticism since these, with intensified duties to its constituents, create interferences that will make efficient administration of this regimented machine impossible.

For any plan of Regimentation to succeed it must have not only powers of rigid discipline but adamant continuity. Does anyone believe that with the interferences of the Congress and the storms of a free press any government can impose discipline and follow a consistent and undeviating course in directing the activities of 125,000,000 highly diversified people? Because such a course is impossible Fascism and Sovietism have suppressed both free speech and representative government. . . .

We cannot extend the mastery of government over the daily life of a people without somewhere making it master of people's souls and thoughts. That is going on today. It is part of all regimentation.

Even if the government conduct of business could give us the maximum of efficiency instead of least efficiency, it would be purchased at the cost of freedom. It would increase rather than decrease abuse and corruption, stifle initiative and invention, undermine the development of leadership, cripple the mental and spiritual energies of our people, extinguish equality of opportunity, and dry up the spirit of liberty and the forces which make progress.

It is a false Liberalism that interprets itself into government dictation, or operation of commerce, industry and agriculture. Every move in that direction poisons the very springs of true Liberalism. It poisons political equality, free thought, free press, and equality of opportunity. It is the road not to liberty but to less liberty. True Liberalism is found not in striving to spread bureaucracy, but in striving to set bounds to it. Liberalism is a force proceeding from the deep realization that economic freedom cannot be sacrificed if political freedom is to be preserved. . . .

☆　　☆　　☆

The National Recovery Administration 1935

One of the pieces of legislation enacted in the spring of 1933 was the creation of the National Recovery Administration. This administration was given the authority to organize a code regulating hours of labor and wages and methods of operation for businesses that voluntarily agreed to sign the code. Roosevelt and his advisors hoped to reduce unemployment by encouraging employers to hire those who needed the work most. The code asked employers to hire only people over sixteen and cut the working day but pay higher wages. A shorter working day would mean that more people could be hired and there would be more jobs. In theory, if more people worked, more people could buy manufactured goods and farm products and wealth would begin to spread.

During the operation of the N.R.A. from 1933 to 1935, the agency did not restore complete prosperity, although some people thought it helped relieve unemployment somewhat. Many businessmen were angered by the legislation because they felt that the federal government was exercising power to which it had no right. In

1935 the Supreme Court, in the case of *Schechter Poultry Corp.* v. *United States*, declared the N.R.A. unconstitutional.

The N.R.A. had marked the beginning of a change in the concept of the power and responsibility of the government. For the N.R.A. was an attempt on the part of the President to relieve the burden of unemployment from individuals who were the victims of an economic system they could not control. Although the Supreme Court was not then willing to allow the government that responsibility, as the years passed this responsibility of the government was accepted.

As you read this document, decide: How had the N.R.A. tried to achieve greater employment? Why was this particular decision reversed? On what grounds was the N.R.A. abolished by the Supreme Court?

(6) . . . the defendants contended (1) that the Code had been adopted pursuant to an unconstitutional delegation by Congress of legislative power; (2) that it attempted to regulate intrastate transactions which lay outside the authority of Congress; and (3) that in certain provisions it was repugnant to the due process clause of the Fifth Amendment.

The defendants are slaughterhouse operators . . . A.L.A. Schechter Poultry Corporation and Schechter Live Poultry Market . . . in Brooklyn, New York City. Defendants ordinarily purchase their live poultry from . . . the West Washington Market in New York City or at the railroad terminals serving the City. . . . They buy the poultry for slaughter and resale. After the poultry is trucked to their slaughterhouse markets in Brooklyn, it is there sold, usually within twenty-four hours, to retail poultry dealers and butchers who sell directly to consumers. The poultry purchased from defendants is immediately slaughtered, prior to delivery. . . . Defendants do not sell poultry in interstate commerce.

The "Live Poultry Code" was promulgated under section 3 of the National Industrial Recovery Act. . . .

The Code fixes the number of hours for work-days. It provides that no employee, with certain exceptions, shall be permitted to work in excess of forty (40) hours in any one week, and that no employee, save as stated, "shall be paid in any pay period less than at the rate of fifty (50) cents per hour." The article containing "general labor provisions" prohibits the employment of any person under sixteen years of age, and declares that employees shall have the right of "collective bargaining," and freedom of choice with respect to labor organizations, in the terms of section 7 (a) of the Act. The minimum number of employees, who shall be employed by slaughterhouse operators, is fixed, the number being graduated according to the average volume of weekly sales. . . .

The seventh article, containing "trade practice provisions," prohibits various practices which are said to constitute "unfair methods of competition." . . .

It is not the province of the Court to consider the economic advantages or disadvantages of such a centralized system. It is sufficient to say that the Federal Constitution does not provide for it. . . .

We are of the opinion that the attempt through the provisions of the Code to fix the hours and wages of employees of defendants in their intrastate business was not a valid exercise of federal power. . . .

On both the grounds we have discussed, the attempted delegation of legislative power and the attempted regulation of intrastate transactions which affect interstate commerce only indirectly, we hold the code provisions here in question to be invalid and that the judgment of conviction must be reversed.

☆   ☆   ☆

Social Security 1935

Roosevelt's "New Deal" had successes as well as failures. Although the Supreme Court declared the N.R.A. unconstitutional (*see pp. 207–209*), not all of Roosevelt's legislation met that fate. In 1935 the Congress passed the Social Security Act to provide a federally operated retirement program for those qualified under the new law.

The Social Security program was the government's attempt to meet a new situation unknown to the nation a hundred years before. America had been an agricultural nation at the time the Constitution was written, and the few who reached old age were cared for on the large farms of their children or relatives. By the 1930's medical advances had increased the number of people who lived to an old age, and we were becoming an urban nation with families divided and young people moving away from home. Thus more and more older people had to support themselves by working because they had been unable to save enough to provide for their old age. The new act tried to provide some security for this group of citizens.

As you read Roosevelt's comments on the law, note how he thinks Social Security will ease the economic difficulties of the nation in the future, as well as how it will help the older group of citizens.

(7) Today a hope of many years' standing is in large part fulfilled. The civilization of the past hundred years, with its startling industrial changes, has tended more and more to make life insecure. Young people have come to wonder what would be their lot when they come to old age. The man with a job has wondered how long the job would last.

This social security measure gives at least some protection to thirty millions of our citizens who will reap direct benefits through unemployment compensation, through old-age pensions and through increased services for the protection of children and the prevention of ill health.

We can never insure one hundred percent of the population against one hundred percent of the hazards and vicissitudes of life, but we have tried to frame a law which will give some measure of protection to the average citizen and to his family against the loss of a job and against poverty-ridden old age.

This law, too, represents a cornerstone in a structure . . . intended to lessen the force of possible future depressions. It will act as a protection to future Administrations against the necessity of going deeply into debt to furnish relief to the needy. The law will flatten out the peaks and valleys of deflation and of inflation. It is, in short, a law that will take care of human needs and at the same time provide for the United States an economic structure of vastly greater soundness.

I congratulate all of you ladies and gentlemen, all of you in the Congress, in the executive departments and all of you who come from private life, and I thank you for your splendid efforts in behalf of this sound, needed and patriotic legislation.

If the Senate and the House of Representatives in this long and arduous session had done nothing more than pass this Bill, the session would be regarded as historic for all time.

☆   ☆   ☆

VIII. Footnotes

[1] *The New York Times*, October 25, 1929. © 1929 by the New York Times Company.

[2] *Congressional Record*, 72nd Congress, 1st Session, 20–26.

[3] *Ibid.*, 98–99.

[4] Samuel I. Rosenman, ed., *The Public Papers and Addresses of Franklin D. Roosevelt* (Random House, New York, 1938) I, 743–755.

[5] Herbert Hoover, *Challenge to Liberty* (Charles Scribner's Sons, New York, 1934) 192–199, 203–204.

[6] 295 U.S. 495.

[7] Rosenman, *Roosevelt*, IV, 324–325.

IX
What Are an Individual's Civil Rights?

One of the most recent upheavals in our nation's internal history, the Negro revolt, has kept the issue of civil rights before the nation's conscience. Negro civil rights has been an issue almost from the time slavery became an established practice. Before the Civil War abolitionists—for example, William Lloyd Garrison—preached that slavery was a moral evil and that the Negro had as much right to citizenship as any other human being.

The history of the United States shows that its citizens were gaining unprecedented freedoms, but the Negro has not shared in this freedom as other groups have. Long before the Civil War, slavery had been protected by law and slaves were considered to be property, not human beings with civil rights. As late as 1857 the Supreme Court, in the famous Dred Scott decision, ruled that slaves had no rights under the Constitution. After the Civil War, Reconstruction legislation did not have a lasting effect, so patterns of segregation and discrimination became an accepted part of daily life. From the 1890's to the 1950's these patterns changed little, having been established by law or habit. Finally, reformers succeeded in passing the 1957 and 1964 Civil Rights Acts, and some progress has been made since then.

As you read this chapter, see how some of the early laws allowed, or even encouraged, segregation and discrimination. Compare the intention of these early laws with that of laws recently passed.

The Dred Scott Decision 1857

One of the most controversial decisions made by the Supreme Court was the ruling in *Dred Scott* v. *Sandford*. Dred Scott was a slave who had been taken by his master into Illinois and the Wisconsin Territory, where slavery had been banned by the Northwest Ordinance of 1787 and the Missouri Compromise of 1820. (This compromise prohibited slavery in the Louisiana Purchase territory north of 36° 30'.) When Dred Scott became the property of an abolitionist, his owner decided to bring a test case into the federal courts to determine whether a slave who lived in a free state or territory was automatically freed. (Dred Scott's owner had decided to free him irrespective of the outcome of the case.)

The Supreme Court ruled against Scott's plea for freedom. Then it proclaimed the startling doctrine that Congress had no power to regulate slavery in the territories; the Missouri Compromise was invalid. Thus slavery could exist in the territories to the Canadian border and the Pacific Ocean. Historically, the decision was explosive: it upset the rather even balance between slave and free states that had existed, since Congress could no longer regulate the spread of slavery; furthermore, it heightened the ill feeling between the North and the South in the critical years before the Civil War *(see pp. 131–141)*.

The Dred Scott decision also has interesting constitutional aspects. As you read the decision, answer these questions about the Court's ruling: Why does the Court feel Negroes do not have the same privileges as other citizens? Under this ruling could Chinese who first entered the country after the ratification of the Constitution have become citizens? Does the Court believe the intention of the Constitution's framers is the means by which to judge a law constitutional? According to this ruling can states change their laws concerning citizenship? On what grounds does the Court rule the Missouri Compromise unconstitutional?

DOCUMENT

(1) The question is simply this: can a negro, whose ancestors were imported into this country, and sold as slaves, become a member of the political community formed and brought into existence by the Constitution of the United States, and as such become entitled to all the rights, and privileges, and immunities, guaranteed by that instrument to the citizens? One of which rights is the privilege of suing in a court of the United States in the cases specified in the Constitution. . . .

It is very clear . . . that no State can, by any act or law of its own, passed since the adoption of the Constitution, introduce a new member into the political community created by the Constitution of the United States. It cannot make him a member of this community by making him a member of its own. And for the same reason it cannot introduce any person, or description of persons, who were not intended to be embraced in this new political family, which the Constitution brought into existence, but were intended to be excluded from it.

The question then arises, whether the provisions of the Constitution, in relation to the personal rights and privileges to which the citizens of a State should be entitled, embraced the negro African race, at that time in this country, or who might afterwards be imported, who had then or should afterwards be made free in any State; and to put it in the power of a single State to make him a citizen of the United States, and endue him with the full rights of citizenship in every other State without their consent? Does the Constitution of the United States act upon him whenever he shall be made free under the laws of a State, and raised there to the rank of a citizen, and immediately clothe him with all the privileges of a citizen in every other state, and in its own courts?

The court thinks the affirmative of these propositions cannot be maintained. And if it cannot, the plaintiff in error [Scott] could not be a citizen of the State of Missouri, within the meaning of the Constitution of the United States, and consequently, was not entitled to sue in its courts.

It is true, every person, and every class and description of persons, who were at the time of the adoption of the Constitution recognized as citizens in the several States, became also citizens of this new political body; but none other; it was formed by them, and for them and their posterity, but for no one else. . . .

And the personal rights and privileges guaranteed to citizens of this new sovereignty were intended to embrace those only who were then members of the several State communities, or who should afterwards by birthright or otherwise become members, according to the provisions of the Constitution and the principles on which it was founded. . . .

It becomes necessary, therefore, to determine who were citizens of the several states when the Constitution was adopted. . . .

In the opinion of the court, the legislation and histories of the times, and the language used in the Declaration of Independence, show, that neither the class of persons who had been imported as slaves, nor their descendants, whether they had become free or not, were then acknowledged as a part of the people, nor intended to be included in the general words used in that memorable instrument. . . . The legislation of the states . . . shows . . . the inferior and subject condition of that race at the time the Constitution was adopted, and long afterward, throughout the thirteen States by which the instrument was framed. . . . It cannot be supposed that they intended to secure to them rights, and privileges, and rank, in the new political body through the Union, which every one of them denied within the limits of its own dominion. . . .

The court is of opinion, that, upon the facts stated in the plea . . . Dred Scott was not a citizen of Missouri within the meaning of the Constitution of the United States, and not entitled as such to sue in its courts. . . .

The Act of Congress, upon which the plaintiff relies, declares that slavery and involuntary servitude, except as a punishment for crime, shall be forever prohibited in all that part of the territory ceded by France, under the name of Louisiana, which lies north of thirty-six degrees thirty minutes north latitude, and not included within the limits of Missouri [Missouri Compromise of 1820]. And the difficulty which meets us at the threshold of this part of the inquiry is, whether Congress was authorized to pass this law under any of the powers granted to it by the Constitution. . . .

At the time when the Territory in question was obtained by cession from France, it contained no population fit to be associated together and admitted as a State; and it therefore was absolutely necessary to hold possession of it as a Territory belonging to the United States until it was settled and inhabited by a civilized community capable of self-government, and in a condition to be admitted on equal terms with the other States as a member of the Union. . . .

Now, as we have already said in an earlier part of this opinion, upon a different point, the right of property in a slave is distinctly and expressly affirmed in the Constitution. The right to traffic in it, like an ordinary article of merchandise and property, was guaranteed to the citizens of the United States, in every state that might desire it, for twenty years. And the government in express terms is pledged to protect it in all future time, if the slave escapes from his owner. . . .

Upon these considerations, it is the opinion of the court that the Act of Congress which prohibited a citizen from holding and owning property of this kind in the territory of the United States north of the line therein mentioned, is not warranted by the Consitution, and is therefore void; and that neither Dred Scott himself, nor any of his family, were made free by being carried into this territory; even if they had been carried there by the owner, with the intention of becoming a permanent resident.

★   ★   ★

The Constitutionality of the 1875 Civil Rights Act 1883

In 1875 Congress passed a Civil Rights Act that provided that persons of "every race and color" should have equal access to inns, to public conveyances, and to theaters and other places of public amusement. Several cases involving this act reached the Supreme Court in 1883. The court declared the act unconstitutional. As these selections from the decision illustrate, the Court held that the Fourteenth Amendment was a prohibition against state action and that this Amendment did not cover such situations as these, which involved discrimination by individuals. The court concluded that "It would be running the slavery argument into the ground, to make it apply to every act of discrimination which a person may see fit to make as to guests he will entertain, or as to the people he will take into his coach or cab or car. . . . If the laws themselves make any unjust discrimination, . . . Congress has full power to afford a remedy. . . ."

There was a strong dissent from the majority opinion, but there was no additional federal legislation aimed at such types of discrimination until the Civil Rights Act of 1964. After reading this decision, reread the Fourteenth Amendment (see pp. 42–43). Why did the Court feel this amendment did not apply to cases of discrimination? How could you argue that the Fourteenth Amendment does apply?

DOCUMENT

(2) These cases are all founded on the 1st and 2nd sections of the Act of Congress, known as the Civil Rights Act, passed March 1, 1875, entitled "An Act to Protect All Citizens in their Civil and Legal Rights." . . . Two of the cases, those against Stanley and Nichols, are indictments for denying to persons of color the accommodations and privileges of an inn or hotel; two of them, those against Ryan and Singleton, are, one an information, the other an indictment, for denying to individuals the privileges and accommodations of a theater, the information against Ryan being for refusing a colored person a seat in the dress circle of Maguire's theater in San Francisco: and the indictment against Singleton being for denying to another person, whose color is not stated, the full enjoyment of the accommodations of the theater known as the Grand Opera House in New York . . . .

It is obvious that the primary and important question in all the cases, is the constitutionality of the law; for if the law is unconstitutional, none of the prosecutions can stand. . . .

. . . Some obnoxious state law, passed or that might be passed, is necessary to be assumed, in order to lay the foundation of any federal remedy in the case; and for the very sufficient reason, that the constitutional prohibition is against *state laws* impairing the obligation of contracts.

And so in the present case, until some state law has been passed or some state action through its officers or agents has been taken, adverse to the rights of citizens sought to be protected by the 14th Amendment, no legislation of the United States under said Amendment, nor any proceeding under such legislation, can be called into activity . . . .

. . . Can the act of a mere individual, the owner of the inn, the public conveyance or place of amusement, refusing the accommodation, be justly regarded as imposing any badge of slavery or servitude upon the applicant, or only as inflicting an ordinary civil injury, properly cognizable by the laws of the State, and presumably subject to redress by those laws until the contrary appears?

After giving to these questions all the consideration which their importance demands, we are forced to the conclusion that such an act of refusal has nothing to do with slavery or involuntary servitude, and that if it is violative of any right of the party, his redress is to be sought under the laws of the State; or if those laws are adverse to his rights and do not protect him, his remedy will be found in the corrective legislation which Congress has adopted, or may adopt, for counteracting the effect of state laws, or state actions, prohibited by the 14th Amendment. It would be running the slavery argument into the ground, to make it apply to every act of discrimination which a person may see fit to make as to the guests he will entertain, or as to the people he will take into his coach or cab or car, or admit to his concert or theater, or deal with in other matters of intercourse or business. Innkeepers and public carriers, by the laws of all the States, so far as we are aware, are bound, to the extent of their facilities, to furnish proper accommodations to all unobjectionable persons who in good faith apply for them. If the laws themselves make any unjust discrimination, amenable to the prohibitions of the 14th Amendment, Congress has full power to afford a remedy, under that Amendment and in accordance with it.

☆   ☆   ☆

Plessy v. Ferguson 1896

Homer A. Plessy, a resident of Louisiana who was part Negro, took a seat on a train car reserved for whites (there were cars reserved for Negroes) and was forcibly ejected from the train and jailed. He had violated an 1890 Louisiana law that provided separate but equal facilities for the different races. This case was finally taken to the Supreme Court of the United States to determine the validity of the Louisiana law. The Supreme Court held that the law was not a violation of the Fourteenth Amendment, and consequently upheld the right of segregation on Southern trains.

This Supreme Court decision, more than any that had preceded it (*see pp. 215–216*), was to have the effect of making segregation the law of the land. Since the Court had ruled that separate facilities on trains were constitutional provided the facilities were equal, the ruling was to mean that separate facilities could be set up in all public places and for all public activities. Schools, parks, restaurants, and even drinking fountains in the South were divided by signs that read "White" and "Colored." Once the Supreme Court had ruled "separate but equal," it was very difficult to prove that the separate facilities were not always equal. For almost sixty years the ruling was to stand.

(3) This was a petition . . . filed in the supreme court of the state by Plessy, the plaintiff in error, against the Hon. John H. Ferguson, judge of the criminal district court for the parish of Orleans, and setting forth in substance the following facts:

That petitioner was a citizen of the United States and a resident of the state of Louisiana, of mixed descent, in the proportion of seven eighths Caucasian and one eighth African blood: that the mixture of colored blood was not discernible in him, and that he was entitled to every recognition, right, privilege, and immunity secured to the citizens of the United States of the white race by its Constitution and laws; that on June 7, 1892, he engaged and paid for a first-class passage on the East Louisiana Railway from New Orleans to Covington, in the same state and thereupon entered a passenger train 'and took possession of a vacant seat in a coach where passengers of the white race were accommodated; that such railroad company was incorporated by the laws of Louisiana as a common carrier, and was not authorized to distinguish between citizens according to their race. But, notwithstanding this, petitioner was required by the conductor, under penalty of ejection from said train and imprisonment, to vacate said coach and occupy another seat in a coach assigned by said company for persons not of the white race, and for no other reason than that petitioner was of the colored race; that upon petitioner's refusal to comply with such order, he was, with the aid of a police officer, forcibly ejected from said coach and hurried off to and imprisoned in the parish jail of New Orleans, and there held to answer a charge made by such officer to the effect that he was guilty of having criminally violated an act of the general assembly of the state, approved July 10, 1890, in such case made and provided. . . .

This case turns upon the constitutionality of an act of the general assembly of the state of Louisiana, passed in 1890, providing for separate railway carriages for the white and colored races. . . .

The 1st section of the statute enacts "that all railway companies carrying passengers in their coaches in this state shall provide equal but separate accommodations for the white and colored races, by providing two or more passenger coaches for each passenger train, or by dividing the passenger coaches by a partition so as to secure separate accommodations: *Provided,* That this section shall not be construed to apply to street railroads. No person or persons shall be permitted to occupy seats in coaches other than the ones assigned to them, on account of the race they belong to."

By the 2d section it was enacted "that the officers of such passenger trains shall have power and are hereby required to assign each passenger to the coach or compartment used for the race to which such passenger belongs; any passenger insisting on going into a coach or compartment to which by race he does not belong, shall be liable to a fine of $25, or in lieu thereof to imprisonment for a period of not more than twenty days in the parish prison, and any officer of any railroad insisting on assigning a passenger to a coach or compartment other than the one set aside for the race to which said passenger belongs, shall be liable to a fine of $25, or in lieu thereof to imprisonment for a period of not more than twenty days in the parish prison; and should any passenger refuse to occupy the coach or compartment to which he or she is assigned by the officer of such railway, said officer shall have power to refuse to carry such passenger on his train, and for such refusal neither he nor the railway company which he represents shall be liable for damages in any of the courts of this state." . . .

While we think the enforced separation of the races, as applied to the internal commerce of the state, neither abridges the privileges or immunities of the colored man, deprives him of his property without due process of law, nor denies him the equal protection of the laws, within the meaning of the 14th Amendment, we are not prepared to say that the conductor, in assigning passengers to the coaches according to their race, does not act at his peril, or that the provision of the 2d section of the act that denies to the passenger compensation in damages for a refusal to receive him into the coach in which he properly belongs, is a valid exercise of the legislative power. Indeed, we understand it to be conceded by the state's attorney that such part of the act that exempts from liability the

218

railway company and its officers is unconstitutional. The power to assign to a particular coach obviously implies the power to determine to which race the passenger belongs, as well as the power to determine who, under the laws of the particular state, is to be deemed a white and who a colored person. This question, though indicated in the brief of the plaintiff in error, does not properly arise in the record of this case, since the only issue made is as to the unconstitutionality of the act, so far as it requires the railway to provide separate accommodations, and the conductor to assign passengers according to their race.

☆   ☆   ☆

The Grandfather Clause 1915

After the Reconstruction period, the Southern state and local governments resorted to various devices to disenfranchise Negroes. These laws were passed to keep them from voting because if Negroes could vote, of course they would support changes in the segregation laws. Since the Fifteenth Amendment prohibited disenfranchisement on the basis of color, the devices chosen included such things as a property tax of some sort or a literacy test (such as being able to read and interpret the Constitution).

The Oklahoma constitution used this type of test on the Constitution as a qualification for voting, and the test was administered so that nearly all Negroes could not pass. All whites, however, including illiterate ones, were exempt from that test in certain instances: if before January 1, 1866, they had been entitled to vote (Negroes could not have voted before that date), or if they had resided in a "foreign nation" (meaning the Confederacy), or if they were sons or grandsons of someone who had voted or resided in a foreign country (hence the title "grandfather clause").

In 1915, in the case of *Guinn* v. *United States,* the Supreme Court invalidated the "grandfather clause" of the Oklahoma constitution on the grounds that it was obviously an attempt to evade the Fifteenth Amendment. As you read, compare the possible results of this ruling with the results of *Plessy* v. *Ferguson (see pp. 216–219).* Does the invalidating of the "grandfather clause" rule out other ways of disenfranchising the Negro?

DOCUMENT

(4) The questions which the court below asks are these:
"1. Was the amendment to the Constitution of Oklahoma, heretofore set forth, valid?

"2. Was that amendment void in so far as it attempted to debar from the right or privilege of voting for a qualified candidate for a member of Congress in Oklahoma unless they were able to read and write any section of the Constitution of Oklahoma, negro citizens of the United States who were otherwise qualified to vote for a qualified candidate for a member of Congress in that state, but who were not, and none of whose lineal ancestors was, entitled to vote under any form of government on January 1, 1866, or at any time prior thereto, because they were then slaves?"

As these questions obviously relate to the provisions concerning suffrage in the original Constitution and the amendment to these provisions which form the basis of the controversy, we state the text of both. The original clause, so far as material, was this:

"The qualified electors of the state shall be male citizens of the United States, male citizens of the state, and male persons of Indian descent native of the United States, who are over the age of twenty-one years, who have resided in the state one year, in the county six months, and in the election precinct thirty days, next preceding the election at which any such elector offers to vote."

And this is the amendment:

"No person shall be registered as an elector of this state or be allowed to vote in any election held herein, unless he be able to read and write any section of the Constitution of the state of Oklahoma; but no person who was, on January 1st, 1866, or any time prior thereto, entitled to vote under any form of government, or who at that time resided in some foreign nation, and no lineal descendant of such person, shall be denied the right to register and vote because of his inability to so read and write sections of such Constitution. Precinct election inspectors having in charge the registration of electors shall enforce the provisions of this section at the time of registration, provided registration be required. Should registration be dispensed with, the provisions of this section shall be enforced by the precinct election officers when electors apply for ballots to vote." . . .

It is true it contains no express words of an exclusion from the standard which it establishes of any person on account of race, color, or previous condition of servitude, prohibited by the 15th Amendment, but the standard itself inherently brings that result into existence since it is based purely upon a period of time before the enactment of the 15th Amendment, and makes that period the controlling and dominant test of the right of suffrage. In other words, we seek in vain for any ground which would sustain any other interpretation but that the provision, recurring to the conditions existing before the 15th Amendment was adopted and the continuance of which the 15th Amendment prohibited, proposed by in substance and effect lifting those conditions over to a period of time after the Amendment, to make them the basis of the right to suffrage conferred in direct and positive disregard of the 15th Amendment. And the same result, we are of opinion, is demonstrated by considering whether it is possible to discover any basis of reason for the standard thus fixed other than the purpose above stated. We say this because we are unable to discover how, unless the prohibitions of the 15th Amendment were considered, the slightest reason was afforded for basing the classification upon a period of time prior to the 15th Amendment. Certainly it cannot be said that there was any peculiar necromancy in the time named which engendered attributes affecting the qualification to vote which would not exist at another and different period unless the 15th Amendment was in view.

While these considerations establish that the standard fixed on the basis of the 1866 test is void, they do not enable us to reply even to the first question asked by the court below . . . .

☆   ☆   ☆

School Desegregation 1954

For almost sixty years following 1896, the *Plessy* v. *Ferguson* ruling was used to uphold state laws that provided "separate but equal" facilities. But in 1954, in the case of *Brown* v. *The Board of Education*, the court reversed itself by declaring that segregation in public schools was unconstitutional. As you read, find out why the Supreme Court decided separate facilities were not equal. Although such "tangible" factors as the quality of teachers and of school buildings may be equal, what intangibles, such as psychological pressures, might be involved? Why does the court think it important to consider education today rather than in 1868 or 1896? What are the aims of education today? How could segregation keep education from attaining those aims?

DOCUMENT

(5) These cases come to us from the States of Kansas, South Carolina, Virginia, and Delaware. They are premised on different facts and different local conditions, but a common legal question justifies their consideration together in this consolidated opinion.

In each of the cases, minors of the Negro race, through their legal representatives, seek the aid of the courts in obtaining admission to the public schools of their community on a nonsegregated basis. In each instance, they have been denied admission to schools attended by white children under laws requiring or permitting segregation according to race. This segregation was alleged to deprive the plaintiffs of the equal protection of the laws under the Fourteenth Amendment. In each of the cases other than the Delaware case, a three-judge federal district court denied relief to the plaintiffs on the so-called "separate but equal" doctrine announced by this court in *Plessy* v. *Ferguson*. . . . Under that doctrine, equality of treatment is accorded when the races are provided substantially equal facilities, even though these facilities be separate. In the Delaware case, the Supreme Court of Delaware adhered to that doctrine, but ordered that the plaintiffs be admitted to the white schools because of their superiority to the Negro schools.

The plaintiffs contend that segregated public schools are not "equal" and cannot be made "equal," and that hence they are deprived of the equal protection of the laws. Because of the obvious importance of the question presented, the Court took jurisdiction. . . .

In approaching this problem, we cannot turn the clock back to 1868 when the Amendment was adopted, or even to 1896 when *Plessy* v. *Ferguson* was written. We must consider public education in the light of its full development and its present place in American life throughout the Nation. Only in this way can it be determined if segregation in public schools deprives these plaintiffs of the equal protection of the laws.

Today, education is perhaps the most important function of state and local governments. Compulsory school attendance laws and the great expenditures for education both demonstrate our recognition of the importance of education to our democratic society. It is required in the performance of our most basic public responsibilities, even service in the armed forces. It is the very foundation of good citizenship. Today it is a principal instrument in awakening the child to cultural values, in preparing him for later professional training, and in helping him to adjust normally to his environment. In these days, it is doubtful that any child may reasonably be expected to succeed in life if he is denied the opportunity of an education. Such an opportunity, where the state has undertaken to provide it, is a right which must be made available to all on equal terms.

We come then to the question presented: Does segregation of children in public schools solely on the basis of race, even though the physical facilities and other "tangible" factors may be equal, deprive the children of the minority group of equal educational opportunities? We believe that it does. . . .

Whatever may have been the extent of psychological knowledge at the time of *Plessy* v. *Ferguson*, this finding is amply supported by modern authority. Any language in *Plessy* v. *Ferguson* contrary to this finding is rejected.

We conclude that in the field of public education the doctrine of "separate but equal" has no place. Separate educational facilities are inherently unequal. Therefore, we hold that the plaintiffs and others similarly situated for whom the actions have been brought are, by reason of segregation complained of, deprived of the equal protection of the laws guaranteed by the Fourteenth Amendment. This disposition makes unnecessary any discussion whether such segregation also violates the Due Process Clause of the Fourteenth Amendment.

Because there are class actions, because of the wide applicability of this decision, and because of the great variety of local conditions, the formulation of decrees in these cases presents problems of considerable complexity. On reargument, the consideration of appropriate relief was necessarily subordinated to the primary question — the constitutionality of segregation in public education. We have now announced that such segregation is denial of the equal protection of the laws. . . .

☆   ☆   ☆

Declaration of Constitutional Principles 1956

When the Supreme Court ordered desegregation of the public schools in *Brown* v. *The Board of Education*, there was far from unanimous agreement that the Supreme Court had made a wise or a constitutional decision. Southerners, who were used to segregation, were reluctant to see their customs changed. But Negro leaders who had worked for years on the legal groundwork for this decision felt it was the beginning, although quite a small one, of a changing era for the members of their race.

Since public school segregation was most rigidly practiced in the South, and because the South would face the first impact of the Court's decision, it is not surprising that Southern congressmen were the first to comment on the decision. Below is a statement by most Southern congressmen stating their objections. As you read, compare these objections with the reasoning in the original decision (*see pp. 221–223*).

DOCUMENT

(6) The unwarranted decision of the Supreme Court in the public school cases is now bearing the fruit always produced when men substitute naked power for established law.

The Founding Fathers gave us a Constitution of checks and balances because they realized the inescapable lesson of history that no man or group of men can be safely entrusted with unlimited power. They framed this Constitution with its provisions for change by amendment in order to secure the fundamentals of government against the dangers of temporary popular passion or the personal predilections of public officeholders.

We regard the decision of the Supreme Court in the school cases as a clear abuse of judicial power. It climaxes a trend in the Federal Judiciary undertaking to legislate in derogation of the authority of Congress, and to encroach upon the reserved rights of the States and the people.

The original Constitution does not mention education. Neither does the 14th amendment nor any other amendment. The debates preceding the submission of the 14th amendment clearly show that there was no intent that it should affect the system of education maintained by the States.

The very Congress which proposed the amendment subsequently provided for segregated schools in the District of Columbia.

When the amendment was adopted in 1868, there were 37 States of the Union. . . . Every one of the 26 States that had any substantial racial differences among its people, either approved the operation of segregated schools already in existence or subsequently established such schools by action of the same law-making body which considered the 14th amendment.

As admitted by the Supreme Court in the public school case (*Brown* v. *Board of Education*), the doctrine of separate but equal schools "apparently originated in *Roberts* v. *City of Boston* (1849), upholding school segregation against attack as being violative of a State constitutional guarantee of equality." This constitutional doctrine began in the North, not in the South, and it was followed not only in Massachusetts, but in Connecticut, New York, Illinois, Indiana, Michigan, Minnesota, New Jersey, Ohio, Pennsylvania and other northern States until they, exercising their rights as States through the constitutional processes of local self-government, changed their school systems.

In the case of *Plessy* v. *Ferguson* in 1896 the Supreme Court expressly declared that under the 14th amendment no person was denied any of his rights if the States provided separate but equal public facilities. This decision has been followed in many other cases. It is notable that the Supreme Court, speaking through Chief Justice Taft, a former President of the United States, unanimously declared in 1927 in *Lum* v. *Rice* that the "separate but equal" principle is "within the discretion of the State in regulating its public schools and does not conflict with the 14th amendment."

This interpretation, restated time and again, became a part of the life of the people of many of the States and confirmed their habits, customs, traditions, and way of life. It is founded on elemental humanity and commonsense, for parents should not be deprived by Government of the right to direct the lives and education of their own children.

Though there has been no constitutional amendment or act of Congress changing this established legal principle almost a century old, the Supreme Court of the United States, with no legal basis for such action, undertook to exercise their naked judicial power and substituted their personal political and social ideas for the established law of the land.

This unwarranted exercise of power by the Court, contrary to the Constitution, is creating chaos and confusion in the States principally affected. It is destroying the amicable relations between the white and Negro races that have been created through 90 years of patient effort by the good people of both races. It has planted hatred and suspicion where there has been heretofore friendship and understanding.

Without regard to the consent of the governed, outside agitators are threatening immediate and revolutionary changes in our public-school systems. If done, this is certain to destroy the system of public education in some of the States.

With the gravest concern for the explosive and dangerous condition created by this decision and inflamed by outside meddlers:

We reaffirm our reliance on the Constitution as the fundamental law of the land.

We decry the Supreme Court's encroachments on rights reserved to the States and to the people, contrary to established law, and to the Constitution.

We commend the motives of those States which have declared the intention to resist forced integration by any lawful means.

We appeal to the States and people who are not directly affected by these decisions to consider the constitutional principles involved against the time when they too, on issues vital to them, may be the victims of judicial encroachment.

Even though we constitute a minority in the present Congress, we have full faith that a majority of the American people believe in the dual system of government which has enabled us to achieve our greatness and will in time demand that the reserved rights of the States and of the people be made secure against judicial usurpation.

We pledge ourselves to use all lawful means to bring about a reversal of this decision which is contrary to the Constitution and to prevent the use of force in its implementation.

In this trying period, as we all seek to right this wrong, we appeal to our people not to be provoked by the agitators and troublemakers invading our States and to scrupulously refrain from disorder and lawless acts.

☆   ☆   ☆

The Civil Rights Act 1957

In 1957 Congress passed the first Civil Rights Act since 1875. The 1875 law had been declared unconstitutional and Congress had shown little intention of attempting to pass a new law in light of the court's ruling. The decision in *Brown* v. *The Board of Education* (*see pp. 221–223*) created a favorable atmosphere for the passage of another civil rights law.

The 1957 law provided for a Civil Rights Commission, whose duty was to collect information about alleged or real cases of violations of federal law or constitutional guarantees in the area of civil rights. It provided that no one should interfere with the rights of qualified electors to vote in elections. And, finally, the Attorney General was authorized to bring civil action against persons who violated any provision of the act.

While the act was an attempt to secure civil rights for the Negro, it had the serious drawback of providing no real way of assuring these rights. The language was vague enough so that it would be difficult, for example, to prove someone had been denied "equal protection under the Constitution." But perhaps the major weakness was that the law did nothing to remove the literacy tests and poll taxes that had been used to keep Negroes from voting.

But whatever the drawbacks of the bill, it was an attempt on the part of Congress to recognize in some small way that inequalities in the system did exist. And this act establishing a Civil Rights Commission to investigate this problem was the forerunner of stronger and more effective legislation.

DOCUMENT

(7) *Duties of the Commission*
      SEC. 104. (a) The Commission shall—
      (1) investigate allegations in writing under oath or affirmation that certain citizens of the United States are being deprived of their right to vote and have that vote counted by reason of their color, race, religion, or national origin; which writing, under oath or affirmation, shall set forth the facts upon which such belief or beliefs are based;
      (2) study and collect information concerning legal develop-

ments constituting a denial of equal protection of the laws under the Constitution; and

(3) appraise the laws and policies of the Federal Government with respect to equal protection of the laws under the Constitution.

(b) The Commission shall submit interim reports to the President and to the Congress at such times as either the Commission or the President shall deem desirable, and shall submit to the President and to the Congress a final and comprehensive report of its activities, findings, and recommendations not later than two years from the date of the enactment of this Act.

(c) Sixty days after the submission of its final report and recommendations the Commission shall cease to exist. . . .

SEC. 131 . . . (b) No person, whether acting under color of law or otherwise, shall intimidate, threaten, coerce, or attempt to intimidate, threaten, or coerce any other person for the purpose of interfering with the right of such other person to vote or to vote as he may choose, or of causing such other person to vote for, or not to vote for, any candidate for the office or President, Vice President, presidential elector, Member of the Senate, or Member of the House of Representatives, Delegates or Commissioners from the Territories or possessions, at any general, special, or primary election held solely or in part for the purpose of selecting or electing any such candidate.

(c) Whenever any person has engaged or there are reasonable grounds to believe that any person is about to engage in any act or practice which would deprive any other person of any right or privilege secured by subsection (a) or (b), the Attorney General may institute for the United States, or in the name of the United States, a civil action or other proper proceeding for preventive relief, including an application for a permanent or temporary injunction, restraining order, or other order. In any proceeding hereunder the United States shall be liable for costs the same as a private person.

(d) The district courts of the United States shall have jurisdiction of proceedings instituted pursuant to this section and shall exercise the same without regard to whether the party aggrieved shall have exhausted any administrative or other remedies that may be provided by law.

☆ ☆ ☆

Desegregation Difficulties 1962

Progress was made in many parts of the South and in the nation at large in desegregating the public schools following the 1954 Supreme Court decision. In some areas there was conflict, and in a few places there was open opposition to the entire concept of desegregation.

One of the most bitter controversies concerned the enrollment of James H. Meredith, a Negro, in the University of Mississippi in the fall of 1962. Governor Ross R. Barnett of Mississippi defied a federal court order to admit Meredith, claiming that a state had the right to "interpose" its power to protect its citizens against an "illegal" exercise of federal power. President John F. Kennedy finally ordered U.S. marshals to the campus of the University of Mississippi to enforce the federal court order, and Meredith was admitted.

The legal aspect of the dispute was debated in the Senate of the United States by Senators James O. Eastland and John Stennis of Mississippi, and Senators Paul H. Douglas of Illinois and Jacob K. Javits of New York.

The following excerpts are taken from the September 26 speech of Senator Eastland and the September 27 address of Senator Douglas. As you read, look up the portions of the Constitution each man refers to. Find other documents in which these points are argued, and compare them with Mr. Eastland's and Mr. Douglas's arguments.

DOCUMENT

(8) MR. EASTLAND. Mr. President, the State of Mississippi has now been placed in the spotlight as a result of the decision rendered by the U.S. Supreme Court on May 17, 1954, in the school integration case. I have warned time and time again that, when a court usurps unto itself powers that are not delegated under the Constitution and laws of the United States and embarks upon a course of illegal action, one illegal usurpation would beget another and that the time would come when the people would be the victims of a judicial oligarchy. Today it is the State of Mississippi that is being made the whipping boy of the heedless and lawless course of conduct that has been pursued by the Federal judiciary since that May 17 decision.

The Governor of Mississippi is charged with the duty and responsibility of seeing that the constitution and statutes of that State are duly and faithfully executed. His power and right to perform this function arises from the sovereign powers that were reserved to the States and to the people under articles 9 and 10 of the amendments to our basic charter [U.S. Constitution]. He deserves and warrants the congratulations of all right-thinking people and those who love and want to keep their hard-won freedom and liberties for interposing himself and frustrating the execution of an illegal and unconstitutional order directed at Mississippi by judicial tyrants who are blind and intoxicated with the alleged power usurped to the Federal judiciary by an unbridled Supreme Court.

MR. DOUGLAS. . . . I like to think of the people of the South as a generous people who, as I say, have been handicapped by the institution of slavery, by the Civil War and by the events which grew out of the Civil War. I do not believe that either I or any member of the so-called civil rights group can be charged with ever reflecting on the character of innate decency of the people of the South. Quite to the contrary. Fortunately, we of the North were spared by climate and history from the evil institution of slavery which still hangs as an albatross around the minds and thoughts of many of the people in the South.

Our great hope is that the saner elements in the South may take control, and that ways will be worked out for peaceful adjustment of these difficulties.

I hope the junior Senator [Stennis] from Mississippi will forgive me if I say that his constant attitude of kindliness and personal fair dealings has, I believe, impressed all of us from the North. And we say in no condescending fashion at all that we believe he represents the true South. If the law is obeyed, as we hope it will be, the final events will be much better than many people in Mississippi now fear. . . .

If I may speak very briefly on the constitutional question, our southern friends constantly appeal to the 10th amendment to the Constitution, which, as we all know, provides—

"The powers not delegated to the United States by the Constitution, nor prohibited by it to the States, are reserved to the States respectively, or to the people."

When the inquiry arises as to the specific power in the Constitution which grants to the Federal Government the right to desegregate schools, or to prevent discrimination in voting or in the use of public facilities, and when such powers cannot be found within the confines of the first 10 amendments, then the assertion is frequently made that there are no such powers. What our good friends ignore are the post-Civil War amendments, not merely the 13th amendment, which abolished chattel slavery, which is recognized, but also the 14th and 15th amendments. The 14th amendment is particularly appropriate. The more I read that amendment, the more I see in it. I hope I may be excused if I repeat the first section:

"All persons born or naturalized in the United States, and subject to the jurisdiction thereof, are citizens of the United States and of the State wherein they reside. No State shall make or enforce any law which shall abridge the privileges or immunities of citizens of the United States; nor shall any State deprive any person of life, liberty, or property without due process of law; nor deny to any person within its jurisdiction the equal protection of the laws."

There are at least four points in that amendment which are essential. First, everyone who is born or naturalized in the United States has a citizenship, not only of the State wherein he resides, but also of the United States as well. There are no first-class citizens or second-class citizens, and no citizens exclusively of Illinois, Mississippi, New York or Alabama. They are citizens of those States, yes, because they reside there. But they are also citizens of the United States. One citizen has the same right as any other citizen.

The next clause provides:

"No State shall make or enforce any law which shall abridge the privileges or immunities of citizens of the United States."

This means that the rights guaranteed under the first 10 amendments of the Constitution, and which under the first 10 amendments are protected against constitutional or national interference, are by this clause also protected against interference by the States or the civil subdivisions of the States.

The Federal Government, therefore, throws this protection around people, to see that these privileges or immunities are not abridged.

Then comes the third phrase:

"Nor shall any State deprive any person of life, liberty, or property without due process of law."

At times in the past the emphasis has been on property, but increasingly the conscience of the country and the opinions of the Court have emphasized life and liberty, along with property. This prohibition against depriving a person of those things without due process of law means that the Federal Government has the right to intervene in order to enforce this protection.

☆　　☆　　☆

Civil Rights Act of 1964

The desegregation difficulties at the University of Mississippi were only a small part of the events that have marked the civil rights struggle. After the Civil Rights Act of 1957, Negroes and white sympathizers took part in thousands of demonstrations demanding equal rights for Negroes in finding public accommodations and in exercising voting rights. The pressure became so intense that in 1964 Congress passed a Civil Rights Act designed to achieve the same general results as had been intended by the voided 1875 Civil Rights Act. The 1964 law again attempted to outlaw segregation in public places, but it specifically mentioned a greater number of places where discrimination was to be banned than the 1875 law had.

In attempting to write a law which would be upheld by the Supreme Court, Congress included places of public accommodation to which the interstate commerce clause of the Constitution applied. By arguing that places of public accommodation were involved in commerce when they served interstate travelers or used goods transported by interstate commerce, Congress found a way of controlling an abuse of individual rights.

More important, however, this law had strong provisions for enforcement. The Attorney General of the United States was permitted to intervene if he saw violations of the act. Although this law did not secure for Negroes all civil rights such as voting and equality of opportunity, it was a step in the struggle for civil rights.

(9) SEC. 201. (a) All persons shall be entitled to the full and equal enjoyment of the goods, services, facilities, privileges, advantages, and accommodations of any place of public accommodation, as defined in this section, without discrimination or segregation on the ground of race, color, religion, or national origin.

(b) Each of the following establishments which serves the public is a place of public accommodation within the meaning of this title if its operations affect commerce, or if discrimination or segregation by it is supported by State action: (1) any inn, hotel, motel, or other establishment which provides lodging to transient guests, other than an establishment located within a building which contains not more than five rooms for rent or hire and which is actually occupied by the proprietor of such establishment as his residence; (2) any restaurant, cafeteria, lunchroom, lunch counter, soda fountain, or other facility principally engaged in selling food for consumption on the premises, including, but not limited to, any such facility located on the premises of any retail establishment; or any gasoline station; (3) any motion picture house, theater, concert hall, sports arena, stadium or other place of exhibition or entertainment; and (4) any establishment (A) (i) which is physically located within the premises of any establishment otherwise covered by this subsection, or (ii) within the premises of which is physically located any such covered establishment, and (B) which holds itself out as serving patrons of such covered establishment.

(c) The operations of an establishment affect commerce within the meaning of this title if (1) it is one of the establishments described in paragraph (1) of subsection (b); (2) in the case of an establishment described in paragraph (2) of subsection (b), it serves or offers to serve interstate travelers or a substantial portion of the food which it serves, or gasoline or other products which it sells, has moved in commerce; (3) in the case of an establishment described in paragraph (3) of subsection (b), it customarily presents films, performances, athletic teams, exhibitions, or other sources of entertainment which move in commerce; and (4) in the case of an establishment described in paragraph (4) of subsection (b), it is physically located within the premises of, or there is physically located within its premises, an establishment the operations of which affect commerce within the meaning of this subsection. For purposes of this section, "commerce" means travel, trade, traffic, commerce, transportation, or communication among the several States, or between the District of Columbia and any State, or between any foreign country or any territory or possession and any State or the District of Columbia, or between points in the same State but through any other State or the District of Columbia or a foreign country.

(d) Discrimination or segregation by an establishment is supported by State action within the meaning of this title if such discrimination or segregation (1) is carried on under color of any law, statute, ordinance, or regulation; or (2) is carried on under color of any custom or usage required or enforced by officials of the State or political subdivision thereof; or (3) is required by action of the State or political subdivision thereof.

(e) The provisions of this title shall not apply to a private club or other establishment not in fact open to the public except to the extent that the facilities of such establishment are made available. . . .

SEC. 206. (a) Whenever the Attorney General has reasonable cause to believe that any person or groups of persons is engaged in a pattern or practice of resistance to the full enjoyment of any of the rights secured by this title, . . . the Attorney General may bring a civil action in the appropriate district court of the United States. . . .

☆ ☆ ☆

Heart of Atlanta Motel
v. United States 1964

The Civil Rights Act of 1964 was controversial, since it was designed to eliminate discrimination in public places. Shortly after the law went into effect, it was tested by the Heart of Atlanta Motel. The case went to the Supreme Court, and the court upheld Congress' belief that public accommodations were a part of interstate commerce.

What did Congress hope to accomplish by this bill? Was interstate commerce really the central issue in the bill? As you read this case, decide why the Court ruled that the action of Congress had been constitutional. Compare this to the decision of the Court after the Civil Rights Act of 1875 (*see pp. 215–216*).

(10) 1. *The Factual Background and Contention of the Parties.* The case comes here on admissions and stipulated facts. Appellant owns and operates the Heart of Atlanta Motel which has 216 rooms available to transient guests. The motel is located on Courtland Street two blocks from downtown Peachtree Street. It is readily accessible to interstate highways 75 and 85 and state highways 23 and 41. Appellant solicits patronage from outside the State of Georgia through various national advertising media, including magazines of national circulation; it maintains over 50 billboards and highway signs within the State, soliciting patronage for the motel; it accepts convention trade from outside Georgia and approximately 75% of its registered guests are from out of State. Prior to passage of the Act the motel had followed a practice of refusing to rent rooms to Negroes, and it alleged that it intended to continue to do so. In an effort to perpetuate that policy this suit was filed.

The Appellant contends that Congress in passing this Act exceeded its power to regulate commerce under Art I, § 8, cl 3, of the Constitution of the United States; that the Act violates the Fifth Amendment because appellant is deprived of the right to choose its customers and operate its business as it wishes, resulting in a taking of its liberty and property without due process of law and a taking of its property without just compensation; and finally, that by requiring appellant to rent available rooms to Negroes against its will, Congress is subjecting it to involuntary servitude in contravention of the Thirteenth Amendment.

The appellees counter that the unavailability to Negroes of adequate accommodations interferes significantly with interstate travel, and that Congress, under the Commerce Clause, has power to remove such obstructions and restraints; that the Fifth Amendment does not forbid reasonable regulation and the consequential damage does not constitute a "taking" within the meaning of that amendment; that the Thirteenth Amendment claim fails because it is entirely frivolous to say that an amendment directed to the abolition of human bondage and the removal of widespread disabilities

233

associated with slavery places discrimination in public accommodations beyond the reach of both federal and state law.

At the trial the appellant offered no evidence, submitting the
case on the pleadings, admissions and stipulation of facts; however,
appellees proved the refusal of the motel to accept Negro transients
after the passage of the Act. . . .

It is admitted that the operation of the motel brings it within
the provision of §201 (a) of the Act and that appellant refused to
provide lodging for transient Negroes because of their race or color
and that it intends to continue that policy unless restrained.

The sole question posed is, therefore, the constitutionality of
the Civil Rights Act of 1964 as applied to these facts. The legislative
history of the Act indicates that Congress based the Act on §5 and
the Equal Protection Clause of the Fourteenth Amendment as well
as its power to regulate interstate commerce under Art I, § 8, cl 3 of
the Constitution. . . .

It is doubtful if in the long run appellant will suffer economic
loss as a result of the Act. Experience is to the contrary where discrimination is completely obliterated as to all public accommodations. But whether this be true or not is of no consequence since
this Court has specifically held that the fact that a "member of the
class which is regulated may suffer economic losses not shared by
others . . . has never been a barrier" to such legislation. . . .

We find no merit in the remainder of appellant's contentions,
including that of "involuntary servitude." As we have seen, 32
States prohibit racial discrimination in public accommodations.
These laws but codify the common-law innkeeper rule which long
predated the Thirteenth Amendment. It is difficult to believe that
the Amendment was intended to abrogate this principle. Indeed,
the Opinion of the Court in the Civil Rights Cases is to the contrary
as we have seen, it having noted with approval the laws of "all the
States" prohibiting discrimination. We could not say that the requirements of the Act in this regard are in any way "akin to African
slavery." . . .

We, therefore, conclude that the action of the Congress in the
adoption of the Act as applied here to a motel which concededly
serves interstate travelers is within the power granted it by the
Commerce Clause of the Constitution, as interpreted by this Court
for 140 years. It may be argued that Congress could have pursued
other methods to eliminate the obstructions it found in interstate
commerce caused by racial discrimination. But this is a matter of
policy that rests entirely with the Congress not with the courts.
How obstructions in commerce may be removed — what means are
to be employed — is within the sound and exclusive discretion of the
Congress. It is subject only to one caveat — that the means chosen by

it must be reasonably adapted to the end permitted by the Constitution. We cannot say that its choice here was not so adapted. The Constitution requires no more.

☆   ☆   ☆

IX. *Footnotes*

[1] 19 Howard 393 ff. (1857).

[2] *United States Supreme Court Reports*, 27 Lawyers' Edition, 1885, 838–844.

[3] *United States Supreme Court Reports*, 41 Lawyers' Edition, 1897, 256–260.

[4] *United States Supreme Court Reports*, 59 Lawyers' Edition, 1915, 1345–1348.

[5] 347 U.S. 483.

[6] *Congressional Record*, 84th Congress, 2nd Session, CII, 4460.

[7] *United States Statutes at Large, 1957* (Government Printing Office, Washington, D.C., 1958) LVII, 635, 637.

[8] *Congressional Record*, 87th Congress, 2nd Session, 20804, 21035.

[9] *United States Statutes at Large, 1964* (Government Printing Office, Washington, D.C., 1965) 243, 245.

[10] *United States Supreme Court Reports*, 13 Lawyers' Edition 2nd, 1965, 260–271.

X

How Does the Constitution Affect Foreign Policy?

The foreign policy of a nation is the sum of the actions and attitudes of that one nation toward other nations of the world. A nation's foreign policy includes the wars it fights, the peace treaties it signs, the trade agreements it makes, the recognition it extends to new governments, and the foreign aid it dispenses. The solutions or actions taken by the United States in regard to these problems make up the history of American foreign affairs.

On reading the Constitution, one finds few provisions which relate directly to foreign policy, because developing a foreign policy in 1787 was not as complex as it would be today. To the framers of the Constitution the problems of Europe simply seemed so far away that they made few specific provisions for the conduct of foreign affairs. Yet the Constitution has proven an amazingly effective document as the basis of our conduct of foreign policy, from the time George Washington acted to establish a place for us as the newest nation in the world until the present time, when we are the most powerful country in the world, with commitments and responsibilities stretching to every corner of the globe.

Our early leaders dealt with foreign nations only as they immediately affected our welfare. Although the early republic was caught up in the rivalry between France and England, the leaders of the new nation maintained neutrality. They bargained with Spain about our use of the Mississippi River, with France about the Louisiana Purchase, and with Britain before and after the War of 1812. But they stayed as separate, as isolated, and as neutral as possible.

Today, however, technological advances in transportation and communication have made the world increasingly small, and this kind of progress creates new problems and responsibilities for the nations of the world. Although people can easily travel from one nation to another and can come to understand the problems of many nations, rapid communication means that unrest, revolution, or war in any part of the world may lead to unrest elsewhere. Fortunately, our Constitution is flexible and allows us to meet these new crises as they develop.

The Constitution does delegate a few powers very specifically. The President is commander in chief of the army and navy, can make treaties with the advice and consent of the Senate, and can appoint ambassadors with senatorial approval. Besides advising the President, the role of Congress is to declare war, to vote money to support the armed forces, and to control foreign trade by setting tariffs and making trade agreements.

These powers are important, and the President and Congress can use them in varying ways to affect the outcome of international events. For instance, Congress advises the President and supports or opposes his policy in foreign affairs. If Congress should oppose the President, it can refuse to vote money to support armed forces the President has ordered to an area of conflict. Or if it feels the President has made a treaty that is not in the best interests of the country, the Senate can refuse to ratify it. Also, Congress can affect the attitude of other nations toward the United States by raising or lowering tariffs on their chief exports to the United States. Thus these powers enable our leaders to employ the checks and balances provided in the Constitution.

One question which recurs through the years, and must be argued anew in each decision, is "To what extent should the United States be involved in the world's affairs?" As you read, decide whether you can find any one time at which the United States fully realized and accepted its involvement. Notice the times when the nation had become involved with, and then stepped back from, the rest of the world. Then notice how our country's leaders since George Washington have used their powers under the Constitution to maneuver in each situation. Notice the ways in which they tried each time to insure freedom for the nations of the world and to advance toward a more perfect union at home.

Washington's Farewell Address 1796

Since England and France were traditional enemies, the young American colonies had difficulty dealing with both countries. The French had aided the colonies during their war for independence, so

France was supposedly a friendly nation. But the new nation, depending on trade for its livelihood, could not afford to antagonize Britain, which controlled the seas. A precarious balance was maintained, even when England and France went to war in 1793.

At this time George Washington was faced with the task of preserving peace and neutrality. Some of his advisors wished to support the new French Republic, whereas others favored alignment with England. But with the United States government facing so many problems of internal organization, it is hardly surprising that Washington had little patience with arguments over difficult alliances and foreign policy. In his Farewell Address Washington cautioned the nation against active involvement in the affairs of European nations, for he realized these involvements might hamper the development of the new country. As you read, summarize how Washington suggests foreign policy should be handled. Was this good advice in 1796? Would it still be good advice now?

DOCUMENT

(1) Observe good faith and justice toward all nations. Cultivate peace and harmony with all. Religion and morality enjoin this conduct. And can it be that good policy does not equally enjoin it? It will be worthy of a free, enlightened, and at no distant period a great nation to give to mankind the magnanimous and too novel example of a people always guided by an exalted justice and benevolence. Who can doubt that in the course of time and things the fruits of such a plan would richly repay any temporary advantages which might be lost by a steady adherence to it? Can it be that Providence has not connected the permanent felicity of a nation with its virtue? The experiment, at least, is recommended by every sentiment which ennobles human nature. Alas! is it rendered impossible by its vices?

In the execution of such a plan nothing is more essential than that permanent, inveterate antipathies against particular nations and passionate attachments for others should be excluded, and that in place of them just and amicable feelings toward all should be cultivated. The nation which indulges toward another an habitual hatred or an habitual fondness is in some degree a slave. It is a slave to its animosity or to its affection, either of which is sufficient to lead it astray from its duty and its interest. Antipathy in one nation against another disposes each more readily to offer insult and injury, to lay hold of slight causes of umbrage, and to be haughty and intractable when accidental or trifling occasions of dispute occur. . . .

238

So, likewise, a passionate attachment of one nation for another produces a variety of evils. Sympathy for the favorite nation, facilitating the illusion of an imaginary common interest in cases where no real common interest exists, and infusing into one the enmities of the other, betrays the former into a participation in the quarrels and wars of the latter without adequate inducement or justification. It leads also to concessions to the favorite nation of privileges denied to others, which is apt doubly to injure the nation making the concessions by unnecessarily parting with what ought to have been retained, and by exciting jealousy, ill will, and a disposition to retaliate in the parties from whom equal privileges are withheld; and it gives to ambitious, corrupted, or deluded citizens (who devote themselves to the favorite nation) facility to betray or sacrifice the interests of their own country without odium, sometimes even with popularity, gilding with the appearances of a virtuous sense of obligation, a commendable deference for public opinion, or a laudable zeal for public good the base or foolish compliances of ambition, corruption, or infatuation. . . .

The great rule of conduct for us in regard to foreign nations is, in extending our commercial relations, to have with them as little *political* connection as possible. So far as we have already formed engagements let them be fulfilled with perfect good faith. Here let us stop.

Europe has a set of primary interests which to us have none or a very remote relation. Hence she must be engaged in frequent controversies, the causes of which are essentially foreign to our concerns. Hence, therefore, it must be unwise in us to implicate ourselves by artificial ties in the ordinary vicissitudes of her politics or the ordinary combinations and collisions of her friendships or enmities.

Our detached and distant situation invites and enables us to pursue a different course. If we remain one people, under an efficient government, the period is not far off when we may defy material injury from external annoyance; when we may take such an attitude as will cause the neutrality we may at any time resolve upon to be scrupulously respected; when belligerent nations, under the impossibility of making acquisitions upon us, will not lightly hazard the giving us provocation; when we may choose peace or war, as our interest, guided by justice, shall counsel.

Why forego the advantages of so peculiar a situation? Why quit our own to stand upon foreign ground? Why, by interweaving our destiny with that of any part of Europe, entangle our peace and prosperity in the toils of European ambition, rivalship, interest, humor, or caprice?

It is our true policy to steer clear of permanent alliances with any portion of the foreign world, so far, I mean, as we are now at liberty to do it; for let me not be understood as capable of patronizing infidelity to existing engagements. I hold the maxim no less applicable to public than to private affairs that honesty is always the best policy. I repeat, therefore, let those engagements be observed in their genuine sense. But in my opinion it is unnecessary and would be unwise to extend them. . . .

The duty of holding a neutral conduct may be inferred, without anything more, from the obligation which justice and humanity impose on every nation, in cases in which it is free to act, to maintain inviolate the relations of peace and amity toward other nations.

The inducements of interest for observing that conduct will best be referred to your own reflections and experience. With me a predominant motive has been to endeavor to gain time to our country to settle and mature its yet recent institutions, and to progress without interruption to that degree of strength and consistency which is necessary to give it, humanly speaking, the command of its own fortunes.

★ ★ ★

Jefferson on the Louisiana Purchase 1802

When the United States gained its independence from England, the land west of the Mississippi River belonged to Spain. The new nation was not worried about Spanish control because Spain had a weak government and little power in the New World. But when President Jefferson heard news that France had gained control of the territory in 1800, he and other Americans were alarmed at the thought of losing the Mississippi. The river was very important to the settlers west of the Appalachian Mountains, since most of their land was drained by it; when farmers wanted to take their crops to the markets in the East, they floated them down the Mississippi and along the coast. Water transport was almost the only kind of heavy transportation in use at that time.

France was a strong nation and could easily use New Orleans to control the traffic on the Mississippi. In 1802, Jefferson sent instructions to Robert R. Livingston, the American minister in Paris, to purchase the New Orleans area from France. The letter quoted below contains Jefferson's explanation to Livingston of his concern about France's control of the Louisiana Territory and his suggestions for ways in which Livingston might proceed.

What interests us most today is how these negotiations mark a change in Jefferson's attitude toward governmental power. Before he became President, Jefferson believed that government should exercise only those powers specifically written in the Constitution (*see pp. 120–121*). But when Jefferson became President and was faced with a situation not covered by the Constitution, he was willing to use his power as President to act in the nation's interest and purchase Louisiana. Thus Jefferson began a long tradition of presidents' taking action in situations of international crisis.

Why would Jefferson be alarmed when Napoleon regained France's former possession in the New World? When he later purchased the territory, would he be acting in ways strictly covered by the Constitution?

DOCUMENT

(2) The cession of Louisiana and the Floridas by Spain to France, works most sorely on the United States. On this subject the Secretary of State has written to you fully, yet I cannot forbear recurring to it personally, so deep is the impression it makes on my mind. It completely reverses all the political relations of the United States, and will form a new epoch in our political course. Of all nations of any consideration, France is the one which, hitherto, has offered the fewest points on which we could have any conflict of right, and the most points of a communion of interests. From these causes, we have ever looked to her as our *natural friend*, as one with which we never could have an occasion of difference. Her growth, therefore, we viewed as our own, her misfortunes ours. There is on the globe one single spot, the possessor of which is our natural and habitual enemy. It is New Orleans, through which the produce of three-eighths of our territory must pass to market, and from its fertility it will ere long yield more than half of our whole produce, and contain more than half of our inhabitants. France, placing herself in that door, assumes to us the attitude of defiance. . . .

If France considers Louisiana, however, as indispensable for her views, she might perhaps be willing to look about for arrangements which might reconcile it to our interests. If anything could do this, it would be the ceding to us the island of New Orleans and the Floridas. This would certainly, in a great degree, remove the causes of jarring and irritation between us, and perhaps for such a length of time, as might produce other means of making the measure permanently conciliatory to our interests and friendships. It would, at any rate, relieve us from the necessity of taking immediate measures for countervailing such an operation by arrangements in another quarter. . . .

☆   ☆   ☆

241

The Monroe Doctrine 1823

In 1823 the administration of James Monroe was faced with an international situation that many people believed was the most critical since the Revolutionary War. Latin-American colonies had revolted and won their independence from Spain. Many Americans feared that France, Russia, and Austria might support Spain's efforts to regain these colonies. The United States also feared problems with Russia, which had planted a few colonies in the area that is now the state of Alaska.

Since Britain was then developing trade with Latin-American countries, she encouraged the United States to oppose intervention in the Western Hemisphere by any other strong European nation. Therefore, Britain offered to make a joint statement with the United States, but Monroe and his cabinet decided against that course. The final result of this crisis was the Monroe Doctrine, a statement issued as part of Monroe's annual message to Congress in December of 1823.

As you read, compare Monroe's attitudes toward foreign policy with Washington's *(see pp. 237–240)*. What Constitutional power permits the President to make such a pronouncement? In what ways could the President enforce his statement?

(3). . . In the wars of the European powers in matters relating to themselves we have never taken any part, nor does it comport with our policy so to do. It is only when our rights are invaded or seriously menaced that we resent injuries or make preparation for our defense. With the movements in this hemisphere we are of necessity more immediately connected, and by causes which must be obvious to all enlightened and impartial observers. The political system of the allied powers is essentially different in this respect from that of America. This difference proceeds from that which exists in their respective Governments; and to the defense of our own, which has been achieved by the loss of so much blood and treasure, and matured by the wisdom of their most enlightened citizens, and under which we have enjoyed unexampled felicity, this whole nation is devoted. We owe it, therefore, to candor and to the amicable relations existing between the United States and those powers to declare that we should consider any attempt on their part to extend their system to any portion of this hemisphere as dangerous to our peace and safety. With the existing colonies or dependencies of any European power we have not interfered and shall not interfere. But with the Governments who have declared their independence and maintained it, and whose independence we have, on great consideration and on just principles, acknowledged, we could not view any interposition for the purpose of oppressing them, or controlling in any other manner their destiny, by any European power in any other light than as the manifestation of an unfriendly disposition toward the United States. . . .

☆   ☆   ☆

The Spanish-American War 1898

In the years following the proclamation of the Monroe Doctrine, the United States was rarely involved in diplomatic conflicts with other nations; most diplomacy was an attempt to gain new territory. For the United States was more concerned with expansion and growth in industry than with international affairs. But by 1890 the United States had become a powerful enough nation to challenge any European nation, and public sentiment led the United States into a temporary involvement in world affairs.

In 1895 a revolt broke out in Cuba against the Spanish colonial government there. The new rebel government quickly gained the support of the American press, which enthusiastically published horrifying stories of Spain's attempts to suppress the rebellion. Prejudice against Spain and the impact of these stories stirred public sentiment to active support of the rebels and to demands for Spain's withdrawal from Cuba. Meanwhile the President had sent the U.S.S. *Maine* to Havana to evacuate Americans if their lives should be in danger. When the *Maine* blew up mysteriously in February of 1898, Congress began to make strong demands that Spain consider granting Cuba independence. But diplomacy failed and Congress drafted resolutions that finally amounted to a declaration of war.

As you read, find evidence that Congress had been influenced by the public sentiment favoring the rebels and condemning Spain.

DOCUMENT

(4) Whereas the abhorrent conditions which have existed for more than three years in the Island of Cuba, so near our own borders, have shocked the moral sense of the people of the United States, have been a disgrace to Christian civilization, culminating, as they have, in the destruction of a United States battleship, with two hundred and sixty-six of its officers and crew, while

243

on a friendly visit in the harbor of Havana, and can not longer be endured, as has been set forth by the President of the United States in his message to Congress of April eleventh, eighteen hundred and ninety-eight, upon which the action of Congress was invited: Therefore,

Resolved . . . First. That the people of the Island of Cuba are, and of right ought to be, free and independent.

Second. That it is the duty of the United States to demand, and the Government of the United States does hereby demand, that the Government of Spain at once relinquish its authority and government in the Island of Cuba and withdraw its land and naval forces from Cuba and Cuban waters.

Third. That the President of the United States be, and he hereby is, directed and empowered to use the entire land and naval forces of the United States, and to call into the actual service of the United States the militia of the several States, to such extent as may be necessary to carry these resolutions into effect.

Fourth. That the United States hereby disclaims any disposition or intention to exercise sovereignty, jurisdiction, or control over said Island except for the pacification thereof, and asserts its determination, when that is accomplished, to leave the government and control of the Island to its people.

☆   ☆   ☆

The Responsibility of an American President 1917

Unfortunately, some American presidents have had to face fateful decisions that would commit their nation to war. Woodrow Wilson made such a soul-searching decision when he decided to ask Congress to declare war on Germany.

Wilson's actions were prompted by America's inescapable involvement in Europe's war, which had begun in 1914. At the outset Wilson tried to keep the United States from siding with either Germany or England, since our ships traded with both nations. England had violated our neutral rights by stopping and searching American ships. But German submarines were more of a threat. They torpedoed British passenger ships on which Americans sailed, and there was a great deal of tension when over 100 Americans died as the *Lusitania* went down in 1915. When in January 1917 the German government informed the United States that unrestricted submarine warfare would begin on any ships approaching England or France,

Wilson broke diplomatic relations with Germany. Then submarines sank several American ships, and Wilson had to decide whether the United States was willing to become involved in a European war.

The difficulties and doubts that beset Wilson the night before he requested that Congress declare war are recorded by a newspaper-man who was with him at the time.

DOCUMENT

(5) The night before he asked Congress for a declaration of war against Germany he sent for me. I was late getting the message and didn't reach the White House till 1 o'clock in the morning. "The old man" was waiting for me, sitting in his study with the typewriter on his table, where he used to type his own messages.

I'd never seen him so worn down. He looked as if he hadn't slept, and he said he hadn't. He said he was probably going before Congress the next day to ask a declaration of war, and he'd never been so uncertain about anything in his life as about that decision. For nights, he said, he'd been lying awake going over the whole situation; over the provocation given by Germany, over the probable feeling in the United States, over the consequences to the settlement and to the world at large if we entered the melee.

He tapped some sheets before him and said that he had written a message and expected to go before Congress with it as it stood. He said he couldn't see any alternative, that he had tried every way he knew to avoid war. "I think I know what war means," he said, and he added that if there were any possibility of avoiding war he wanted to try it. "What else can I do?" he asked. "Is there anything else I can do?"

I told him his hand had been forced by Germany, that so far as I could see we couldn't keep out.

"Yes," he said, "but do you know what that means?" He said war would overturn the world we had known; that so long as we remained out there was a preponderance of neutrality, but that if we joined with the Allies the world would be off the peace basis and onto a war basis.

It would mean that we should lose our heads along with the rest and stop weighing right and wrong. It would mean that a majority of people in this hemisphere would go war-mad, quit thinking and devote their energies to destruction. The President said a declaration of war would mean that Germany would be beaten and so badly beaten that there would be a dictated peace, a victorious peace.

"It means," he said, "an attempt to reconstruct a peace-time civilization with war standards, and at the end of the war there will be no bystanders with sufficient power to influence the terms. There won't be any peace standards left to work with. There will only be war standards."

The President said that such a basis was what the Allies thought they wanted, and that they would have their way in the very thing that America had hoped against and struggled against. W. W. was uncanny that night. He had the whole panorama in his mind. He went on to say that so far as he knew he had considered every loophole of escape and as fast as they were discovered Germany deliberately blocked them with some new outrage.

Then he began to talk about the consequences to the United States. He had no illusions about the fashion in which we were likely to fight the war.

He said when a war got going it was just war and there weren't two kinds of it. It required illiberalism at home to reinforce the men at the front. We couldn't fight Germany and maintain the ideals of Government that all thinking men shared. He said we would try it but it would be too much for us.

"Once lead this people into war," he said, "and they'll forget there ever was such a thing as tolerance. To fight you must be brutal and ruthless, and the spirit of ruthless brutality will enter into the very fiber of our national life, infecting Congress, the courts, the policeman on the beat, the man in the street." Conformity would be the only virtue, said the President, and every man who refused to conform would have to pay the penalty.

He thought the Constitution would not survive it; that free speech and the right of assembly would go. He said a nation couldn't put its strength into a war and keep its head level; it had never been done.

☆   ☆   ☆

Wilson's Call to Arms 1917

On April 2, 1917, Wilson called Congress into special session, and with a note of anguish asked Congress for a declaration of war. Congress acted promptly and declared war on Germany on April 6, 1917.

(6) I have called the Congress into extraordinary session because there are serious, very serious, choices of policy to be made, and made immediately, which it was neither right nor constitutionally permissible that I should assume the responsibility of making.

On the third of February last I officially laid before you the extraordinary announcement of the Imperial German Government that on and after the first day of February it was its purpose to put aside all restraints of law or of humanity and use its submarines to sink every vessel that sought to approach either the ports of Great Britain and Ireland or the western coasts of Europe or any of the ports controlled by the enemies of Germany within the Mediterranean. That had seemed to be the object of the German submarine warfare earlier in the war, but since April of last year the Imperial Government had somewhat restrained the commanders of its undersea craft in conformity with its promise then given to us that passenger boats should not be sunk and that due warning would be given to all other vessels which its submarines might seek to destroy, when no resistance was offered or escape attempted, and care taken that their crews were given at least a fair chance to save their lives in their open boats. The precautions taken were meagre and haphazard enough, as was proved in distressing instance after instance in the progress of the cruel and unmanly business, but a certain degree of restraint was observed. The new policy has swept every restriction aside. Vessels of every kind, whatever their flag, their character, their cargo, their destination, their errand, have been ruthlessly sent to the bottom without warning and without thought of help or mercy for those on board, the vessels of friendly neutrals along with those of belligerents. Even hospital ships and ships carrying relief to the sorely bereaved and stricken people of Belgium, though the latter were provided with safe conduct through the proscribed areas by the German Government itself and were distinguished by unmistakable marks of identity, have been sunk with the same reckless lack of compassion or of principle. . . .

It is a war against all nations. American ships have been sunk, American lives taken, in ways which it has stirred us very deeply to learn of, but the ships and people of other neutral and friendly nations have been sunk and overwhelmed in the waters in the same way. There has been no discrimination. The challenge is to all mankind. Each nation must decide for itself how it will meet it. The choice we make for ourselves must be made with a moderation of counsel and a temperateness of judgment befitting our character and our motives as a nation. We must put excited feeling away. Our motive will not be revenge or the victorious assertion of the physical might of the nation, but only the vindication of right, of human right, of which we are only a single champion. . . .

With a profound sense of the solemn and even tragical character of the step I am taking and of the grave responsibilities which it involves, but in unhesitating obedience to what I deem my constitutional duty, I advise that the Congress declare the recent course of the Imperial German Government to be in fact nothing less than war against the government and people of the United States; that it formally accept the status of belligerent which has thus been thrust upon it; and that it take immediate steps not only to put the country in a more thorough state of defense but also to exert all its power and employ all its resources to bring the Government of the German Empire to terms and end the war. . . .

We have no quarrel with the German people. We have no feeling towards them but one of sympathy and friendship. It was not upon their impulse that their government acted in entering this war. It was not with their previous knowledge or approval. It was a war determined upon as wars used to be determined upon in the old, unhappy days when peoples were nowhere consulted by their rulers and wars were provoked and waged in the interest of dynasties or of little groups of ambitious men who were accustomed to use their fellow men as pawns and tools. Self-governed nations do not fill their neighbour states with spies or set the course of intrigue to bring about some critical posture of affairs which will give them an opportunity to strike and make conquest. Such designs can be successfully worked out only under cover and where no one has the right to ask questions. . . .

It will be all the easier for us to conduct ourselves as belligerents in a high spirit of right and fairness because we act without animus, not in enmity towards a people or with the desire to bring any injury or disadvantage upon them, but only in armed opposition to an irresponsible government which has thrown aside all considerations of humanity and of right and is running amuck. We are, let me say again, the sincere friends of the German people, and shall desire nothing so much as the early re-establishment of intimate relations of mutual advantage between us,—however hard it may be for them, for the time being, to believe that this is spoken from our hearts.

It is a distressing and oppressive duty, Gentlemen of the Congress, which I have performed in thus addressing you. There are, it may be, many months of fiery trial and sacrifice ahead of us. It is a fearful thing to lead this great peaceful people into war, into the most terrible and disastrous of all wars, civilization itself seeming to be in the balance. But the right is more precious than peace, and we shall fight for the things which we have always carried nearest our hearts,—for democracy, for the right of those who submit to authority to have a voice in their own governments, for the rights and liberties of small nations, for a universal dominion of right by such a concert of free peoples as shall bring peace and safety to all nations and make the world itself at last free. To such a task we can dedicate our lives and our fortunes, everything that we are and everything that we have, with the pride of those who know that the day has come when America is privileged to spend her blood and her might for the principles that gave her birth and happiness and the peace which she has treasured. God helping her, she can do no other.

☆   ☆   ☆

Woodrow Wilson's Support of the League of Nations 1919

President Woodrow Wilson's major postwar ambition was to help create an international organization designed to prevent future wars. In 1919 the President was chief delegate of the United States to the Paris Peace Conference to discuss terms of peace. The Covenant of the League of Nations, as the peace organization was called, was part of the text of the Treaty of Versailles which ended the war officially. Wilson then had to submit the Treaty to the Senate of the United States for its approval. Within a short time opposition developed within the Senate, opposition strong enough to block the necessary two-thirds vote of approval. Wilson then decided to appeal to the citizenry by making a speaking tour to explain the importance of America's entrance into the League of Nations.

At Pueblo, Colorado, on September 25, 1919, Wilson delivered what may have been his most effective speech. Following this speech, Wilson suffered a physical collapse. Then opposition in the Senate defeated the Treaty and ended all hope of United States entry into the League of Nations.

Wilson's tour was an attempt to overcome what was from his point of view an unwise rejection of the League. Many senators had refused to vote for the League because they felt the United States should isolate itself from the affairs of Europe as George Washington had counseled in 1796 (see pp. 237–240). The Senate was within its constitutional rights to refuse to consent to the treaty, but this refusal and the President's failure to gain popular support to defeat Senate opposition were to have serious results. Because the United States was a powerful nation and had refused to join the League, the League lacked the support and authority of one important world leader. Only twenty years later, the United States was again to fight a European war; the weakened League of Nations had been unable to prevent its outbreak.

As you read from Wilson's speech at Pueblo, note what importance Wilson attaches to Article 10. Would Article 10 help prevent wars? How would this be so?

(7) . . . as I have crossed the Continent I have perceived more and more that men have been busy creating an absolutely false impression of what the treaty of peace and the covenant of the league of nations contain and mean. . . .

When you come to the heart of the covenant, my fellow citizens, you will find it in article 10. . . . Article 10 provides that every member of the league covenants to respect and preserve the territorial integrity and existing political independence of every other member of the league as against external aggression. Not against internal disturbance. There was not a man at that table who did not admit the sacredness of the right of self-determination, the sacredness of the right of any body of people to say that they would not continue to live under the Government they were then living under, and under article 11 of the covenant they are given a place to say whether they will live under it or not. For . . . article 11 . . . makes it the right of any member of the league at any time to call attention to anything, anywhere, that is likely to disturb the peace of the world or the good understanding between nations upon which the peace of the world depends. . . .

Yet article 10 strikes at the taproot of war. Article 10 is a statement that the very things that have always been sought in imperialistic wars are henceforth foregone by every ambitious nation in the world. I would have felt very lonely, my fellow countrymen, and I would have felt very much disturbed if, sitting at the peace table in Paris, I had supposed that I was expounding my own ideas. . . . I proposed nothing whatever at the peace table at Paris that I had not sufficiently certain knowledge embodied the moral judgment of the citizens of the United States. I had gone over there with, so to say, explicit instructions. Don't you remember that we laid down 14 points which should contain the principles of the settlement? They were not my points. In every one of them I was conscientiously trying to read the thought of the people of the United States, and after I uttered those points I had every assurance given me that could be given me that they did speak the moral judgment of the United States and not my single judgment. Then when it came to that critical period just a little less than a year ago, when it was evident that the war was coming to its critical end, all the nations engaged in the war accepted those 14 principles explicitly as the basis of the armistice and the basis of the peace. In those circumstances I crossed the ocean under bond to my own people and to the other governments with which I was dealing. The whole specification of the method of settlement was written down and accepted beforehand, and we were architects building on those specifications. . . .

You will say, "Is the league an absolute guaranty against war?"

No; I do not know any absolute guaranty against the errors of human judgment or the violence of human passion. . . .

☆   ☆   ☆

Recognition of the Soviet Union 1933

In 1917 the Russian Revolution overthrew the monarchy. By November of that year Lenin, Trotsky, and their Communist associates were in power. But the United States and many other nations did not believe these men could establish a lasting government. The Communists repudiated capitalism and tried to break up land ownership. As their policies became clear, many people in the United States were opposed to them.

Although other nations began recognizing the U.S.S.R. (as Russia was renamed after the Revolution) during the 1920's, the United States showed its disapproval of many Russian policies by withholding formal recognition. (Refusing to recognize a government or to appoint an ambassador is an example of how the President could attempt to affect international events by showing American disapproval.) After several years under Communist government, however, it became clear that the regime was in full and actual control of the country. Then, regardless of the disapproval many Americans still felt for their policies and theories, when Franklin Roosevelt became President, the United States recognized the U.S.S.R.

DOCUMENT

(8) *President Roosevelt to the Soviet Commissar for Foreign Affairs (Litvinov)*

Washington, November 16, 1933.

My Dear Mr. Litvinov: I am very happy to inform you that as a result of our conversations the Government of the United States has decided to establish normal diplomatic relations with the Government of the Union of Soviet Socialist Republics and to exchange ambassadors. I trust that the relations now established between our peoples may forever remain normal and friendly, and that our nations henceforth may cooperate for their mutual benefit and for the preservation of the peace of the world.

    I am [etc.]

Franklin D. Roosevelt

The Soviet Commissar for Foreign Affairs (Litvinov) to President Roosevelt

Washington, November 16, 1933.

My Dear Mr. President: I am very happy to inform you that the government of the Union of Soviet Socialist Republics is glad to establish normal diplomatic relations with the Government of the United States and to exchange ambassadors.

I, too, share the hope that the relations now established between our peoples may forever remain normal and friendly, and that our nations henceforth may cooperate for their mutual benefit and for the preservation of the peace of the world.

I am [etc.]

Maxim Litvinoff

The Soviet Commissar for Foreign Affairs (Litvinov) to President Roosevelt

Washington, November 16, 1933.

My Dear Mr. President: I have the honor to inform you that coincident with the establishment of diplomatic relations between our two governments it will be the fixed policy of the Government of the Union of Soviet Socialist Republics:

1. To respect scrupulously the indisputable right of the United States to order its own life within its own jurisdiction in its own way and to refrain from interfering in any manner in the internal affairs of the United States, its territories or possessions.

2. To refrain, and to restrain all persons in government service and all organizations of the Government or under its direct or indirect control, including the organizations in receipt of any financial assistance from it, from any act overt or covert liable in any way whatsoever to injure the tranquillity, prosperity, order, or security of the whole or any part of the United States, its territories or possessions, and in particular from any act tending to incite or encourage armed intervention, or any agitation or propaganda having as an aim, the violation of the territorial integrity of the United States, its territories or possessions, or the bringing about by force of a change in the political or social order of the whole or any part of the United States, its territories or possessions.

3. Not to permit the formation or residence on its territory of any organization or group—and to prevent the activity on its territory of any organization or group, or of representatives or officials of any organization or group—which makes claim to be the Government of, or makes attempt upon the territorial integrity of, the United States, its territories or possessions; not to form, subsidize, support or permit on its territory military organizations or groups

252

having the aim of armed struggle against the United States, its territories or possessions, and to prevent any recruiting on behalf of such organizations and groups.

4. Not to permit the formation or residence on its territory of any organization or group — and to prevent the activity on its territory of any organization or group, or of representatives or officials of any organization or group — which has as an aim the overthrow or the preparation for the overthrow of, or the bringing about by force of a change in, the political or social order of the whole or any part of the United States, its territories or possessions.

I am [etc.]

Maxim Litvinoff

President Roosevelt to the Soviet Commissar for Foreign Affairs (Litvinov)

Washington, November 16, 1933.
My Dear Mr. Litvinov: I am glad to have received the assurance expressed in your note to me of this date that it will be the fixed policy of the Government of the Union of Soviet Socialist Republics:

[Here follows repetition of the four numbered paragraphs in Mr. Litvinov's note printed *supra*.]

It will be the fixed policy of the Executive of the United States within the limits of the powers conferred by the Constitution and the laws of the United States to adhere reciprocally to the engagements above expressed.

I am [etc.]

Franklin D. Roosevelt

☆　　☆　　☆

Destroyer-Bases Agreement 1940

After the League of Nations proposal was defeated in the Senate, the United States settled down to enjoy ten years of prosperity (*see pp. 194–195*). The nation became involved in its own affairs, and when the depression hit, internal problems kept most Americans from concerning themselves with menacing actions in the rest of the world.

In 1931 Japan invaded and conquered Manchuria; when the weak League of Nations attempted to censure Japan, Japan walked out of the League. Mussolini had gained control of the government of Italy and emphasized military training for Italian youth. Hitler gained control of Germany in 1933 and began to rearm the country. Mussolini conquered Ethiopia and Hitler occupied the Rhineland. In

1936 Hitler and Mussolini formed an alliance and began a systematic domination of nearby countries.

In 1937 all these European problems seemed remote from America, and Congress attempted to make sure that these problems stayed in Europe and Asia by passing the Neutrality Act. One reason the United States had become involved in the First World War, many people reasoned, was its refusal to stop shipping arms to the nations that were fighting. The Neutrality Act was designed to avoid this kind of involvement again in future world conflicts.

But the Neutrality Act of 1937 did nothing to improve the situation in Europe. In early 1938 Hitler took over Austria. Then Hitler began his plan to annex Czechoslovakia. He demanded that the Sudetenland, with its large German-speaking population, unite with Germany, and England and France thought Hitler should be pacified to avoid war. Six months later, Germany took the rest of Czechoslovakia as well. After Hitler took Czechoslovakia, Mussolini annexed Albania. In September of 1939, when Germany invaded Poland, World War II began. In early 1940 Germany invaded and conquered Norway, Denmark, Holland, Belgium, and Luxembourg. By June of 1940, when it was clear that France would soon fall, Roosevelt gave an address at the University of Virginia in which he said, "the hand that held the dagger has struck it into the back of its neighbor." How different this was from the hopeful attitude of the Neutrality Act of 1937!

On June 22, 1940, France surrendered to Germany and only England stood in the way of a complete German victory. Hitler ordered his forces to prepare for the invasion of Britain, an event which everyone believed would be attempted during the summer or early fall of 1940. The British desperately needed small ships, particularly destroyers, to protect their shores from the small vessels which might bring invaders across the narrow waters of the English Channel.

Americans feared that if Britain fell to the Germans, this country would be protected from a possible German thrust at North America only by the Atlantic Ocean and the United States Navy. This fear helped Franklin D. Roosevelt and Winston Churchill devise a scheme to benefit both their countries. The United States exchanged fifty destroyers for a lease on some British bases in the western Atlantic that could be fortified to defend our eastern coast.

The accord was reached by an executive agreement between the two nations. This agreement illustrates the value of the President's having such a power. The President saw Germany as a threat to the security of the United States, but there was still a great deal of feeling in the United States that neutrality was the best policy. On a treaty, the President could have faced defeat after a two-thirds vote in the Senate, but by using his power of executive agreement in a less important matter, the President did not have to face the Senate, and he was free to make plans to protect the nation if attack came.

(9) *The British Ambassador (Lothian) to the Secretary of State*
Washington, September 2, 1940.

Sir: I have the honour under instructions from His Majesty's Principal Secretary of State for Foreign Affairs to inform you that in view of the friendly and sympathetic interest of His Majesty's Government in the United Kingdom in the national security of the United States and their desire to strengthen the ability of the United States to cooperate effectively with the other nations of the Americas in the defence of the Western Hemisphere, His Majesty's Government will secure the grant to the Government of the United States, freely and without consideration, of the lease for immediate establishment and use of naval and air bases and facilities for entrance thereto and the operation and protection thereof, on the Avalon Peninsula and on the southern coast of Newfoundland, and on the east coast and on the Great Bay of Bermuda.

Furthermore, in view of the above and in view of the desire of the United States to acquire additional air and naval bases in the Caribbean and in British Guiana, and without endeavouring to place a monetary or commercial value upon the many tangible and intangible rights and properties involved, His Majesty's Government will make available to the United States for immediate establishment and use naval and air bases and facilities for entrance thereto and the operation and protection thereof, on the eastern side of the Bahamas, the southern coast of Jamaica, the western coast of St. Lucia, the west coast of Trinidad in the Gulf of Paria, in the island of Antigua and in British Guiana within fifty miles of Georgetown, in exchange for naval and military equipment and material which the United States Government will transfer to His Majesty's Government.

All the bases and facilities referred to in the preceding paragraphs will be leased to the United States for a period of ninety-nine years, free from all rent and charges other than such compensation to be mutually agreed on to be paid by the United States in order to compensate the owners of private property for loss by expropriation or damage arising out of the establishment of the bases and facilities in question.

His Majesty's Government, in the leases to be agreed upon, will grant to the United States for the period of the leases all the rights, power, and authority within the bases leased, and within the limits of the territorial waters and air spaces adjacent to or in the vicinity of such bases, necessary to provide access to and defence of such bases, and appropriate provisions for their control.

Without prejudice to the above-mentioned rights of the United States authorities and their jurisdiction within the leased areas, the adjustment and reconciliation between the jurisdiction of the authorities of the United States within these areas and the jurisdiction of the authorities of the territories in which these areas are situated shall be determined by common agreement.

The exact location and bounds of the aforesaid bases, the necessary seaward, coast and anti-aircraft defences, the location of sufficient military garrisons, stores and other necessary auxiliary facilities shall be determined by common agreement.

His Majesty's Government are prepared to designate immediately experts to meet with experts of the United States for these purposes. Should these experts be unable to agree in any particular situation, except in the case of Newfoundland and Bermuda, the matter shall be settled by the Secretary of State of the United States and His Majesty's Secretary of State for Foreign Affairs.

I have [etc.]

Lothian

The Secretary of State to the British Ambassador (Lothian)

Washington, September 2, 1940.

Excellency: I have received your note of September 2, 1940, of which the text is as follows:

[Here follows text of note printed *supra*.]

I am directed by the President to reply to your note as follows:

The Government of the United States appreciates the declarations and the generous action of His Majesty's Government as contained in your communication which are destined to enhance the national security of the United States and greatly to strengthen its ability to cooperate effectively with the other nations of the Americas in the defense of the Western Hemisphere. It therefore gladly accepts the proposals.

The Government of the United States will immediately designate experts to meet with experts designated by His Majesty's Government to determine upon the exact location of the naval and air bases mentioned in your communication under acknowledgment.

In consideration of the declarations above quoted, the Government of the United States will immediately transfer to His Majesty's

Government fifty United States Navy destroyers generally referred to as the twelve hundred-ton type.

Accept [etc.]

Cordell Hull

☆   ☆   ☆

The Yalta Agreement 1945

The United States entered the war when Japan attacked Pearl Harbor in December of 1941. Alliances changed during the war, but by 1945 the Axis powers of Germany, Italy, and Japan were fighting against the major Allied powers of the United States, Great Britain, the Soviet Union, and China. In an effort to chart the course of the war's final stages and the peace that was to follow, the leaders of the Allies met on several occasions. The final meeting before the surrender of Germany and Japan, attended by Roosevelt, Winston Churchill, and Joseph Stalin, was held at Yalta on the Crimean peninsula in February of 1945 and resulted in a pact known as the Yalta agreement.

The agreement, parts of which follow, has been a source of controversy. Many have argued that Roosevelt and Churchill had no moral right or legal authority to make any commitment about the disposition of the various territories. Others claim that Communist successes in China and other areas would have resulted anyway. At the time, Britain and the United States felt that they had to have Russian support against Japan, whatever the cost, and that Russia would honor her commitments.

Whether the agreement was a good or bad one, it demonstrates how an American president can influence the affairs of the world through his power to make personal agreements. Although the Yalta agreement was not binding, notice the important effect it had on the outcome of events.

DOCUMENT

(10) The Premier of the Union of Soviet Socialist Republics, the Prime Minister of the United Kingdom and the President of the United States of America have consulted with each other in the common interests of the peoples of their countries and those of liberated Europe. They jointly declare their mutual agreement to concert during the temporary period of instability in liberated Europe the policies of their three governments in assisting the peoples liberated from the domination of Nazi Germany and

the peoples of the former Axis satellite states of Europe to solve by democratic means their pressing political and economic problems.

The establishment of order in Europe and the rebuilding of national economic life must be achieved by processes which will enable the liberated peoples to destroy the last vestiges of Nazism and Fascism and to create democratic institutions of their own choice. . . .

III *Dismemberment of Germany*

It was agreed that Article 12 (a) of the Surrender Terms for Germany should be amended to read as follows:

The United Kingdom, the United States of America and the Union of Soviet Socialist Republics shall possess supreme authority with respect to Germany. In the exercise of such authority they will take such steps, including the complete disarmament, demilitarisation and dismemberment of Germany as they deem requisite for future peace and security. . . .

VII *Poland*

The following declaration on Poland was agreed by the Conference:

A new situation has been created in Poland as a result of her complete liberation by the Red Army. This calls for the establishment of a Polish Provisional Government which can be more broadly based than was possible before the recent liberation of Western Poland. The Provisional Government which is now functioning in Poland should therefore be reorganized on a broader democratic basis with the inclusion of democratic leaders from Poland itself and from Poles abroad. This new Government should then be called the Polish Provisional Government of National Unity.

. . . . This Polish Provisional Government of National Unity shall be pledged to the holding of free and unfettered elections as soon as possible on the basis of universal suffrage and secret ballot. In these elections all democratic and anti-Nazi parties shall have the right to take part and to put forward candidates. . . .

The three Heads of Government consider that the Eastern frontier of Poland should follow the Curzon Line with digressions from it in some regions of five to eight kilometres in favour of Poland. They recognise that Poland must receive substantial accessions of territory in the North and West. They feel that the opinion of the new Polish Provisional Government of National Unity should be sought in due course on the extent of these accessions and that the final delimitation of the Western frontier of Poland should thereafter await the Peace Conference. . . .

Agreement Regarding Japan

The leaders of the three Great Powers—the Soviet Union, the United States of America and Great Britain—have agreed that in

258

two or three months after Germany has surrendered and the war in Europe has terminated the Soviet Union shall enter into the war against Japan on the side of the Allies on condition that:

1. The status quo in Outer-Mongolia (The Mongolian People's Republic) shall be preserved;

2. The former rights of Russia violated by the treacherous attack of Japan in 1904 shall be restored, viz:

(a) the southern part of Sakhalin as well as the islands adjacent to it shall be returned to the Soviet Union,

(b) the commercial port of Dairen shall be internationalized, the preeminent interests of the Soviet Union in this port being safeguarded and the lease of Port Arthur as a naval base of the U.S.S.R. restored,

(c) the Chinese-Eastern Railroad and the South-Manchurian Railroad which provides an outlet to Dairen shall be jointly operated by the establishment of a joint Soviet-Chinese Company, it being understood that the preeminent interests of the Soviet Union shall be safeguarded and that China shall retain full sovereignty in Manchuria;

3. The Kuril islands shall be handed over to the Soviet Union.

It is understood, that the agreement concerning Outer-Mongolia and the ports and railroads referred to above will require concurrence of Generalissimo Chiang Kai-Shek. The President will take measures in order to obtain this concurrence on advice from Marshal Stalin.

The Heads of the three Great Powers have agreed that these claims of the Soviet Union shall be unquestionably fulfilled after Japan has been defeated.

For its part the Soviet Union expresses its readiness to conclude with the National Government of China a pact of friendship and alliance between the U.S.S.R. and China in order to render assistance to China with its armed forces for the purpose of liberating China from the Japanese yoke.

★ ★ ★

The Charter of
the United Nations 1945

In 1941, Prime Minister Churchill and President Roosevelt had met off the coast of Newfoundland. There they signed the Atlantic Charter, reaffirming the principles of peaceful self-government and a collaboration of all nations. Then, several months later, the United States entered the war and people began to feel that perhaps it could all have been avoided if the United States had supported these same principles in the League of Nations twenty years before.

As leaders began to think about the end of hostilities, the Allies met at Dumbarton Oaks to confer on specifications for a charter for a peace organization. In the United States, both political parties had agreed to support such a project for peace. Preliminaries were discussed at Yalta. Then, in April 1945, a formal conference in San Francisco was attended by fifty nations; after much discussion, in June of that year, the Charter was signed and the United Nations came into existence.

The Charter was then presented to the various nations. On July 2, President Harry Truman presented the Charter to the Senate for ratification, saying:

> It is the product of many hands and many influences. It comes from the reality of experience in a world where one generation has failed twice to keep the peace. The lessons of that experience have been written into the documents. . . .
>
> Improvements will come in the future as the United Nations gain experience with the machinery and methods which they have set up. It can be improved—and, as the years go by, it will be—just as our own Constitution has been improved. . . .
>
> I urge ratification. I urge prompt ratification.*

The Senate then proceeded to debate ratification. Most public sentiment was in favor of a league for peace, and the Charter was finally ratified on July 28, 1945, with a vote of 89 to 2. During the debate, however, several important questions had been raised to clarify the relations between the United States and other nations of the world. As you read, think about these issues which were faced by the senators:

Will the Charter prohibit our falling back on the Monroe Doctrine and hinder our agreements for inter-American defense just concluded at Chapultepec? Does the Constitution give the President the right to make troops available for external peace-keeping in the world? Would the use of these troops be "declaring war" (a Congressional power) or merely police action (a Presidential prerogative)? Are there any circumstances under which the UN may interfere in the internal affairs of sovereign states? Finally, to use the phrase of Senator Vandenberg of Michigan, how can the UN best become the "Town Meeting of the World"?

*Congressional Record, 79th Congress, First Session (U.S. Government Printing Office, Washington, D.C., 1945) 7118–7119.

(11) Chapter I

Purposes and Principles

Article I The Purposes of the United Nations are:

1. To maintain international peace and security, and to that end: to take effective collective measures for the prevention and removal of threats to the peace, and for the suppression of acts of aggression or other breaches of the peace, and to bring about by peaceful means, and in conformity with the principles of justice and international law, adjustment or settlement of international disputes or situations which might lead to a breach of the peace;

2. To develop friendly relations among nations based on respect for the principle of equal rights and self-determination of peoples, and to take other appropriate measures to strengthen universal peace;

3. To achieve international cooperation in solving international problems of an economic, social, cultural, or humanitarian character, and in promoting and encouraging respect for human rights and for fundamental freedoms for all without distinction as to race, sex, language, or religion; and

4. To be a center for harmonizing the actions of nations in the attainment of these common ends.

Article 2 The Organization and its Members, in pursuit of the Purposes stated in Article 1, shall act in accordance with the following Principles.

1. The Organization is based on the principle of the sovereign equality of all its Members.

2. All Members, in order to ensure to all of them the rights and benefits resulting from membership, shall fulfill in good faith the obligations assumed by them in accordance with the present Charter.

3. All Members shall settle their international disputes by peaceful means, in such a manner that international peace and security, and justice, are not endangered.

4. All Members shall refrain in their international relations from the threat or use of force against the territorial integrity or political independence of any state, or in any other manner inconsistent with the Purposes of the United Nations.

5. All Members shall give the United Nations every assistance in any action it takes in accordance with the present Charter, and shall refrain from giving assistance to any state against which the United Nations is taking preventive or enforcement action.

6. The organization shall ensure that states which are not Members of the United Nations act in accordance with these Principles so far as may be necessary for the maintenance of international peace and security.

7. Nothing contained in the present Charter shall authorize the United Nations to intervene in matters which are essentially within the domestic jurisdiction of any state or shall require the Members to submit such matters to settlement under the present Charter; but this principle shall not prejudice the application of enforcement measures under Chapter VII.

Chapter II
Membership

Article 3 The original Members of the United Nations shall be the states which, having participated in the United Nations Conference on International Organization at San Francisco, or having previously signed the Declaration by United Nations of January 1, 1942, sign the present Charter and ratify it in accordance with Article 110.

Article 4 1. Membership in the United Nations is open to all other peace-loving states which accept the obligations contained in the present Charter and, in the judgment of the Organization, are able and willing to carry out these obligations. . . .

Article 6 A Member of the United Nations which has persistently violated the Principles contained in the present Charter may be expelled from the Organization by the General Assembly upon the recommendation of the Security Council.

Chapter III
Organs

Article 7 1. There are established as the principal organs of the United Nations: a General Assembly, a Security Council, an Economic and Social Council, a Trusteeship Council, an International Court of Justice, and a Secretariat.

2. Such subsidiary organs as may be found necessary may be established in accordance with the present Charter. . . .

Chapter VII
Action with Respect to Threats to the Peace, Breaches of the Peace, . . .

Article 39 The Security Council shall determine the existence of any threat to the peace, breach of the peace, or act of aggression and shall make recommendations, or decide what measures shall be taken in accordance with Articles 41 and 42, to maintain or restore international peace and security. . . .

Article 41 The Security Council may decide what measures not involving the use of armed force are to be employed to give effect to its decisions, and it may call upon the Members of the United

Nations to apply such measures. These may include complete or partial interruption of economic relations and of rail, sea, air, postal, telegraphic, radio, and other means of communication, and the severance of diplomatic relations.

Article 42   Should the Security Council consider that measures provided for in Article 41 would be inadequate or have proved to be inadequate, it may take such action by air, sea, or land forces as may be necessary to maintain or restore international peace and security. Such action may include demonstrations, blockade, and other operations by air, sea, or land forces of Members of the United Nations.

Article 43   1. All Members of the United Nations, in order to contribute to the maintenance of international peace and security, undertake to make available to the Security Council . . . armed forces, assistance, and facilities, including rights of passage, necessary for the purpose of maintaining international peace and security. . . .

Article 48   1. The action required to carry out the decisions of the Security Council for the maintenance of international peace and security shall be taken by all the Members of the United Nations or by some of them as the Security Council may determine. . . .

Article 51   Nothing in the present Charter shall impair the inherent right of individual or collective self-defense if an armed attack occurs against a Member of the United Nations, until the Security Council has taken the Measures necessary to maintain international peace and security. Measures taken by Members in the exercise of this right of self-defense shall be immediately reported to the Security Council and shall not in any way affect the authority and responsibility of the Security Council under the present Charter to take at any time such action as it deems necessary in order to maintain or restore international peace and security. . . .

Chapter VIII
Regional Arrangements
Article 52   1. Nothing in the present Charter precludes the existence of regional arrangements or agencies for dealing with such matters relating to the maintenance of international peace and security as are appropriate for regional action, provided that such arrangements or agencies and their activities are consistent with the Purposes and Principles of the United Nations.

2. The Members of the United Nations entering into such arrangements or constituting such agencies shall make every effort to achieve pacific settlement of local disputes . . . before referring them to the Security Council. . . .   ☆   ☆   ☆

North Atlantic Treaty Organization 1949

The spirit of cooperation between the United States, Great Britain, and the Soviet Union that seemed to characterize Yalta soon disappeared (*see pp. 257–259*). Even as the Allies met, the Russian armies were moving across eastern Europe, freeing the countries from Nazi control but planting Communist governments in their stead, despite Stalin's agreement at Yalta to hold free elections. Through protests and negotiations, Russia continued an expansionist policy. Finally, in 1946, Winston Churchill observed in a historic speech: "From Stettin in the Baltic to Trieste in the Adriatic, an iron curtain has descended across the continent." When Communist pressure also threatened Greece and Turkey, the United States sent aid. Western Europe, too, became fully convinced of the Soviet threat when all of Czechoslovakia's government was taken over by a Communist coup.

In March 1948, after the fall of Czechoslovakia, diplomats of five European nations agreed in Brussels that an attack upon one would be an attack upon all. Still, these nations knew that their agreement was not enough to contain the Soviet Union. Therefore in April 1949, after the Berlin blockade, these and other European nations and the United States signed the stronger North Atlantic Treaty. Thus the United States became further involved abroad.

For most of its history the United States had followed the advice Washington had given in his Farewell Address (*see pp. 237–240*) and had avoided entangling alliances. While there was still a great deal of feeling that the United States would do well to avoid future European conflicts, the President and many congressmen realized that the United States lived in an age in which isolation could have even more serious consequences than alliance.

In 1947 the United States had already signed the Rio treaty, promising with other American nations to defend one another in case of attack. A similar regional treaty with European countries was not quite so frightening. The debate for European alliance was long, but in July of 1949 the Senate agreed and the United States, Britain, France, Italy, Norway, Denmark, Belgium, the Netherlands, Luxembourg, Portugal, Iceland, and Canada signed the North Atlantic Treaty for their mutual defense. They also established the North Atlantic Treaty Organization to develop defense plans and work out the possibilities of a combined army. (Later Greece, Turkey, and West Germany joined NATO.)

Compare this action of the United States with its attitude toward the League of Nations following the First World War. How does this action differ?

(12) PREAMBLE

The Parties to this Treaty reaffirm their faith in the purposes and principles of the Charter of the United Nations and their desire to live in peace with all peoples and all governments.

They are determined to safeguard the freedom, common heritage and civilization of their peoples, founded on the principles of democracy, individual liberty and the rule of law.

They seek to promote stability and well-being in the North Atlantic area.

They are resolved to unite their efforts for collective defense and for the preservation of peace and security.

They therefore agree to this North Atlantic Treaty: . . . .

Article 3 In order more effectively to achieve the objectives of this Treaty, the Parties, separately and jointly, by means of continuous and effective self-help and mutual aid, will maintain and develop their individual and collective capacity to resist armed attack.

Article 4 The Parties will consult together whenever, in the opinion of any of them, the territorial integrity, political independence or security of any of the Parties is threatened.

Article 5 The Parties agree that an armed attack against one or more of them in Europe or North America shall be considered an attack against them all; and consequently they agree that, if such an armed attack occurs, each of them, in exercise of the right of individual or collective self-defense recognized by Article 51 of the Charter of the United Nations, will assist the Party or Parties so attacked by taking forthwith, individually and in concert with the other Parties, such action as it deems necessary, including the use of armed force, to restore and maintain the security of the North Atlantic area.

Any such armed attack and all measures taken as a result thereof shall immediately be reported to the Security Council. Such measures shall be terminated when the Security Council has taken the measures necessary to restore and maintain international peace and security. . . .

Article 10 The Parties may, by unanimous agreement, invite any other European state in a position to further the principles of this Treaty and to contribute to the security of the North Atlantic area to accede to this Treaty. . . .

                                              ☆   ☆   ☆

Vietnam Resolution of Support 1964

Immediately following the Second World War, Southeast Asia became a center of conflict. The area known as French Indochina was racked by wars and civil war. By 1954 the French had ended their colonial rule with the Geneva agreement that temporarily divided Indochina into North Vietnam (ruled by a Communist government) and the independent, neutral nations of South Vietnam, Cambodia, and Laos. But fighting continued as guerilla forces, later known as the Viet Cong, tried to overthrow the government of South Vietnam. By 1961 the United States was actively involved, aiding the government in resisting the pressures of the Viet Cong.

Then, during the summer of 1964, naval units of North Vietnam attacked vessels of the United States Navy sailing in international waters in the Gulf of Tonkin. The naval vessels had been ordered to defend themselves. Using his powers as commander in chief of the army, the President ordered limited air strikes in retaliation. By not declaring war formally, he hoped to prevent a large war's developing out of a small conflict. In this rather tense situation Congress passed a resolution to strengthen the position of the President in the Vietnam conflict. The Gulf of Tonkin resolution indicated the unity of Congress behind presidential policy in critical times when a formal war declaration was not considered desirable.

(13) Whereas naval units of the Communist regime in Vietnam, in violation of the principles of the Charter of the United Nations and of international law, have deliberately and repeatedly attacked United States naval vessels lawfully present in international waters, and have thereby created a serious threat to international peace; and

Whereas these attacks are part of a deliberate and systematic campaign of aggression that the Communist regime in North Vietnam has been waging against its neighbors and the nations joined with them in the collective defense of their freedom; and

Whereas the United States is assisting the peoples of southeast Asia to protect their freedom and has no territorial, military or political ambitions in that area, but desires only that these peoples should be left in peace to work out their own destinies in their own way: Now, therefore, be it

Resolved by the Senate and House of Representatives of the United States of America in Congress assembled, That the Congress approves and supports the determination of the President, as Commander in Chief, to take all necessary measures to repel any armed attack against the forces of the United States and to prevent further aggression.

Sec. 2. The United States regards as vital to its national interest and to world peace the maintenance of international peace and security in southeast Asia. Consonant with the Constitution of the

United States and the Charter of the United Nations and in accordance with its obligations under the Southeast Asia Collective Defense Treaty, the United States is, therefore, prepared, as the President determines, to take all necessary steps, including the use of armed force, to assist any member or protocol state of the Southeast Asia Collective Defense Treaty requesting assistance in the defense of its freedom.

SEC. 3. This resolution shall expire when the President shall determine that the peace and security of the area is reasonably assured by international conditions created by action of the United Nations or otherwise, except that it may be terminated earlier by concurrent resolution of the Congress.

☆   ☆   ☆

Senate Debate on Vietnam 1966

After the Gulf of Tonkin resolution in support of the President (see pp. 265–267), the fighting in Vietnam continued. There was a great deal of controversy over the course the United States should pursue. Some people felt that United States troops should withdraw, others felt peace through negotiations should be an immediate goal, and some wanted to use as much force as necessary to win the war. In 1965 the key word was "escalation," a word that meant sending more men to Vietnam and having America pilots bomb cities in North Vietnam.

In the beginnning of 1966 the senators were discussing appropriations to support Vietnam forces. Before the vote was taken, the Senate aired many of the conflicting views of its members and the nation. One of these conflicts, mentioned in this excerpt from the January 31st session of the Senate, involves the fact that the President had ordered bombing of North Vietnam to begin again after a month's respite.

The importance of this debate – and of most others for that matter – is not the final vote of the Senate; as expected, the Senate voted the money the President requested. But debate allows for all opinions to be heard; these opinions, both popular and unpopular, are offered to the President and to the American people. In this way the Senate can advise the President on his policies, and the Senate can attempt to influence popular opinion to gain support of or opposition to a particular issue.

As you read, decide: On what issues do the senators disagree? How much of this is disagreement about how the war should be conducted?

(14) MR. YOUNG of North Dakota. . . . With our limited resources, both in manpower and financially, we should not be picking out an area to fight the Communists where they have all the advantages and we all the disadvantages as is the case in Vietnam.

The administration has been totally unrealistic on this war situation, and I believe it has been something less than frank with the American people in not giving them all the information they are entitled to have and in not telling them all that we would have to encounter in fighting a war in southeast Asia.

Approximately 2 years ago we were advised by top officials of the administration that the war would be over in a few months. They should know better than that, I believe that the public could and should be told now at least some of the problems we face. . . .

For example, the estimate of 600,000 troops we will need in southeast Asia is a conservative one and is something that our people should be told. . . .

For myself, I see no alternative at this time but to support the President in the decision he has made — at least for the time being. . . .

MR. COOPER. I am one of those who believe that the bombing should not have been resumed, at least at present. . . . But the most important factor, was whether resumption would lead to . . . extensions of conflict. . . .

MR. LONG of Louisiana. Mr. President, I believe that the President had no choice about resuming bombing and the other efforts being made by this Nation to assist South Vietnam.

This nation is there because the Communist aggressors are there. This is a part of world struggle that has continued since 1946, an effort by Communists to subjugate by force everything they can subjugate, an effort to take over everything that they can take over. . . .

We did what we could to help South Vietnam sustain itself. It was faced with constant aggression to the point where our naval vessels were in the area and were attacked on the high seas by torpedo boats of North Vietnam.

At that point we voted for a resolution. We said that we approved measures directing a strike back at aggression in the area. We approved of such additional measures as the President might deem necessary to resist aggression in that area.

What did the President do? At that time we struck back at the bases from which the enemy vessels were operating in the waters in the vicinity of North Vietnam. That was an act of war. But we did not start it. They did. We struck back. We authorized the President to take such additional measures as he deemed necessary.

Those people were sending down organized forces from North Vietnam and South Vietnam. The President sent in forces to help South Vietnam sustain itself. . . .

We hope to limit that struggle and keep it within bounds and we hope for a peaceful settlement.

We will discover that when North Vietnam thinks they are in a position to defeat us before the entire world, with two other Communist powers behind them. They are not going to let us out of there, short of defeating us, if they can.

When we are in a war we should fight to win. That is what we have done in the past in any fight when we wished to prevail. . . .

If the United States cannot stand fast against Communist aggression, does anyone think that India is going to stand against Communist China? Does anyone think that Pakistan or Indonesia is going to stand against Communist China? Who is going to stand against Communist China when they see that they cannot count on the United States to stand by with fortitude?

I yield to the Senator from North Carolina. . . .

MR. ERVIN. Does the Senator from Louisiana agree with the Senator from North Carolina that the President has done and is doing everything in his power to obtain a settlement by negotiation and thus far he has been unable to find anybody willing to negotiate with him?

MR. LONG of Louisiana. He has done exactly that.

MR. ERVIN. Does not the Senator from Louisiana agree with the Senator from North Carolina that communism is determined to extinguish the light of liberty all over the face of the earth?

MR. LONG of Louisiana. That is my opinion. If the Communists feel that they can extinguish the light of liberty, they will do everything they can to get rid of it. They are seeking by every means to prevail.

MR. ERVIN. Before putting to you my next question I would like to make this plain: If I had been running the United States all by myself during recent years, I would not have placed any American servicemen in South Vietnam. But the question confronting America at this hour is not whether we should put our servicemen in South Vietnam. They are already there. Are we not in the position which Grover Cleveland called a condition and not a theory?

MR. LONG of Louisiana. We are. We have committed ourselves in Vietnam.

MR. ERVIN. Does not the Senator from Louisiana agree with me in the proposition that if history teaches anything, it teaches that even the most righteous man cannot live in peace unless it pleases his wicked neighbor for him to do so? Does not the Senator from Louisiana agree with me in the proposition that if North Vietnam

269

and those who back North Vietnam would stop furnishing men and weapons and equipment, the war would cease?

MR. LONG of Louisiana. I believe the Senator is correct about that. He is correct.

☆ ☆ ☆

X Footnotes

[1]James D. Richardson, ed., *Messages and Papers of the Presidents* (Government Printing Office, Washington, D.C., 1897) I, 213–224.

[2]H. A. Washington, ed., *The Writings of Thomas Jefferson* (Taylor & Maury, Washington, D.C., 1854) IV, 431–434.

[3]James D. Richardson, *A Compilation of the Messages and Papers of the Presidents, 1789–1897* (Government Printing Office, Washington, D.C., 1896–1899) II, 218.

[4]*U.S. Statutes at Large*, XXX, 738–739.

[5]J. L. Heaton, *Cobb of "The World"* (E.P. Dutton and Co., New York, 1924) 268–270.

[6]*Congressional Record*, 65th Congress, Special Session, 1st Session, LV, 102–104.

[7]*Congressional Record*, October 6, 1919, LVIII, 6424–6427.

[8]*Foreign Relations of the United States, 1933* (Government Printing Office, Washington, D.C., 1949) 805.

[9]*Foreign Relations of the United States, 1940* (Government Printing Office, Washington, D.C., 1958) III, 73–75.

[10]*A Decade of American Foreign Policy, Basic Documents, 1941–49* (Government Printing Office, Washington, D.C., 1950) 27–34.

[11]*Charter of the United Nations*, Department of State Publication 2353, III, 1–85.

[12]*North Atlantic Treaty*, Department of State, Gen. For. Pol. Ser., 8 (Government Printing Office, Washington, D.C., 1949).

[13]*Congressional Record*, 88th Congress, 2nd Session, CX, xiv, 18471.

[14]*Congressional Record*, 89th Congress, 2nd Session, CXII, xv, 1499–1500.

Selected Readings for Teachers and Students

* *Indicates books that may be of special interest to students*

II

* Churchill, Winston S. *A History of the English Speaking Peoples: The New World*. Dodd, Mead & Co., New York, 1956.

Clark, George N. *The Later Stuarts, 1660–1714*. Oxford University Press, New York, 1955.

Davies, Godfrey. *The Early Stuarts, 1603–1660*. Oxford University Press, New York, 1959.

Morpurgo, J. E., ed. *Life Under the Stuarts*. British Book Centre, New York, 1951.

Notestein, Wallace. *The English People on the Eve of Colonization, 1603–1630*. Harper & Brothers, New York, 1954.

Ogg, David. *England in the Reign of Charles II*, 2 vols. Oxford University Press, New York, 1955.

* Schrag, Peter, ed. *The European Mind and the Discovery of the New World*. D. C. Heath and Co., Boston, 1965.

Trevelyan, G. M. *England under the Stuarts*. Barnes & Noble, New York, 1957.

III

* American Heritage. *Book of the Revolution*. American Heritage Publishing Company, New York, 1958.

* Bowen, Catherine Drinker. *John Adams and the American Revolution*. Little, Brown and Co., Boston, 1950.

Gipson, Lawrence H. *The Coming of the Revolution*. Harper & Row, Publishers, New York, 1962.

Malone, Dumas. *Jefferson the Virginian*. Little, Brown and Co., Boston, 1948.

McIlwain, C. H. *The American Revolution: A Constitutional Interpretation*. Cornell University Press, Ithaca, New York, 1958.

Miller, J. C. *Origins of the American Revolution*. Little, Brown and Co., Boston, 1943.

Morgan, Edmund S. *The Puritan Dilemma, the Story of John Winthrop*. Little, Brown and Co., Boston, 1958.

* Morison, Samuel E. *Builders of the Bay Colony*. Houghton Mifflin Co., Boston, 1963.

* Morris, Richard B. *The American Revolution: A Short History*. D. Van Nostrand Company, Princeton, New Jersey, 1955.

* Rozwenc, E. C., and Bauer, F. E., Jr., eds. *Liberty and Power in the Making of the Constitution*. D. C. Heath and Co., Boston, 1963.

Savelle, Max. *Seeds of Liberty*. University of Washington Press, Seattle, 1957.

* Schultz, Donald P., ed. *Conflict and Consensus in the American Revolution*. D. C. Heath and Co., Boston, 1964.

* Squire, Marjorie J., ed. *British Views of the American Revolution*. D. C. Heath and Co., Boston, 1965.

271

Van Doren, Carl. *Benjamin Franklin*. Viking Press, New York, 1956.

Wright, Louis B. *Cultural Life of the American Colonies: 1607–1763*. Harper & Brothers, New York, 1957.

IV

* Bauer, F. E., Jr., ed. *Liberty and Power in the Making of the Constitution*. D. C. Heath and Co., Boston, 1963.

Beard, Charles A. *The Supreme Court and the Constitution*. Prentice-Hall, Englewood Cliffs, New Jersey, 1962.

Beloff, Max. *Thomas Jefferson and American Democracy*. Collier-Macmillan Library Service, New York, 1949.

* Bowers, Claude G. *Jefferson and Hamilton*. Houghton Mifflin Co., Boston, 1933.

* Corwin, Edward S. *John Marshall and the Constitution*. Yale University Press, New Haven, Conn., 1919.

Jensen, Merrill. *The Articles of Confederation*. University of Wisconsin Press, Madison, Wisc., 1959.

* Krout, J. A. and Fox, D. R. *The Completion of Independence, 1790–1830*. The Macmillan Company, New York, 1944.

Rossiter, Clinton. *Alexander Hamilton and the Constitution*. Harcourt, Brace & World, Inc., New York, 1964.

* Schrag, Peter. *The Ratification of the Constitution and the Bill of Rights*. D. C. Heath and Co., Boston, 1964.

* Van Doren, Carl. *The Great Rehearsal: The Story of the Making and Ratifying of the Constitution*. The Viking Press, New York, 1948.

Warren, Charles. *The Making of the Constitution*. Harvard University Press, Cambridge, Mass., 1928.

White, Leonard D. *The Federalists*. The Macmillan Company, New York, 1961.

V

* Baker, Gary G., ed. *Andrew Johnson and the Struggle for Presidential Reconstruction, 1865–1868*. D. C. Heath and Co., Boston, 1966.

Bancroft, Frederick. *Calhoun and the South Carolina Nullification Movement*. Johns Hopkins Press, Baltimore, 1928.

* Bowers, Claude G. *The Tragic Era: The Revolution after Lincoln*. Houghton Mifflin Co., Boston, 1929.

* Brown, R. H., ed. *The Missouri Compromise: Political Statesmanship or Unwise Evasion?* D. C. Heath and Co., Boston, 1964.

* Commager, Henry S., ed. *Photographic History of the Civil War*, 5 vols. Thomas Yoseloff, New York, 1957.

* Craven, Avery. *The Coming of the Civil War*, 2nd ed., rev. University of Chicago Press, Chicago, 1957.

* Dodd, William E. *The Cotton Kingdom*. Yale University Press, New Haven, Conn., 1919.

* Dowdey, Clifford. *Land They Fought For: The South as the Confederacy.* Doubleday & Company, Garden City, New York, 1955.

Dumond, Dwight L. *The Secession Movement, 1860–1861.* Octagon Books, Inc., New York, 1963.

Frederick, Wayne A., ed. *Slavery and the Breakdown of the American Consensus.* D. C. Heath and Co., Boston, 1964.

* Jenkins, William S. *Pro-Slavery Thought in the Old South.* Peter Smith, Gloucester, Mass., 1959.

Miller, John C. *Crisis in Freedom: The Alien and Sedition Acts.* Little, Brown and Co., Boston, 1964.

* Randall, J. G., and Donald, D. *The Civil War and Reconstruction,* 2nd ed. D. C. Heath and Co., Boston, 1961.

* Stampp, Kenneth. *The Peculiar Institution: Slavery and the Antebellum South.* Alfred A. Knopf, Inc., New York, 1956.

* Turner, Frederick J. *The United States, 1830–1850.* W. W. Norton & Co., New York, 1965.

VI

* Bauer, Frederick E., Jr., ed. *Democracy in the Age of Jackson.* D. C. Heath and Co., Boston, 1965.

Commager, Henry S. *The Era of Reform, 1830–1860.* D. Van Nostrand Co., Princeton, New Jersey, 1960.

Faulkner, Harold U. *The Quest for Social Justice, 1898–1914.* The Macmillan Company, New York, 1931.

Fish, Carl R. *The Rise of the Common Man, 1830–1850.* The Macmillan Company, New York, 1937.

Flexner, Eleanor. *Century of Struggle: The Woman's Rights Movement in the United States.* Harvard University Press, Cambridge, Mass., 1959.

Kraditor, A. S. *The Ideas of the Woman Suffrage Movement, 1890–1920.* Columbia University Press, New York, 1965.

Lutz, Alma. *Susan B. Anthony.* Beacon Press, Boston, 1959.

* Schlesinger, Arthur M., Jr. *Age of Jackson.* Little Brown and Co., Boston, 1945.

Williamson, Chilton. *American Suffrage, from Property to Democracy, 1760–1860.* Princeton University Press, Princeton, New Jersey, 1960.

VII

* Allen, Frederick L. *The Great Pierpont Morgan.* Harper & Brothers, New York, 1949.

* Blum, John M. *The Republican Roosevelt.* Harvard University Press, Cambridge, Mass., 1954.

* Buck, Solon J. *The Agrarian Crusade.* Yale University Press, New Haven, Conn., 1930.

* Faulkner, Harold U. *The Quest for Social Justice, 1898–1914.* The Macmillan Company, New York, 1931.

Fine, Sidney. *Laissez Faire and the General-Welfare State, 1865–1901.* University of Michigan Press, Ann Arbor, Mich., 1956.

273

Hofstadter, Richard. *The Age of Reform: from Bryan to F. D. R.* Alfred A. Knopf, Inc., New York, 1955.

* Holbrook, Stewart H. *The Age of the Moguls.* Doubleday & Company, Garden City, New York, 1953.

Josephson, Hannah. *The Golden Threads: New England's Mill Girls and Magnates.* Little, Brown and Co., Boston, 1949.

Kirkland, Edward C. *Dream and Thought in the Business Community, 1860–1900.* Quadrangle Books, Chicago, 1964.

Latham, Earl, ed. *John D. Rockefeller, Robber Baron or Industrial Statesman?* D. C. Heath and Co., Boston, 1949.

* Link, Arthur S. *Woodrow Wilson and the Progressive Era, 1910–1917.* Harper & Brothers, New York, 1954.

* Riis, Jacob A. *How the Other Half Lives: Studies among the Tenements of New York.* Peter Smith, Gloucester, Mass., 1959.

* Rozwenc, E. C., and Roehm, A. W., eds. *The Entrepreneur in the Gilded Age.* D. C. Heath and Co., Boston, 1965.

* Schlesinger, A. M. *The Rise of the City, 1878–1898.* The Macmillan Company, New York, 1933.

* Steffens, Lincoln. *The Shame of the Cities.* Sagamore Press, New York, 1957.

* Tarbell, Ida M. *The History of the Standard Oil Company,* 2 vols. The Macmillan Co., New York, 1925.

* ———. *The Nationalizing of Business, 1878–1898.* The Macmillan Company, New York, 1936.

* Traverso, Edmund. *The 1920's: Rhetoric or Reality?* D. C. Heath and Co., Boston, 1964.

VIII

Allen, Frederick L. *Only Yesterday.* Harper & Brothers, New York, 1931.

Burns, James H. *Roosevelt: The Lion and the Fox.* Harcourt, Brace & World, New York, 1956.

Freidel, Frank, ed. *The New Deal and the American People.* Prentice-Hall, Englewood Cliffs, New Jersey, 1964.

Leuchtenburg, William E. *Franklin D. Roosevelt and the New Deal, 1932–1940.* Harper & Row, Publishers, New York, 1963.

* Merrill, Edward H., ed. *Responses to Economic Collapse: The Great Depression of the 1930's.* D. C. Heath and Co., Boston, 1964.

Mitchell, Broadus. *Depression Decade, 1929–1941.* Holt, Rinehart and Winston, New York, 1947.

Rauch, Basil. *The History of the New Deal, 1933–1938.* Peter Smith, Magnolia, Mass., 1944.

Rozwenc, E. C., and Lyons, T.T., eds. *Presidential Power in the New Deal.* D. C. Heath and Co., Boston, 1963.

Schlesinger, A. M., Jr. *The Age of Roosevelt: The Coming of the New Deal.* Houghton Mifflin Co., Boston, 1959.

———. *The Age of Roosevelt: The Crisis of the Old Order.* Houghton Mifflin Co., Boston, 1957.

Warren, Harris G. *Herbert Hoover and the Great Depression*. Oxford University Press, New York, 1959.

* Wecter, Dixon. *The Age of the Great Depression, 1929–1941*. The Macmillan Co., New York, 1948.

IX

* Ames, William C., ed. *The Negro Struggle for Equality in the Twentieth Century*. D. C. Heath and Co., Boston, 1965.

Donald, Henderson H. *The Negro Freedman*. Henry Schuman, Inc., New York, 1952.

Filler, Louis. *The Crusade Against Slavery, 1830–1860*. Harper & Brothers, New York, 1960.

* Franklin, John H. *From Slavery to Freedom: A History of American Negroes*. Alfred A. Knopf, Inc., New York, 1956.

Humphrey, Hubert H. *School Desegregation*. Thomas Y. Crowell Co., New York, 1964.

James, Joseph B. *The Framing of the Fourteenth Amendment*. University of Illinois Press, Urbana, Illinois, 1965.

Logan, Rayford W. *The Negro in the United States*. D. Van Nostrand Co., Princeton, New Jersey, 1957.

Muse, Benjamin. *Ten Years of Prelude*. Viking Press, New York, 1964.

* Silberman, Charles E. *Crisis in Black and White*. Random House, New York, 1964.

Stampp, K. M. *The Peculiar Institution*. Alfred A. Knopf, Inc., New York, 1956.

Wish, Harvey, ed. *Slavery in the South*. Farrar, Straus & Giroux, New York, 1964.

Ziegler, Benjamin M., ed. *Desegregation and the Supreme Court*. D. C. Heath and Co., Boston, 1958.

X

Bailey, Thomas A. *Woodrow Wilson and the Peacemakers*, 2 vols. The Macmillan Company, New York, 1947.

* Chase, E. P. *The United Nations in Action*. McGraw-Hill Book Co., New York, 1950.

Churchill, Winston S. *The Second World War*, 6 vols. Houghton Mifflin Co., Boston, 1959.

* Dulles, Foster R. *America's Rise to World Power, 1898–1954*. Harper & Brothers, New York, 1955.

* Eisenhower, Dwight D. *Crusade in Europe*. Doubleday & Co., Garden City, New York, 1948.

* Falk, Edwin A. *From Perry to Pearl Harbor*. Doubleday & Co., Garden City, New York, 1943.

Feis, Herbert. *Churchill, Roosevelt, and Stalin: The War They Waged and the Peace They Sought*. Princeton University Press, Princeton, New Jersey, 1957.

* Kennan, George F. *American Diplomacy, 1900–1950.* University of Chicago Press, Chicago, 1951.

Langer, W. L., and Gleason, S. E. *The Challenge to Isolation: 1937–1940.* Harper & Brothers, New York, 1952.

Link, Arthur S. *Wilson the Diplomatist.* Johns Hopkins Press, Baltimore, 1957.

* Marshall, Charles B. *The Limits of Foreign Policy.* Holt, Rinehart & Winston, New York, 1954.

May, Ernest R. *The World War and American Isolationism, 1914–1917.* Harvard University Press, Cambridge, Mass., 1959.

* Millis, Walter. *The Martial Spirit: A Study of Our War with Spain.* Houghton Mifflin Co., Boston, 1937.

Perkins, Dexter. *A History of the Monroe Doctrine,* rev. ed. Little, Brown and Co., Boston, 1955.

Pratt, Julius W. *Expansionists of 1898.* Quadrangle Books, Chicago, 1964.

Rostow, Walt W. *The United States in the World Arena.* Harper & Brothers, New York, 1960.

* Rozwenc, E. C. and Lindfors, Kenneth, eds. *Containment and the Origins of the Cold War.* D. C. Heath and Co., Boston, 1967.

* Rozwenc, E. C., and Lyons, Thomas, eds. *Realism and Idealism in Wilson's Peace Program.* D. C. Heath and Co., Boston, 1965.

* Slosson, P. W. *The Great Crusade and After, 1914–1928.* The Macmillan Co. New York, 1930.

* Wilbur, W. Allan, ed. *The Monroe Doctrine.* D. C. Heath and Co., Boston, 1965.